100 BIZARRE ANIMALS

MIKE UNWIN

First published August 2010
Bradt Travel Guides Ltd
23 High Street, Chalfont St Peter, Bucks SL9 9QE, England
www.bradtguides.com
Published in the USA by The Globe Pequot Press Inc,
PO Box 480, Guilford, Connecticut 06437-0480

ISBN: 978 1 84162 300 9

British Library Cataloguing in Publication Data
A catalogue record for this book is available from the British Library

Front cover above: star-nosed mole (Ken Catania)
Front cover below, left to right: magnificent frigatebird (Tui De Roy/Minden Pictures/FLPA),
Parson's chameleon (Ingo Arndt/Minden Pictures/FLPA); mudskipper (Jurgen & Christine Sohns/FLPA),
shoebill (Konrad Wothe/Minden Pictures/FLPA), mandrill (ImageBroker/Imagebroker/FLPA)

Back cover: axolotl (Jane Burton/Photoshot)

Designed and formatted by Chris Lane at Artinfusion
Maps by Chris Lane and David McCutcheon

Production managed by Jellyfish Print Solutions; printed in India

Foreword

If you've never seen a star-nosed mole before, the photo on the cover will make you blink in disbelief. Or take the pangolin, bustling around like an animated artichoke, or the sabre-toothed sausage that is the naked mole rat. Every page of this book introduces you to fresh absurdities. You cannot fail to smile at Mike Unwin's descriptions of a bat with a 'megaphone for a muzzle', which 'honks to bonk', or the risk that a wombat's attacker might be crushed to death by its prey's backside. Then there's the 'shocking experience for any predator: one minute you're casually investigating an old stick; the next you're being rushed by a hissing, gaping lunatic brandishing a bright yellow umbrella.'

The humour turns to fascination, however, when the animal's bizarre appearance or behaviour is explained. Mike is a passionate naturalist as well as a delighted observer, and the fact that these animals have survived at all points to how successfully they have adapted to its environment. They look or act odd because they need to hide or escape from enemies, attract mates, or find food.

Wildlife enthusiasts all have their favourite encounters: a big cat, maybe, or perhaps a family of mountain gorillas. But for me it was finding a leaf-nosed snake in Madagascar. I can still recall the mixture of enchantment and astonishment that such an utterly bizarre creature could exist, and my extraordinary luck at seeing one. Had it not moved, its camouflage would have been perfect.
Now top of my wish list is a pangolin. And you?

Hilary Bradt

Contents

Foreword   3
The call of the weird   6

1 GETTING AROUND   8

Introduction to locomotion   9
Animals 1–19   12

2 GRABBING A BITE   34

Introduction to feeding   35
Animals 20–43   38

3 STAYING ALIVE   66

Introduction to self-defence and survival   67
Animals 44–62   70

4 SHOWING OFF   90

Introduction to display   91
Animals 63–77   94

5 PASSING IT ON   114

Introduction to breeding   115
Animals 78–89   118

6 LIVING TOGETHER   130

Introduction to social behaviour   131
Animals 90–100   134

Conservation contacts   149
Acknowledgements   150
Index   151

◀ *North Island brown kiwi: a bird that breaks all the rules.*

The call of the weird

Bizarreness, like beauty, is in the eye of the beholder. That much quickly became apparent while I was compiling the list of species that make up this book. No two people I consulted could agree on which animals they found the most bizarre. For some, nothing could beat the desert horned lizard, which squirts blood out of its eyes in self-defence. Others were left speechless by the scarlet throat balloon of a frigatebird. What was nature *on* when she produced freaks like these? Surely it must be some kind of joke.

There seems to be, however, a general consensus that the weirdest creatures are shrouded in obscurity. Those animals that elicit the most gasps and grimaces are generally little-known creatures hidden in remote corners of the planet. It is as though we suspect that weirdness truly flourishes only when nature escapes our scrutiny. Thus the giraffe-necked weevil of Madagascar's rainforests is, consistently, a jaw-dropper – as is the hagfish, found in deep oceans worldwide and known as the 'ugliest fish in the world'. In both cases the name surely helps, too.

Creatures also seem to take us aback when they subvert our expectations. A frog that can jump ten times its own length leaves us unmoved. That's old hat. But a frog that can fly? You'll find it here – along with a lizard that walks on water, a kangaroo that climbs trees, a fish that walks on land, a bird with claws on its wings and *two* mammals that lay eggs.

There are many creatures, by contrast, whose extraordinary traits were deemed – by popular opinion – too familiar to make the final cut. Nobody today considers an elephant bizarre. Its image accompanies us in one form or another from cradle to grave, whether as cuddly toy, cartoon character or curio. Yet imagine if scientists returned tomorrow from some remote jungle clutching a few blurred images of the first jumbo ever seen. That nose! Those ears! The sheer size! It would quickly be denounced as a hoax; offered, perhaps, as an exclusive to the *National Enquirer*.

Apologies, then, to elephants. Also to puffins, peacocks, porcupines and the myriad of other amazing creatures that have become part of our daily frame of reference. And spare a thought for *Camponotus saunderi* – a Malaysian ant that deters enemies by detonating poison glands on its abdomen and thus spontaneously, and fatally, combusting. Sadly, there wasn't room for all.

And yet, we all know what familiarity breeds. Hence this book includes one or two creatures that, at first glance, may seem out of place but, upon a closer look, are up there with the most outlandish. Take the Eurasian swift, well known to millions of people. It's an impressive flyer, you might think, but hardly 'bizarre'. Not, that is, until you find out more about its life. Mating in mid-air? Flying for years without landing? Feeding entirely on 'aerial plankton', which it gathers by the hundred into a food ball and regurgitates to its young? How weird do you want?

Such extraordinary life stories show the surprises that lurk behind the everyday. They also explain why this book is not concerned only with how animals look. Like beauty, again, bizarreness is more than skin-deep. Granted, our first impression of an animal is invariably its appearance – which is why the front cover features a gallery of the grotesque. There is something undeniably compelling about

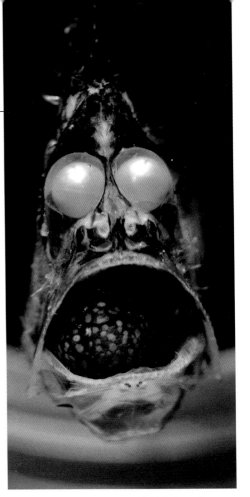

▲ *Here's looking at you! A hatchet fish is just one of countless peculiar critters that lurk in the ocean depths – though perfectly normal to its fellow hatchet fish.*

the outsized conk of a shoebill, the goggle eyes of a mudskipper or the painted grimace of a mandrill. And some creatures, such as chameleons, seem to have all bases covered: rotating turret eyes, kitchen-tong hands, curly tail, outrageous colour scheme and a tongue that stretches the length of its body.

Appearance can lose its novelty, though. It's often what the animal does that is even more astounding – and which explains many of the selections in this book. The black heron, for instance, is a perfectly standard-looking member of the heron family, with its serpentine neck, long legs and stabbing bill. But it becomes utterly unrecognisable when it flings out its wings into a bizarre, umbrella-shaped canopy with which to lure fish. The banded archerfish, which may be nothing special to look at, has evolved a unique weapon: the ability to spray a jet of water with such power and accuracy that it knocks insect prey off its perch and into the water.

In the end, what exactly do we mean by 'bizarre'? We know that it suggests something strange or unusual – something 'abnormal', perhaps. But we have no yardstick for the normal other than that with which we are most familiar. The first Europeans to see kangaroos were astonished by these large animals that bounced. They'd seen nothing like that in Europe. And yet, in Australia, of course, hopping had evolved millions of years earlier as the energy-efficient locomotive method of choice for dozens of macropod species. To these animals, the wandering earthbound sheep introduced by those same Europeans must have appeared decidedly odd.

So bizarreness, ultimately, reflects a subjective value judgement. There is no scientific rationale behind the selection of species in this book. Those that made it had something that caught the eye or imagination – something unusual enough to jolt our idea of the normal in nature. In the end, though, it's a personal choice, and I make no apologies for the arbitrariness of the selection.

But of course there is nothing arbitrary about the evolution of these animals themselves. Nature has not set about producing a freak show purely for our amusement. Each trait that we find extraordinary, from the outsized toes of a jacana to the headstand of a fog-basking beetle, is an adaptation honed by the forces of natural selection to equip an animal for its environment.

Each of the six chapters in this book groups animals by a common theme: from locomotion, feeding and self-defence to display, breeding and living together. This approach reveals the astonishing range of solutions that the animal kingdom has found to common problems. And the more bizarre the animal is in our eyes, often the more perfectly suited it is to the task in hand.

Keen-eyed readers will spot that some of the animals in this book, such as chameleons, dung beetles and frogfish, actually represent a group of species – a genus, or even a family – rather than just one. This is simply because, in some cases, it was easier to do justice to an animal's bizarreness, both in words and pictures, by tackling it within the spectrum of its relatives.

The 'Status' listed in each animal's 'At a glance' box refers to their conservation status as recognised by the International Union for Conservation of Nature (IUCN), from Least Concern through to Critically Endangered. These designations speak for themselves. They illustrate the fact that, bizarre or not, many of these animals will not be with us much longer unless we take urgent steps to safeguard them and their habitat.

Ultimately, this book is more celebration than freak show. Its pageant of weird and wonderful animals is testimony to the sheer richness and variety of life on our planet. It would have been easy to choose 100 more. There's one that springs immediately to mind: a large ape that, bizarrely, walks upright. It is almost completely naked – once you strip away the multi-coloured material in which it cocoons itself daily – and seems most unsuited to its natural habitat, being slow, cumbersome and especially vulnerable to the elements. It is not yet endangered, in fact it is thriving, but most peculiar of all, it has evolved a unique capacity to destroy its own environment. Keep an eye out: this species is not hard to spot.

▼ Apologies to the golden-rumped elephant-shrew, one of numerous worthy contenders that failed to make the final cut.

1 GETTING AROUND

Run, hop, crawl, burrow, swim, flap, glide, slither: animals have a myriad of ways to do the locomotion. Granted, a few aquatic creatures, such as sea anemones, may pass their adult lives anchored to one spot, simply twitching tentacles to filter food from the current. But for the rest, survival generally depends upon getting from A to B.

Doing the locomotion

Locomotion, loosely, is movement that gets you from one place to another on purpose. Animals that locomote are described as 'motile', whereas those that sit in one place, as plants do, are 'sessile'. There are many good reasons why it pays to get around: finding food, securing a mate, avoiding danger and securing habitat are among the most pressing.

Locomotion is loosely defined as movement that gets you from one place to another on purpose. There are two basic ways of doing this: 'axial' locomotion is when an animal modifies its own shape in order to move forward – as with an eel, that sends a rhythmic ripple down the length of its body; 'appendicular' locomotion involves using appendages, such as legs, wings or fins, to engage forcefully with the environment. The latter also takes muscle power.

▲ *Many caterpillars employ the 'looper' method to get around, first anchoring their head in position then bringing their rear end forward to join it.*

The form that these appendages take depends upon the medium through which the animal moves. Every environment poses its own mechanical challenges, and specialised modifications and techniques are required to overcome gravity, drag, inertia and other obstacles of physics. The sheer variety of ways in which nature has risen to these challenges is breathtaking. And some – at least to our eyes – are decidedly bizarre.

Legging it

Legs are nature's best answer to the challenge of moving forward over a surface. Whether in batches of two, four, six, eight or the countless limbs of a millipede, they provide both support and propulsion to everything from elephants to ants. You push your feet against the ground and – following Newton's third law – the ground produces an equal and opposite force that gets you on your way. Do it with each leg in turn and, hey presto, you're walking. Sounds straightforward enough. But, as always in nature, it is the exceptions that prove the rule.

The barred mudskipper (page 32), for instance, is not blessed with legs but, driven by the urge to stroll around on land, has decided that fins will do just as well. Thus this small fish skitters around on the mangroves as though it had feet, and has evolved a semi-terrestrial lifestyle to match.

You'd have thought that, with eight legs, any spider should be able to outrun its predators. But what if that predator is a hunting wasp? The desert-dwelling cartwheeling spider (page 33) puts on a life-saving burst of speed by rolling up its legs into a wheel and tumbling down the dune-slope to escape its pursuer. And, when it comes to rapid, the greater roadrunner (page 26) is a veritable cheetah among birds. Eschewing its facility for flight, it chases down its prey on foot at speeds that would test an Olympic sprinter.

High life

Treetops are a medium all of their own. Neither really land nor air, they present arboreal animals

▼ *Verreaux's sifaka is adapted for life in the treetops but can cross open ground by bounding upright on its hind legs.*

▲ *The raft spider spreads its legs across the water's surface to avoid breaking the surface tension.*

– wings – that can generate enough lift to propel an animal upward and forward beyond the clutches of gravity and drag. Birds are the undisputed masters of the air, and none more so than the Eurasian swift (page 24). So aerial is this creature that it feeds, mates and even sleeps on the wing, with youngsters known to remain airborne for a staggering four years without once touching down.

Watersports

Water offers more resistance than air, which is why most aquatic creatures have evolved such a streamlined shape to power themselves through it. For many, the tail provides the thrust: most fish move theirs from side to side, while dolphins and other cetaceans undulate theirs up and down. For other creatures, including sea turtles, penguins and seals, it is the front flippers that do most of the work. The blobfish (page 33), however, is anything but streamlined. This deepwater species relies on having a body mass that is less dense than water to hover – shapelessly – just above the seabed, waiting for its food to drift past.

with abundant food – but also the tricky obstacle of gravity to overcome. Thus a three-toed sloth (page 18) has evolved grappling-iron claws with which to anchor itself securely among the branches, while the sucker-footed bat (page 15), uses adhesive pads to 'glue' itself firmly to palm leaves, making it one of the only bats to sleep the right way up.

For a sloth, there's no rush; the leaves it eats are going nowhere. Not so for a western tarsier (page 12), however, which feeds at night on insects that whizz around the canopy. Thus this mini primate has evolved prodigiously long back legs that propel it in great frog-like leaps after its prey.

Such treetop agility is rather less associated with kangaroos. Nonetheless, tree-kangaroos (page 17),

finding a vacant niche in monkey-free Australasia, have embraced the high life, and can happily leap down to the ground further than most kangaroos can bounce across it.

Taking off

There comes a point when even the greatest jumpers have to admit defeat. Thus the colugo (page 16) is one of a number of mammals to develop a flap of skin called a gliding membrane that provides enough air-resistance to glide serious distances from one tree to the next. And it's not only mammals: amazingly, there are flying frogs (page 31) and even flying snakes (page 30) that use similar adaptations to much the same effect.

Gliding is not really flying, however, but falling slowly. True flight requires specially modified limbs

Aquatic creatures needn't stay down below, either. For those with the right technique and equipment the water's surface also offers a means of getting around. These creatures, such as pond skaters, are usually small enough to avoid breaking the surface tension. But not all of them: the green basilisk (page 28), though a perfectly capable swimmer, has embraced the more biblical challenge of running on water; while the African jacana (page 21) has evolved enormously long toes that can traverse the thinnest of lily pads without it sinking beneath the surface.

We humans may pride ourselves on our advanced transport technology. But from helicopters (dragonflies) to tube trains (moles), there is really no means of getting around that wasn't first patented by the animal kingdom, and no corner of the planet that animals haven't reached.

1. Western tarsier

Tarsius bancanus

The huge bug eyes of this pocket-sized primate, each one bigger than its own brain, are surely nature's most outlandish night goggles. Add to this a pair of outsized back legs – built for superhero leaps through the forest tangle – and you have the nemesis of every creepy-crawly that braves the jungle moonlight.

Big foot

Tarsiers get their name from the elongated tarsus bones in their unusually long feet – an adaptation that allows them exceptional reach and grip as they leap around their rainforest home. Suction pads on the toes bring adhesion to this grip, though the second and third toes of the front feet also bear long curved claws for grooming the silky coat.

Only when a tarsier springs from its perch can you appreciate the full length of those hind legs, which are twice as long as its head and body combined. Though no bigger than a squirrel, this diminutive creature can leap more than 2m – roughly 40 times its own length – from one vertical hold to another, enabling it to negotiate the tangled canopy at an impressive lick.

The forelegs are much shorter than the hind legs but have similarly elongated toes. These are adapted not only for securing acrobatic handholds but also for grasping struggling prey. In fact, a tarsier's front middle toe is longer than its upper arm. A thin, tufted tail completes the anatomy of the arboreal athlete, giving it balance among the branches and support at its daytime roost.

The eyes have it

A tarsier's boggle eyes are the largest, proportionally, of any mammal; on us they would be apple-sized. Unlike those of many nocturnal creatures, however, they do not have a *tapetum lucidum* – the reflective layer that helps gather light in darkness. Instead, their sheer size does this job more than adequately. An adaptation to the fovea, found elsewhere only in the higher primates, allows the pinpoint depth perception required for capturing elusive prey.

These eyes do not revolve in their sockets. But a tarsier can turn its head almost 180° in both directions, allowing it, like an owl, to look directly behind itself. This habit is sufficiently unnerving for the indigenous Iban people of Borneo to fear the tarsier as an ill omen. Indeed, a hiding tarsier discovered by a predator will suddenly reveal its eyes as a ploy to spook its assailant.

Ears are also vital to the night hunter. A tarsier's membranous, bat-like ears are constantly twitching as they zero in on the slightest rustle among the leaves. A tarsier does much of its hunting by hearing alone. During the death tussle with prey it usually closes its eyes to avoid any risk of damage.

Tarsiers are highly unusual among primates in that they subsist almost entirely upon animal protein. Their diet comprises mostly large invertebrates, such as crickets and moths, which they grip with their front toes and dispatch with bites to the head. They may also take small vertebrates, including lizards, birds, bats and even poisonous snakes.

Fast learners

A pair of tarsiers is monogamous and gives birth to a single baby after a six-month gestation. This baby weighs 20–30g, which may sound small but, being about one-quarter of its mother's weight, makes it proportionally the biggest newborn infant of any mammal. It emerges fully furred, open-eyed and ready to go – able to hunt for itself after just 42 days.

Tarsiers form close-knit family units of mother, father and offspring. Females are responsible for most childcare, while males perform territorial duties, marking out their home range of 1–2ha using urine or secretions from a scent gland. Adults forage alone, setting out at dusk, but keep in contact using piercing, high-pitched calls that can carry for 100m. A courting male and female utter softer calls during their breathless chases through the canopy.

Out of order?

Tarsiers have long confused taxonomists. For years they were classified as 'prosimians', along with the similar-looking bushbabies, lemurs and other more primitive primates. Recent studies, however – notably of their teeth and eyes – suggest that tarsiers are descended from a separate, older line and are actually more closely related to today's 'anthropoid' primates, the monkeys and apes.

Today the western tarsier, which inhabits the tropical forests of Borneo and Sumatra, is one of at least four species. It is not considered endangered, though widespread logging and commercial pesticides continue to eat away at its habitat. The other species are found on the nearby islands of Sulawesi and the Philippines, but studies of tarsier calls now suggest there may well be more species – and indeed more genera – than scientists previously recognised.

At a glance

Size: head and body length 10–15cm; hind legs 20–25cm; tail 20–25cm
Weight: 80–160g
Food: large insects and other invertebrates; occasionally small vertebrates, including lizards, birds, bats and snakes
Reproduction: 1 young, born in February–March after 6-month gestation
Habitat: primary and secondary rainforest up to 900m; also dense bamboo, plantations and large gardens
Distribution: southern Sumatra (Indonesia); Borneo (including Kalimantan, Sarawak and Sabah)
Status: Least Concern

2. Bald uakari

Cacajao calvus

Bald is beautiful – or so the follically challenged (this author, for one) would have us believe. If so, then the shocking red pate of this South American monkey makes it one of the pin-ups of the animal world. Local people may not have had beauty in mind, however, when they nicknamed it *mono angles*, or 'English monkey', inspired by the first sunburnt natives of Blighty to visit their homeland.

Flushed with success

Whatever your idea of beauty, the flaming face of a uakari is certainly attractive to its own species. Indeed, good colour vision is one feature that distinguishes South American monkeys from their Old World cousins. Mature males are balder and redder of face than their juniors, with their deep-set eyes and prominent skull creating an intense expression. The colour fades in individuals out of condition, suggesting that baldness and redness are indicative of health and breeding prowess.

Tear your gaze from its bonce and you'll see this is a medium-sized, long-limbed monkey with a coarse, shaggy coat. The body colour varies across four different subspecies, from a rich orange-chestnut in the red uakari (*C. c. rubinculus*) to a pale cream in the white uakari (*C. c. calvus*). The tail is unusually short for a South American monkey, just one-third of the body length, and is not prehensile.

Above the flood

Uakaris live in flooded forest, where they move along lofty arboreal walkways. They favour trees 20–25m in height, which is where they find the seeds and fruit that form the bulk of their diet – often foraging in the outermost branches then carrying back their booty to a less precarious position in order to eat it. During the dry season they may supplement their diet with nectar and invertebrates – especially caterpillars.

These monkeys are very agile, despite their lack of a prehensile tail, and will often suspend themselves by a single limb while feeding. They sometimes descend to forage on the ground – males especially – but are quick to return to the trees at the first hint of danger.

Social skills

Uakari troops generally number 15–30 individuals and occasionally up to 100 or more. While foraging they may extend this sociability to include other species, including woolly monkey (*Lagothrix* spp), squirrel monkey (*Saimiri* spp) and white-fronted capuchin (*Cebus albifrons*): the more eyes the better when the formidable harpy eagle is cruising the canopy for victims.

Like most monkeys, uakaris have an eloquent lexicon of facial expressions, and often flaunt the bald scalp as an intimidation display. Pair bonds are reinforced with mutual grooming, though being both a polygamous and promiscuous species these bonds are hardly binding. A female gives birth to a single infant once every two years after a six-month gestation.

Uakaris are highly endangered, restricted to a small area of Amazonian rainforest in western Brazil and neighbouring Peru. Their habitat is shrinking daily under the onslaught of logging and in some regions they are also hunted – although in certain areas of Brazil their human-like physiognomy has made eating them taboo.

At a glance

Size: head and body length 36–37cm; tail 15cm
Weight: 2–3kg
Food: seeds and fruits; also flowers and occasionally insects
Reproduction: 1 young, born after 6-month gestation
Habitat: tropical evergreen swamp forest
Distribution: Amazon Basin, in western Brazil, Peru and Columbia
Status: Vulnerable

3. Madagascar sucker-footed bats

Myzopoda spp

Catching a kip while upright does not generally cause a stir. After all, everything from giraffe to Grenadier Guard seems to have perfected the art. But in the upside-down world of bats it is a positively outrageous stunt – and two species in Madagascar have evolved a unique means of pulling it off. The clue is in the name.

Hanging on

The suckers in question are tiny horseshoe-shaped pads located on the bats' wrists and ankles. Onto these the bat secretes an adhesive liquid from special glands, creating a bond strong enough to suspend its entire body from a smooth vertical surface – specifically that of the palm leaves in which it roosts.

Were it not for these bizarre appendages, sucker-footed bats would resemble many other small insectivorous bats, with their wrinkled face, dense brown fur and large rounded ears. They feed primarily on small moths, which they capture at night by echolocation, using those big ears to pick up the returning signals from their unusually long calls. Their long wings allow a particularly agile flight in order to pursue this elusive diet, and their tail, which is longer than that of most bats, protrudes from the flight membrane to help support the bat in its upright roost.

Seeing double

Old World sucker-footed bats are confined to the island of Madagascar and are unrelated to the *Thyroptera* sucker-footed bats of South America, which probably evolved their sucker feet independently. For years scientists knew of only one species, *Myzopoda aurita*, which inhabits the rainforest of the east coast. But there was great excitement in 2007 when a second, *M. schliemanni*, was discovered in the dry deciduous forest of the west coast. The new species was distinguished by the structure of its skull and the greyish tinge to its fur.

This was a significant discovery, and not only because Madagascar had turned up yet another new mammal. It suggested that this genus of bats, once thought to be close to extinction, might be doing rather better than had been feared. And there are further grounds for optimism in the bats' choice of roost. Both species favour the long leaves of the traveller's palm (*Ravanela madagascariensis*), which thrives in degraded areas. This suggests that sucker-footed bats might be well placed to survive the rampant deforestation that has devastated so much of the island's other wildlife.

Nonetheless, there is no room for complacency. Scientists are currently undertaking new research into the distribution of both sucker-footed bat species, using radio-tracking to determine their movements and assess their populations.

At a glance

Size: head and body length 57mm; tail 48mm; forearm 46–50mm
Food: small moths, caught on the wing
Reproduction: little known
Habitat: rainforest (*M. aurita*); dry deciduous forest (*M. schliemanni*)
Distribution: Madagascar: east coast (*Myzopoda aurita*); west coast (*M. schliemanni*)
Status: Least Concern

4. Malayan colugo (flying lemur)
Cynocephalus variegatus

Never trust a nickname. This bizarre animal is not a lemur and neither can it fly. Nonetheless, its gliding prowess is unequalled among airborne mammals, allowing it to cover astonishing distances from one tree to the next.

Nature's hang-glider

The nocturnal colugo is the size of a cat, with a dog-like muzzle and tiny ears. Large, forward-facing eyes give it the good night vision and depth perception it needs to leap around the canopy at night. Meanwhile its mottled grey-brown, white-spotted fur provides perfect camouflage when lying up by day among the lichen-covered tree trunks of its rainforest home.

Most striking, however, is its patagium – or gliding membrane. This loose fold of skin stretches from throat to tail, swathing the colugo's body like a cloak while at rest but extending like a kite when it takes off on one of its breathtaking glides. It is more complete than that of other gliding mammals, reaching to the tips of all four feet and tail, and even covering the gaps between the toes.

On the ground the colugo would be pretty much helpless. But this is immaterial as this animal lives entirely in trees. By day it roosts, using its sharp claws to cling to a trunk or hang, hammock-like, beneath a branch. At dusk it sets out in search of the flowers, fruit and sap on which it feeds. It hops rather clumsily up a tree, hugging the trunk with its forelegs, then launches itself onto the forest breeze. It can glide a staggering 70m or more to the next tree, hardly losing any height in the process.

Colugo confusion

Scientists remain uncertain about exactly where the colugo belongs in the great filing cabinet of mammalian taxonomy. The latest DNA evidence, however, suggests it is descended from the same line as the Anthropoidea – today's monkeys and apes – and that it may well be among their closest living relatives.

Whatever its lineage, this animal is certainly an anomaly. Among other unusual features are its peculiar dentition and the highly undeveloped state of the newborn youngster – a feature it shares with marsupials. A baby colugo arrives after a gestation of just 60 days and weighs just 35g at birth. The female carries it under her body for up to six months – even while gliding – using her patagium as a papoose. She is able to conceive again while still nursing.

The Malayan colugo is widespread across Malaysia, Thailand, Borneo and much of Indonesia. Populations are currently thought to be secure, though, as for many rainforest species, deforestation is always a threat. Scientists recognise three other species, one of which – the Philippine colugo – is confined to the Philippines. Here it makes up 90% of the diet of the critically endangered Philippine eagle, which suggests that colugos may be more diurnal in habit than was once thought.

At a glance

Size: head and body length 32–42cm; tail 22–27cm; 'wingspan' 70cm
Weight: 1–1.75kg
Food: leaves, flowers, fruit and sap
Reproduction: single offspring, born after 60 days; 35g at birth
Habitat: primary and secondary rainforest and plantations; exclusively arboreal
Distribution: Malaysia, Thailand and Borneo, as well as Java, Sumatra and other Indonesian islands
Status: Least Concern

5. Goodfellow's tree-kangaroo

Dendrolagus goodfellowi

'Tree-kangaroo' sounds oxymoronic – like 'cliff dolphin', perhaps, or 'pond camel'. But these strange marsupials do, indeed, belong to the same family as their better-known namesakes – the ones that stick to terra firma as they bounce around the Outback.

Pads, paws and claws

Tree-kangaroos resemble a cross between cat, kangaroo and koala. Their furry frame clearly reflects the basic kangaroo body plan, but they have shorter hind limbs than their terrestrial relatives, plus bigger, padded front paws and strong claws – all adaptations for climbing rather than bounding. The thick, muscular tail is also proportionally longer, providing balance in the treetops.

Goodfellow's tree-kangaroo is one of 12 species. It inhabits the rainforests of New Guinea and is distinguished from other species by its striking chestnut-and-gold coat, which is striped down the back and barred across the tail (hence the alternative name of 'ornate tree-kangaroo'). No two individuals have exactly the same pattern.

One giant leap

Like all its kind, this tree-kangaroo feeds high in the canopy. It climbs by wrapping its front limbs around a tree trunk and hopping upwards with its back legs. Coming down is trickier, but it will sometimes take a short cut by leaping to a lower branch. Indeed tree-kangaroos have been known to jump an astonishing 18m to the ground and land completely unharmed. Once down, they hop along rather ineptly, having to lean forward in order to balance their long tail.

The leaves of the silkwood (*Flindersia pimenteliana*) are the staple diet of this species, along with shoots, creepers, ferns and some fruit. Its teeth are adapted to tearing foliage, while its enlarged fore-stomach, fizzing with bacteria, acts as a fermentation chamber to break down all that cellulose.

Tiny tot

Goodfellow's tree-kangaroo, like all kangaroos, gives birth to a minuscule, almost embryonic offspring. This butter bean-sized baby emerges after a gestation of just 21–38 days. Its eyes, hind legs and tail are undeveloped, but its front legs are strong enough to haul itself up to the mother's pouch, where it latches onto one of her four teats. Here it stays for eight to ten months until it grows large enough to venture out. For the next year or so it will continue to poke its head inside for the occasional suckle, though by this time its mother may already be nursing a new tiny youngster on a different teat.

Mature Goodfellow's tree-kangaroos lead solitary lives, each male defending a territory that overlaps that of several females. They have few natural enemies, but – like many of their kind – they are seriously threatened by both uncontrolled hunting and habitat loss.

At a glance

Size: head and body length 58–78cm (male larger than female); tail 84.5cm
Weight: 7.5kg
Food: leaves (especially silkwood), flowers, fruit and sap
Reproduction: single offspring (just 5–15mm long)
Habitat: rainforest at 680–2,865m
Distribution: New Guinea
Status: Endangered

6. Brown-throated three-toed sloth

Bradypus variegatus

What's the rush? Speed, sloths teach us, is not always of the essence. Indeed, for these extraordinary creatures – clocking just 4m per minute flat out – it is not even an option. And yet, ecologically speaking, they are arguably the most successful large mammals in tropical America.

Suspended animation

The lugubrious, flattened face of a sloth bears an uncanny resemblance to ET, as it cranes outwards, rotating up to 220° on its extra neck vertebrae. But Spielberg's loveable extra-terrestrial would have struggled to phone home with a sloth's wicked 10cm-long claws. These are the grappling hooks by which it clambers around the treetops. So sure is its grip that a sloth has been found still hanging securely from its branch, stone dead.

The claws on the front legs distinguish three-toed sloths (*Bradypus* spp) from the slightly larger two-toed sloths (*Choloepus* spp). Both genera have three claws on the hind legs, however, suggesting that 'three-fingered' and 'two-fingered' would have made rather better names.

A three-toed sloth is the size of a large house cat, with a dense layer of short fur covered by a layer of longer, coarser hairs. This outer coat is – uniquely among mammals – green, due to the algae that grow in longitudinal grooves on each hair. Indeed, with moths, beetles and other mini-beasts infesting its coat, the sloth is an ecosystem all its own.

This animal is helpless on the ground, having to sink its front claws into the earth in order to haul its body ponderously forward. But it is a surprisingly good swimmer, and in flooded forest will sometimes drop into the water to reach the next tree.

nature is all about conserving what little energy they have. Studies have found that most individuals do not travel more than 48m in an average day, two-thirds of which they will spend sleeping. Also – and unusually among mammals – sloths can allow their body temperature to fall, so they need not burn energy to keep warm but can simply raise their temperature by sunbathing in the crown of a tree.

You might think this sluggish lifestyle would leave sloths lagging far behind in the race for survival. Yet in ecological terms they outpace the competition, making up over one-quarter of the mammal biomass in some parts of their range. This is partly because each individual inherits its diet from its mother, feeding on a very particular combination of plant species that it is unlikely to share with a neighbour. Thus several individuals can co-exist without competition – a factor that puts them at an advantage over other canopy herbivores, such as howler monkeys.

Hanging in there

Brown-throated three-toed sloths breed throughout the year. A single infant weighing just 300–400g is born after a six-month gestation and immediately clings beneath its mother's body. After one month it stops nursing and switches to a diet of leaves. However, it continues to hitch a ride for another six months or more. Once it finally strikes out alone it occupies a portion of its mother's home range that she has purposefully left vacant.

Adults are solitary. They communicate by wiping a glandular secretion onto branches and visiting one another's dung middens. However, they can also make a long, shrill whistle – described by local people as 'ai-ai' and sometimes likened to a woman's scream.

The brown-throated three-toed sloth occurs in tropical forest from Honduras to northern

Argentina, and does perfectly well in disturbed areas. It is the most common and widespread of four species, all of which occupy mutually exclusive ranges. The pale-throated three-toed sloth (*B. tridactylus*) is found in northeast South America and sports an orange patch on the back of the male. The endangered maned three-toed sloth (*B. torquatus*) is confined to the Bahia forests of coastal Brazil. The pygmy three-toed sloth (*B. pymaeus*), rarer still, is found only on the tiny island of Isla Escudo de Veraguas, off Panama.

Slow burn

Sloths are the ultimate plant-eaters of the mammal world. They use their simple peg-like teeth (just molars; no canines or incisors) to tear off leaves, which they then digest extremely slowly in their multi-compartmented and disproportionately large stomachs. Indeed, a sloth's stomach when full may account for one-third of its weight. Not surprisingly, defecation is a serious business and a sloth tends to perform the honours just once a week, usually descending to the foot of the tree.

Such a slow-release diet means that sloths have a very low metabolic rate: just 40–45% of what is normal for a mammal of their weight. Their torpid

At a glance

Size: head and body length 56–60cm; tail 6–7cm
Weight: 3.5–4.5kg
Food: diet is 99% leaves, comprising many different species
Reproduction: single offspring
Habitat: rainforest and montane forest; dry, deciduous and disturbed
Distribution: Honduras to northern Argentina
Status: Least Concern

7. Torrent duck
Merganetta armata

Nature, Aristotle once said, abhors a vacuum. Thus even the most apparently inhospitable environmental niche will have its tenant. This bizarre bird is a case in point: it has earned its name by its death-defying stunts among the raging rapids of the Andes, making it truly the white-water rafter of wildfowl.

Sink or swim
Torrent ducks are endemic to South America, where they inhabit fast-flowing mountain streams along the spine of the continent, from Venezuela to Chile. They range widely, from sea level (in the south) up to 4,500m, appearing wherever the water is white and conditions look, frankly, hazardous.

Even if they behaved a little more conventionally, however, these slim ducks would be distinctive. The males sport a boldly striped head and neck and a bright-red bill. The smaller females, by contrast, are neatly decked out in rich chestnut. Both sexes have a long and unusually stiff tail, which serves as a powerful rudder in the turbulent waters.

Torrent ducks make for a remarkable spectacle as they plunge headfirst into the maelstrom. Just as you fear they must have drowned or been dashed to pieces on the rocks, they bob up to the surface again, apparently unconcerned. They will even feed directly under the roaring cascade of a waterfall.

The reason for such derring-do is the ducks' diet, which comprises small aquatic invertebrates such as stonefly larvae that are themselves specially adapted to these conditions. With no natural competitors, they have this food all to themselves.

Taking the plunge
Torrent ducks are highly territorial and form long-term pair bonds, communicating through a shrill whistle (in the male) or a throaty 'queech' (the female). They nest close beside the water, usually in a hidden crevice or cave among the overhanging rocks, which they line with down. The clutch of three to four eggs takes 43–44 days to incubate – among the longest period of any duck.

It's when these eggs hatch that the duck's life of adventure sports really begins: the hatchlings often have no choice of exit other than a headlong jump from their precipitous nest, usually crashing down onto the rocks or spray many metres below. True to type they invariably pop up again with no ill effects.

Torrent ducks are not considered threatened. However, they are declining in many areas – especially towards the north of their range – due to the pollution and exploitation of the waterways. They also suffer competition for food from introduced trout. The global population is estimated at 20,000–35,000.

At a glance

Size: length 40–46cm
Weight: 440g (male); 330g (female)
Food: aquatic invertebrates, such as stonefly larvae, and occasionally fish
Reproduction: 3–4 eggs
Habitat: clear, fast-flowing, rocky mountain streams in paramo grasslands and humid montane forest
Distribution: the Andes, from Venezuela to Tierra del Fuego
Status: Least Concern

8. African jacana
Actophilornis africana

Walking on water is not as hard as you might imagine – as long as you have the right feet for the job. The African jacana has a pair of whoppers. It also has no time for gender stereotypes, with girls very much on top when it comes to allocating domestic chores.

Lily-trotter

This moorhen-sized bird is a common and conspicuous sight around the fringes of lakes and wetlands across sub-Saharan Africa. Its bold livery of chestnut, yellow, black and white, combined with its histrionic behaviour, make it unmistakable.

Even more striking, once you see them, are the extraordinarily long toes on which a jacana picks its way across floating vegetation. These outsized digits spread out to distribute its weight, allowing it to move with ease across the water's surface – hence its nickname of lily-trotter. Admittedly, it doesn't walk on the actual water, but at times it certainly appears to. Occasional sinking is not a problem: jacanas swim well, and may plunge below the surface to escape a predator.

Food comprises aquatic invertebrates such as insects, snails and tiny crabs. Jacanas forage over the water's surface and around the edge, picking through the vegetation. Often they will lift the edge of a lily to snap up any goodies underneath, with quick stabs of their sharp, bright-blue bill.

Girl power

The jacana's love life arguably causes more ripples than its toes. This species is a rare example of a polyandrous bird, ie: one in which a single female breeds with several males. In fact a female jacana assembles a harem of up to four consorts, and by breeding with each in turn produces multiple clutches – up to eight or nine in one season – with an average of four eggs per clutch. Such fecundity may be explained by the fact that numerous predators, from otters to monitor lizards, like nothing better than to snack upon jacana eggs. Thus a lost clutch can be replaced at short notice.

With the female busy attracting suitors and laying eggs, parental duties are down to the male. He incubates the clutch for 23–26 days, and then looks after the chicks for another 18 days after they hatch, sheltering them under his wings when necessary. The youngsters can find their own food within hours of hatching and can fly at 35–40 days.

This arrangement may sound cushy for the female jacana. But her life is one of constant stress and strife, fighting off rival females with designs on her harem and territory. Indeed jacanas are very aggressive birds, and their running battles across the water's surface and leg-trailing aerial pursuits are a noisy feature of many African wetlands. These battles can lead to injury and exhaustion.

The African jacana is one of eight different species in the family Jacanidae, with others found in tropical Asia and Latin America. Although these birds resemble rails or moorhens in their habits and appearance, they actually belong to the order Charadriiformes along with plovers and sandpipers.

At a glance

Size: length 28cm
Weight: 140–250g (female larger)
Food: aquatic invertebrates, including insects, snails and crustaceans
Reproduction: 3–4 eggs; multiple clutches
Habitat: low-lying swamps, lakes, lagoons and slow-flowing rivers, with plentiful floating and fringing vegetation
Distribution: sub-Saharan Africa, except for areas of rainforest or desert
Status: Least Concern

9. Hoatzin

Opisthocomus hoazin

Where to start with this bizarre bird? Some have suggested the Jurassic, as it bears an uncanny resemblance to *Archaeopteryx*, the ancestor of all feathered things. While taxonomists continue to argue the toss about the hoatzin's lineage, however, there's no disputing its weirdness: this bird has claws on its wings and, effectively, a stomach in its throat. What's more, it stinks.

Prehistoric pheasant?

The hoatzin certainly looks prehistoric. Its pheasant-sized body is chestnut-bronze above and buff below, with streaky markings down the neck, a spiky, fiery crest and blood-red, reptilian eyes set in a bare, bright-blue face. The short rounded wings are designed for brief bursts of frantic flapping – enough to get it across a river – and the long, black tail offers balance in the treetops.

Home for this bird is the swamp forests and waterways of tropical South America. It prefers quiet backwaters and oxbows with overgrown riverbanks, and is usually to be found in the lower and middle branches of overhanging vegetation.

Gut-wrenching

Hoatzins feed primarily on the leaves of marsh plants, such as arums, and will also take some fruits and flowers. They have evolved a digestive system unique among birds to cope with this cellulose-heavy diet. This is known as 'foregut fermentation'. In simple terms, the food ferments and breaks down in the bird's enlarged and modified crop, before passing to the stomach.

This technique has its drawbacks. First, the hoatzin has had to reduce some of its key flying gear – the pectoral muscles and sternum – in order to accommodate the enlarged crop, which explains why its aerial abilities are so limited. Second, all that fermentation stinks: the bird smells like manure.

Hoatzins feed by both day and night. They clamber awkwardly through the foliage, often betraying their presence with a wheezy call that has been likened to a heavy smoker's cough. A feathered lump at the base of their crop helps them balance on a branch when roosting. If disturbed, they may attempt to deter an assailant by raising their wings to reveal round, black eye markings.

Get-out claws

So what about the hoatzin's celebrated wing claws? Well, admittedly, you won't see them on adults. This extraordinary feature, again unique among birds, is confined to the nestlings, which hatch with two claws on each wing – one each on the first and second digits. It is vital to the youngsters' survival.

Hoatzins, you see, construct their flimsy stick nest in an exposed position overhanging the water – often clearly visible to predators, such as snakes or passing raptors. When danger appears suddenly the adults will flap away and abandon the chicks to their fate. The chicks, however, have an exit strategy: they simply drop from the nest into the water below, drift a little way downstream, then use their claws – along with their bill and feet – to haul themselves back out and return to the nest when the danger has passed.

An average brood for a pair of hoatzins is two chicks, the youngsters hatching from the creamy, speckled eggs after an incubation of 28–32 days.

Their wing claws are serviceable immediately, but disappear as they mature into adult plumage. Young hoatzins take three years to reach breeding maturity.

In the meantime they act as 'helpers' for their parents, babysitting the next brood of youngsters and feeding them a 'pea soup' of regurgitated, fermented leaves. Yum.

All alone

The taxonomy of the hoatzin has proved more contentious than that of almost any other living bird. Once grouped with the galliformes (game birds), subsequent theories have seen it allied with first cuckoos, then turacos and now doves. Neither DNA evidence nor the fossil record has been able to provide anything conclusive and, amid general confusion, many scientists are happy to leave the hoatzin as the sole member of its own sub-order: Opisthocomi.

Whatever this bird may or may not be, it is not currently threatened. Populations remain reasonably stable in most parts of its range – though, like all rest species, it is vulnerable to habitat loss.

Historically the hoatzin has suffered some exploitation for feathers and eggs, though its reputedly foul taste keeps it off most menus.

At a glance

Size: length 61–66cm
Weight: 816g
Food: leaves of aquatic and waterside plants, notably *Philidendron* spp; also fruit and flowers
Reproduction: 2 eggs (occasionally 3); incubation 28–32 days
Habitat: flooded forest, mangroves, rivers, backwaters and oxbows
Distribution: northern South America: Venezuela south to Bolivia, Peru and Amazonian Brazil
Status: Least Concern

10. Eurasian swift

Apus apus

This abundant bird cuts a familiar dash as it heralds summer in thrilling rooftop flypasts across Europe. So familiar, you might think, that it hardly warrants a place in a book of the bizarre. Yet there is more to this high-altitude daredevil than meets the eye.

Magnificent flying machine

The swift is a master flyer. Everything about that rakish silhouette – the long, sickle wings and cigar-shaped fuselage of a body – screams aerodynamics. And there seems to be no extra clutter, such as legs, to spoil the streamlining. Indeed its family name, Apodidae, means 'without feet', and although swifts do have tiny, vestigial legs, these are incapable of locomotion, their needle-clawed toes being merely hooks to grip the vertical surfaces on which the birds briefly alight.

But for swifts the sky is more than just a convenient means of getting from A to B. So completely is this bird adapted to an aerial existence that it both feeds and mates on the wing. It even sleeps there, power-napping on autopilot in

a zone of cool air high above the ground. Indeed, were it not for the tiresome necessity of breeding, a swift would no more need to leave the air than would a fish the water.

Feeding on the wing is made easier by a cavernous gape that allows swifts to scoop up tiny airborne insects and spiders from the aerial plankton that drifts through our summer skies. One bird may capture over 10,000 of these prey items a day, sometimes storing them in 'food balls', which it takes back to the nest to feed its young. This diet, however, fluctuates with the weather, so swifts must often fly great distances to find suitable feeding conditions. And in winter they have to migrate from Europe to the sunnier, insect-rich climes of sub-Saharan Africa. Thus a swift that lives to 20 years will have flown nearly six million kilometres in its lifetime; the equivalent of seven return journeys to the moon.

Born to fly

Eurasian swifts nest mostly in the roof cavities of old buildings, such as church towers. Out of town they may also use cliffs, quarries or natural tree holes. A pair builds together, using materials such as straw and feathers that they gather on the wing and cement in place with saliva. They also rotate

incubation duties for the two to three eggs. The young usually fledge after about 36 days. But in lean times they may exhibit another of this bird's remarkable traits by going into a state of torpor – their vital processes slowing down, as in hibernation – thus extending the fledging process to 50 days or even longer.

It is once the youngsters leave the nest, however, that the most mind-boggling chapter of their story gets under way. Within days these fledglings are heading off alone to Africa. Given that it takes swifts four years to reach breeding maturity, this means that most will not touch down at all – not so much as a two-minute breather – from the moment they leave their natal nest to the first time they build a new one of their own. In other words they spend a staggering four continuous years on the wing. How's that for air miles?

At a glance

Size: body length 16–17cm; wingspan 36–38cm
Weight: 40–50g
Food: small flying insects and aerial spiders
Reproduction: 2–3 eggs; incubation 18–19 days
Habitat: flies over all habitats; nests mostly in old buildings in towns
Distribution: summers across Europe and central Asia, except high Arctic and deserts; winters in sub-Saharan Africa, ranging widely in search of food
Status: Least Concern

11. Oilbird

Steatornis caripensis

Trinidadians call the oilbird *Diablotin*, or 'little devil'. This may seem rather harsh for such an inoffensive vegetarian. Yet so unusual is the behaviour of this night bird that a little superstition is hardly surprising.

Extra sensory perception

The oilbird's large eyes, long tail and white-spotted, brown plumage resemble those of a nightjar, and indeed it has long been lumped alongside nightjars in the order Caprimulgiformes. But it differs in its larger size, its distinctive hooked bill and – most significantly – some very peculiar habits. In fact it is the sole member of its own family: the Steatornithidae.

Oilbirds roost in caves by day and feed in the forest by night. In other words they are more or less always in the dark. They have risen to this challenge with some remarkable adaptations. Those big eyes, for a start, are the most light-sensitive of any bird, with millions of tiny rods (the photo-receptor cells) packed together in a tier arrangement similar to that of some deep-sea fish.

And then there's echolocation. Like bats, oilbirds can navigate around the murky gloom of their roosting caves by emitting a continuous stream of high-pitched noise that bounces back from the walls – though unlike in bats, these noises are audible to us. The only other birds that can do this are the cave-dwelling swiftlets of southeast Asia.

The oilbird's diet of fruit is unique among nocturnal birds, and its keen sense of smell – again, very unusual in birds – helps sniff out the ripe figs and palm nuts on which it feeds. It plucks this food in flight, using its long wings to hover around the tree canopy and fine feathers around the bill, known as rictal bristles, as whisker-like feelers. Some individuals may forage for more than 100km in one night, and oilbird droppings play an important role in the dispersal of certain plants.

Baby oil

Oilbirds are monogamous and breed together in large colonies, each pair laying two to four eggs in a nest of droppings on a rock ledge. Adults feed their nestlings on fruit pulp. This protein-poor diet is very unusual for young birds, but baby oilbirds digest their food so slowly that they can eke out every last nutrient, including 80% of the lipids (fats). In fact they grow huge: up to half as large again as their parents. It is this fat-storing ability of the youngsters that has given the oilbird its name. Indians once knocked them from their nests, then boiled down the bodies to render their fat, which they used as oil for torches.

Oilbirds are no longer harvested, although disturbance to their breeding caves has caused a decline in some regions. Trinidad is the only Caribbean island on which they breed, but they also occur across much of northern South America, from Colombia to Bolivia. The Guacharo (oilbird) Cave in Venezuela, where German explorer Von Humboldt first studied this bird in 1799, was the country's first national monument.

At a glance

Size: body length 41–48cm; wingspan 91cm
Weight: 415g (adult); up to 650g (juvenile)
Food: fruit, such as figs and palm nuts
(36 food species identified in Trinidad)
Reproduction: 2–4 eggs; incubation 1 month
Habitat: woodland forest with suitable large caves for roosting and breeding
Distribution: northern South America, including Colombia, Venezuela, Peru, Bolivia, Ecuador and Guyana; also Trinidad
Status: Least Concern

12. Greater roadrunner

Geococcyx californianus

A 'beep beep!' alarm call may be a fanciful notion, but in other respects Warner Brothers were spot on: this comical, ground-dwelling cuckoo is the Usain Bolt of flying birds, dashing across the desert floor at speeds of up to 30km/h. Flying, in fact, is a last resort, as those stubby wings are good for only a few airborne seconds at a time.

Desert rooster

The greater roadrunner is the larger of two similar species and looks more like a long-tailed chicken than your average cuckoo. Its streaky dark-and-cream plumage is set off by a jaunty, cocked tail and perky crest. It has a big bill, stout legs and – like all cuckoos – zygodactyl toes, ie: two facing forward and two back.

Roadrunners live in the desert scrublands of the southern United States and northern Mexico, hence their local nickname of 'chaparral cock'. They are well adapted to the arid conditions, able to reabsorb water from their faeces before excreting it and also to use special glands in front of their eyes – like those of many ocean-going birds – to eliminate salt from their water intake.

Deserts can also be freezing. Thus roadrunners sunbathe on the morning after a cold night, fluffing out their back feathers to expose the black skin underneath and absorb more solar energy.

Snakes alive

Roadrunners capture their prey in lightning dashes, running with head and tail stretched out parallel to the ground. Their victims range from large invertebrates, such as scorpions, to rodents, small birds and reptiles.

At a glance

Size: length 52–60cm; wingspan ±50cm
Weight: 220–340g
Food: large invertebrates; small vertebrates, including rodents, birds and reptiles
Reproduction: 2–8 eggs
Habitat: desert and 'chaparral' scrub
Distribution: southern USA (including California, Arizona, New Mexico and Texas); northern Mexico
Status: not currently threatened

They will happily tackle a venomous snake – even a rattlesnake – seizing it by the tail and whip-cracking its head against the ground; two birds may team up to deal with a big one.

The fleetness is not just of foot: these opportunist hunters have reflexes fast enough to pluck a dragonfly or hummingbird from the air. There is even a record of a roadrunner leaping up from its hiding place to snatch a low-flying swift. Food goes down whole – and usually headfirst. One end of a large meal may sometimes be left dangling from the bird's bill for a while, slipping down gradually as the rest is digested inside.

Speed also helps roadrunners to escape – not only from Wile E Coyote, but from a range of predators that includes skunks, house cats, raccoons and birds of prey. A clattering of the bill sounds the alarm when danger is close. But these birds are incorrigibly curious and will approach humans without fear.

Two's company
Greater roadrunners mate for life. In spring a male performs a flamboyant courtship display, wagging his wings and dangling a food offering to tempt his partner close. He calls with a series of descending coos (not beep beep!), and makes a low whirring sound at the height of the excitement.

Roadrunners are not habitual brood parasites, like some cuckoos, although they have been known to lay their eggs in the nest of both common raven and northern mockingbird. Generally they build a saucer-shaped, stick nest of their own low down in a bush or cactus. The male gathers most of the materials, while the female does the bulk of the construction work.

The clutch of two to eight pale eggs is laid over three days. Hatching is staggered, which means that later arrivals cannot usually compete with their older siblings; casualties may even be eaten by the parents. The youngsters fledge after about 18 days, but will hang around for another two weeks or so, cadging food.

In areas with a single, spring rainy season, such as the Sonoran and Mojave deserts of California, roadrunners breed just once. But in the Arizona Sonoran Desert, where rains also fall in summer, they may raise a second brood in September.

Road safety
The greater roadrunner is not uncommon. Ironically, though, its greatest threat may come from roads – not just traffic, which claims its fair share of victims, but also the proliferation of new highways in prime habitat, which fragments populations. This latter problem already looks set to drive the species from southern coastal California.

A more natural threat comes in the form of hard winters. Roadrunners do not migrate, so a serious ice-over in the desert can prove more deadly than any pesky coyote.

13. Green basilisk
Basiliscus plumifrons

No prizes for guessing how this creature acquired its local name of *largato de Jesus Christo*. Yes, it's another walker on water. But unlike jacanas (see page 21), it dispenses with waterweed support and goes the whole hog.

Stone face

The name basilisk comes from the creature of Greek mythology – part lion, part snake and part rooster – whose stare could reputedly turn victims to stone. Thankfully this medium-sized lizard, a member of the iguana family, has not yet mastered that particular trick. Nonetheless its bright-green, extravagantly crested appearance does have something of the mythical dragon about it.

The male is more showy than the female, sporting a double crest on the head (hence the alternative name of plumed basilisk), plus a spiky fin down the spine and tail that it can raise and flaunt in courtship. All this ornamentation, however, may well escape your attention when the lizard drops from an overhanging branch to perform its eye-popping party trick

before your very eyes – scampering away at breakneck speed across the water's surface.

The secret is all in the hind feet. A basilisk's outer toes are fringed with scales that flare out like webbing when its foot hits the water then fold up when it withdraws. Thus each foot slaps down large, preserving the surface tension of the water, but withdraws small, creating an air pocket that allows it to escape without adhesion. For a high-speed burst of 4–5m – running at roughly 20 steps a second and with its whip-like tail extended as a counter-balance – the basilisk can resist gravity and keep going across the surface. As gravity comes into effect it sinks beneath the water – or reaches the bank. But by this time it will have made good its escape. Basilisks are accomplished swimmers and, if necessary, can remain under water for 30 minutes.

Branch line

Green basilisks live in tropical forests alongside watercourses. The water itself is not their habitat but more a means of dodging trouble or getting from A to B. Most of their time is spent in overhanging branches, where they feed on everything from fruits and other plant matter, to large insects and small vertebrates. Like many lizards, they can store fat in their tail for harder times.

A female lays up to 20 eggs in a shallow trench that she digs in moist soil. Having covered them up she has nothing

more to do with them. The youngsters emerge after eight to ten weeks, immediately ready to climb, swim and – yes – run across the water. In fact, being lighter than adults they can run even further. However, they tend to avoid predators by lying doggo, their excellent camouflage making them very hard to spot among the overhanging riverine vegetation.

The green basilisk is one of four species in the genus *Basiliscus*, all of which are confined to Central and northern South America. It is widespread and abundant in the wild, with many natural predators – from snakes to birds of prey.

At a glance

Size: length 60–80cm (female smaller)
Weight: 200g
Food: omnivorous, from fruit to insects, worms and other small reptiles
Reproduction: up to 20 eggs buried in a shallow trench; 3–4 clutches per year
Habitat: tropical rainforest along waterways
Distribution: Central America, from southern Mexico to Panama; introduced to Florida
Status: Least Concern

14. Shovel-snouted lizard

Meroles anchietae

This is another reptile that has evolved fancy footwork as a survival strategy. Its dance floor is the scorching sand dunes of the Namib Desert. And in its 'strictly come thermo-dancing' routine, style wins more points than speed.

The heat is on

Shovel-snouted lizards are found only in the sand dunes of the Namib. They are unremarkable at first glance: small, slim and mottled sandy in colour, with a pearly sheen to their head. The snout is indeed shovel-shaped – flattened, with a sharp, cutting edge – and enables the lizard to dig rapidly beneath the surface of the sand. This is a useful trick when surface temperatures can exceed 50°C.

Like all reptiles, this lizard absorbs heat from its surroundings. It sleeps at night beneath the sand then emerges during the day when the sun has warmed the surface. On cool days it may stay above ground for most of the day, while on hot days – especially when dry winds are blowing – it often prefers to remain buried.

Desert tango

Hiding below the sand is all very well, but this lizard has to eat. And as its food consists of insects and windblown seeds, it must from time to time brave the blistering dune surface in order to grab a bite. When the going gets too hot there are various ways to escape: it can corkscrew head-first down into the cooler sand below or race up to the crest of a dune to catch the breeze. Or it can dance.

The 'thermoregulatory dance' of the shovel-snouted lizard is a comical business. It lifts its body from the sand on stiff legs, as though stilt walking, then raises its diagonally opposite front and hind legs into the air – alternating in pairs – while holding its tail aloft. In this way no part of the body remains in contact with the surface for too long. The routine may look bizarre, but it's life and death to an overheating lizard.

Other ways in which this remarkable reptile has adapted to desert survival include the ability to break down accumulated fats into water. And like many Namib species, it can also derive life-giving moisture from the ocean fog.

Male shovel-snouted lizards defend a territory with four or five females. They have no particular breeding season, though tend to be most productive between December and March. A female lays a single egg three or four times a year – sometimes, after good rains, producing a clutch of two.

She chooses a sheltered site in the eddy of a dune slip-face where she digs her egg chamber in a patch of firm sand. Hatchlings reach breeding maturity within four to six months.

At a glance

Size: length 10–11cm
Weight: 4–5g
Food: insects and windblown plant matter, such as grass seeds
Reproduction: female lays 1 egg, occasionally 2, 3–4 times a year
Habitat: desert sand dunes
Distribution: Namib Desert, from Namibia to southern Angola
Status: Least Concern

15. Paradise tree snake

Chrysopelea paradisi

A flying snake? Surely such lurid nonsense belongs in nightmares and Hollywood B-movies. But it's true – this astonishing reptile can launch itself more than 100m through the air from tree to tree. Strictly speaking it's not flying but gliding. But whatever you call it, it's pretty impressive.

Lift-off

A glimpse of this reptile disappearing into the tree canopy gives no hint of its hidden talent. There are no wings or other flying gear in evidence. It is simply a small, slim snake, decked out in black and green, with an ornate floral pattern printed in red or yellow along its spine.

In fact you are unlikely to get much more than a glimpse, as this is a highly arboreal snake and its intricate patterning makes for excellent camouflage. But follow one up into the branches and you might just witness its party trick at first hand. Because, when pressed by predators, this snake takes to the air.

This physics behind this feat baffled scientists for years. The secret lies in the snake's broad belly scales, which are flexible at their centre. When gliding, the snake sucks in its long belly to make an inverted 'C' shape, with the stiffened outer edges of these scales forming a long flap down either side.

This effectively turns its body into a flattened concave strip, with the extra surface area providing enough air resistance to float out on the breeze.

A snake about to launch will dangle from a high branch in a 'J' shape then push itself off with a muscular thrust from the coils at the rear. Once airborne it undulates in S-bends, as though swimming, and can direct itself in any direction. The trajectory is always gently downwards – the snake cannot gain height – and landing is a pretty clumsy business. Nonetheless it is technically a more accomplished glider than any gliding mammal, such as a flying squirrel. The smaller the snake, the further it can travel.

Mild-mannered

The paradise tree snake preys on small vertebrates, especially arboreal lizards, which it captures with a venomous bite to the neck using short fangs at the back of the mouth. This venom is too mild to pose any threat to humans. Females lay 15–20 eggs, and the hatchlings are miniature, more brightly marked versions of the adults, able to glide from the moment they leave the egg.

This species is one of five that make up the *Chrysopelea* genus, also known as flying snakes, which is endemic to southeast Asia. The genus, in turn, belongs to the large Colubridae family, or 'typical snakes'. A misnomer perhaps: this remarkable reptile may be many things, but 'typical' it is not.

At a glance

Size: length up to 120cm
Food: small vertebrates, especially arboreal lizards
Reproduction: 15–20 eggs
Habitat: tropical forest, mangroves, gardens and plantations
Distribution: southeast Asia, including Burma, Thailand, Malaysia, Indonesia and the Philippines
Status: Least Concern

16. Wallace's flying frog

Rhacophorus nigropalmatus

At a glance

Size: length up to
8–10cm
Food: insects
and other
invertebrates, especially arboreal lizards
Reproduction: makes 'bubble nest' of foam,
from which tadpoles drop into pool below
Habitat: tropical and subtropical lowland
forest, including old secondary forest,
up to 600m
Distribution: Malay peninsula, Borneo and
Sumatra (Indonesia)
Status: Least Concern

This frog gets the first part of its name from the Victorian naturalist Alfred Russel Wallace, whose expeditions into southeast Asia in the 1850s were a decisive influence on Darwin's *Origin of Species*. There can be few more bizarre examples of where evolution can lead – as indicated in the second part of its name.

Check canopy

There must be something about the rainforests of southeast Asia that persuades normally land-bound creatures to take to the air. This shiny, bright-green frog, which lives high in the tree canopy, is not content with hopping around like your average amphibian. Instead it makes prodigious flying leaps from tree to tree.

Wings come in the form of huge webbed feet, which the frog effectively uses as parachutes. These feet are webbed right to the tips, with bold black and yellow markings that serve to increase their visual impact when unfurled. If threatened by a predator – or simply when getting from branch A to tree trunk B – it kicks out into space using its powerful back legs, and spreads the webbing between its toes to turn itself into a four-legged kite. A membrane of skin between the front and back limbs helps increase the surface area and thus the air resistance.

With a good leap, and a prevailing wind, the frog can cover over 15m in one glide. As it approaches touchdown it flattens its trajectory for a smoother impact. 'Sucker pads' on the tips of its toes allow a secure grip upon the branch.

Grounded

Despite its daredevil high life in the treetops and the air, Wallace's flying frog must come to the ground to breed. A female produces a sticky fluid that she whips into a foam and attaches to vegetation overhanging a pool on the forest floor. Inside this 'bubble nest' she lays her eggs, which the male then fertilises with his sperm. When the embryos develop into tadpoles, the nest falls apart and they drop into the pool below. Here they mature, until they are ready to make the ascent into the canopy.

Wallace's tree frog is not the only frog species capable of gliding in this way, but it is one of the largest and most impressive. Like most frogs, it feeds primarily on insects and other small invertebrates. It is abundant within its range and not considered threatened – though it is fond of breeding in wallows left by the Sumatran rhino, so the steep decline of this endangered mammal may have reduced its breeding options.

17. Barred mudskipper

Periophthalmus argentilineatus

A fish that walks? Sounds no more likely than a pig that flies. Yet this extraordinary, boggle-eyed little creature does just that. Sometimes it even flings itself into the air, as though with the sheer exhilaration of being on terra firma.

Amphibian ambitions

The barred mudskipper, identified by the vertical silvery stripes on its flanks, is the best known and most widespread of 39 mudskipper species. All belong to the subfamily Oxudercinae, part of the large Gobiidae family of fish. In terms of lifestyle, however, these bizarre creatures seem more amphibian than fish. They inhabit the intertidal zone among mangroves on tropical shores, but instead of retreating with the tide, as other fish do, they hop out onto the mud, where they use their modified pectoral fins as legs to get around. Indeed they spend up to three-quarters of their time out of the water, often perching on mangrove roots to scan their surroundings.

The secret is in the breathing. Mudskippers, like true amphibians, practise 'cutaneous breathing', which means they can absorb oxygen through their skin, and through the lining of the mouth (mucosa) and throat (pharynx) – as long as they keep themselves moist. Like all fish, they have gills located behind the head, but while on land they seal these to keep the water in, which provides a permanent, portable oxygen supply – rather like an aqualung.

The boggle eyes perched on top of a mudskipper's head allow a panoramic view of its terrain, either when semi-submerged or out and about. Each eye

moves independently of the other. With no tear ducts for lubrication, they must constantly roll back into the head to keep moist. This applies pressure to the gill chambers and thus helps reoxygenate the water stored there.

Battles and burrows

The territorial disputes of barred mudskippers make for an entertaining spectacle. A male performs acrobatic antics at the mouth of his burrow – flapping, posturing, erecting his showy dorsal fins and even somersaulting into the air – in order to repel rivals. With luck this display will also attract a female.

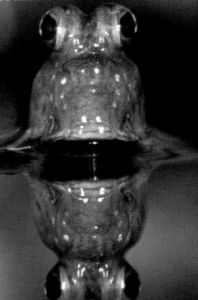

The breeding pair then enters the burrow together. The female lays her eggs in the egg chamber – a side-branch dug by the male off the main burrow – and promptly leaves. He then fertilises the eggs and settles down for the long vigil of the single parent. Other fish spawn could not survive the suffocating conditions beneath the mud but the

At a glance

Size: up to 9cm
Food: crustaceans, fish eggs and other small marine creatures
Reproduction: lays eggs in burrow beneath the mud; male responsible for all parental care
Habitat: mudflats and tidal creeks of mangroves on tropical coastlines
Distribution: east coast of Africa to southern Japan, Australasia and Oceania
Status: Least Concern

male mudskipper takes down a mouthful of air to sustain his brood. He stands guard over the burrow until hatching time approaches. Then, on a rising night tide, he swims down to remove the air bubble. The burrow floods, the eggs hatch and the tiny fry swim free.

This strange story doesn't end there. Mudskipper larvae, rather like those of flatfish, must undergo a profound metamorphosis on the way to adulthood. They hatch as normal-looking, free-swimming fish. It is not until 30 days later that their body mutates into its unique amphibious form.

18. Blobfish

Psychrolutes marcidus

The name sounds like something from a children's cartoon, but then that's exactly what this bizarre fish looks like. Hardly a pin-up – in fact, little more than a shapeless mass of jelly with a mouth at one end – its locomotion requirements are less about how to get around than how to stay in one place.

Under pressure

Blobfish inhabit the seas around Australia and Tasmania. But few people ever see one other than as an unfortunate casualty in the nets of a deep-sea trawler. This is because they live deep on the seabed, far out of sight.

At depths of 800m or more the pressure is 80 times greater than at the surface. This far down, the gas-filled swim bladder that provides buoyancy for most fish is useless, as the gas

At a glance

Size: up to 30cm
Food: scavenges food floating above the seabed
Habitat: seabed, at depths of 600–1,200m
Distribution: endemic to Australia, from Broken Bay, NSW, to southern Australia and Tasmania
Status: vulnerable to deep water trawling

becomes too compressed. So the blobfish has dispensed with this feature. Instead its body consists of gelatinous flesh that is less dense than the water itself. It has little muscle structure to speak of so wastes no energy in muscular movement but simply hovers above the sea floor, where it swallows food items that float past.

The blobfish belongs to the flatheads family (Psychrolutidae), which, in turn, is part of the Scorpaeniformes order of scorpionfish and flatheads.

19. Cartwheeling spider

Carparachne aureoflava

Here's yet another weirdo from the Namib Desert: the only animal on the planet to turn itself into a wheel and roll downhill. Indeed, it's quite possible that this spider was first to discover the advantages of the wheel and we humans have merely been reinventing it ever since.

Wasp attack

The cartwheeling spider belongs to the large Sparassidae group of huntsman spiders. It lies in wait for its prey in a long, silk-lined burrow that it digs 40–50cm into the face of a sand dune.

But hunter becomes hunted when a Pompilid wasp arrives on the scene. This ruthless predator paralyses spiders with its sting and lays its egg inside their body – a hideous fate indeed, as the wasp larva hatches within the still-living spider and consumes it from the inside out.

Cartwheeling spiders are at their most vulnerable when their burrow collapses and they come to the surface to build another. A roving wasp that spots the new excavation will buzz over and follow the spider in. It is able to shift a staggering ten litres of sand – 80,000 times its own weight – in pursuit of its victim.

Thus the exposed spider is highly vulnerable. If it runs the speedy wasp will quickly overhaul it. So it rolls up its legs and tilts its body on its side to form a wheel shape, then simply trundles off down the dune slope. It can cover a considerable distance in this way, whizzing along at an amazing 20 rotations per second. Fast enough, with luck, to throw the wasp off the scent.

At a glance

Size: 18–24mm
Food: insects
Habitat: desert sand dunes
Distribution: endemic to the Namib Desert, Namibia
Status: Least Concern

2 GRABBING A BITE

Animals cannot simply manufacture their own food, as plants do, but must go out and find it. Happily, there is scarcely a millimetre of our planet that does not offer nourishment to one creature or another. But getting hold of it can sometimes be tricky. This is where evolution has gone to town, producing countless innovative – and often extraordinary – ways in which animals can catch a bite.

▲ *This African rock python will swallow its crocodile victim headfirst and whole.*

Tooled up

First, of course, every animal in search of a meal needs the right tools for the job. Natural selection has fashioned a veritable DIY store of jaws, teeth, mandibles and other mouthparts. Take the bird's bill. This lightweight keratinous appendage probably first evolved to help birds get airborne, being proportionally much lighter than teeth and jawbones. But on this one simple template, nature has since fashioned a cornucopia of variations to exploit every ecological niche, from the colossal fish-scoop of the shoebill (page 47) to the outsized blade of the black skimmer (page 50).

Other implements help reach, pluck, crush, grab or kill. Thus the pickaxe claws of an aardvark (page 41) can hack into a rock-hard termite mound, while the uniquely attenuated middle finger of an aye-aye (page 45) can winkle out grubs from crevices. And nimble digits are superfluous when your tongue, like that of a giant anteater (page 38), can shoot out further than any of your limbs.

Senses also play their part. The conventional ones are often impressive enough: an owl can capture a vole in pitch darkness by hearing alone; a polar bear can sniff out a hidden seal pup from kilometres away. But many animals also deploy sensory equipment that, at least by human standards, seems decidedly weird. A hammerhead shark (page 60), for instance, can locate prey by its

electrical currents, while an Amazon river dolphin water simply by detecting the echoes of its own relentless clicks and squeaks.

Green machines

Animals' feeding adaptations have evolved according to their diet. First up are the veggies. All food comes originally from plants, which manufacture – via photosynthesis – the sugars and other compounds that kick-start every food chain. Those animals that munch plants at source are known, in ecological terms, as 'primary consumers'.

Browsing and grazing their way across the planet, large herbivores spend much of their life feeding in order to derive enough energy from their relatively nutrient-poor diet. Grindstone molars help them crush fibrous food, and ruminants – such as sheep, cattle and giraffes – effectively eat it twice, first breaking it down in stomach number one, then bringing it back up for further processing in the mouth (chewing the cud) before finishing the job in stomach number two. Rodents, meanwhile, use chisel-like incisors to split open seeds, birds wield their bills to shatter nuts and strip fruit, and the mandibles of locusts can nibble leaves on an industrial scale.

◄ *A Eurasian jay may retrieve more than 80% of the 5,000 or more acorns it caches beneath the ground.*

Red in tooth and claw

Carnivores are the secondary consumers. In other words, they consume the animals that eat the plants. But animals need catching. Thus predators such as cats have evolved not only the weaponry to dispatch their prey (lethal claws and stabbing canines) but also the strategies that allow them to capture it, from the high-speed pursuit of the cheetah to the stealthy stalk of the leopard.

Again, these strategies take some ingenious forms. Among fish-eaters, for instance, the black heron (page 48) makes an umbrella of its wings to lure tiddlers into the shade, while the archerfish (page 58) shoots down prey from overhanging foliage with its own water cannon. And as techniques have become ever more refined, so tools have kept pace – witness the stick-thin jaws of the gharial (page 52) that allow it to sweep its head sideways to grab its prey.

Snakes, all of which are carnivores, exhibit some of nature's most outlandish feeding adaptations, including the ability to detach their own jawbones in order to engulf prey items larger than their own head – the African egg-eating snake (page 56) offering a particularly impressive example. Many also use venom, of course, injecting it via syringe-like fangs to disable prey for the big swallow. Other venom merchants range from wasps and spiders to

the lethal cone snail (page 65), which fires poison darts into unsuspecting prey along a modified tube-like proboscis.

Hunting is not all about the chase, however. Many canny predators wait for prey to come to them. Some, such as the orchid mantis (page 65) and the mata mata (page 54), disguise themselves so effectively that victims never know what hit them. Others dangle temptation in the path of their prey: the flashlight fish (page 63) 'switches on' a bioluminescent organ to lure curious crustaceans, while the frogfish (see page 59) dangles a fleshy lure that proves fatally irresistible to smaller fry.

Each to its own

Every feeding challenge for animals has produced ever more ingenious solutions. Animals that sustain themselves from liquids, for example, have developed highly specialised mouthparts – from the nectar-sipping lance of the sword-billed hummingbird (page 49) to the plankton-filtering baleen of the blue whale. The humble housefly even liquefies its

▲ A housefly digests food outside its body using its enzyme-rich saliva.

food before eating it, secreting onto the meal a dollop of enzyme-rich saliva then sucking the solution back into its body. Yum.

Many animals get a little help from others. Such strategies range from the innocent hitchhiking of the carmine bee-eater, which rides on the back of a bustard to snap up insects disturbed around the larger bird's feet, to the downright piracy of a great skua, which snatches its meal from the mouths of hapless gannets. The skua's behaviour is known as 'kleptoparasitism'.

True parasites, however, include animals such as ticks, which attach themselves to a large mammal 'host' and feed on its blood.

Some of these solutions disgust us: the carrion-eating hyena, for instance, whose gut is adapted to processing putrid meat; or the parasitic wasps, whose larvae eat their way out of the still-living bodies of paralysed caterpillars. Others impress us, such as the ants that farm aphids for their honeydew or the jays that cache 5,000 acorns beneath the ground as a winter food store. And many – such as the python that swallows a whole antelope, horns and all – simply astound us.

But before we pass judgement on animal table manners we'd do well to remember that every creature can only nourish itself using the means evolution has placed at its disposal. Besides, our own sophisticated species – with all its GM crops, fishing fleets, battery farms and fridge-freezers – still somehow manages to let more than half its population go hungry.

▼ Humpback whales feed together on krill that they have trapped at the surface using a 'net' of bubbles.

20. Giant anteater
Myrmecophaga tridactyla

There's nothing you could call 'normal' about this animal. A vacuum-cleaner nozzle for a face, a witch's broom for a tail and meat hooks for claws: it could have been assembled from cast-offs at your local dump. Yet each of these bizarre features has evolved to play a vital part in its survival.

Shaping up

The giant anteater is by far the largest of the four anteater species – all of which are endemic to Central and South America – and may exceed 2m in length. Its coarse, straw-like fur varies from brown to grey in colour and is emblazoned with a broad black 'scarf' that stretches from throat to shoulder, and dark 'wristbands' around the pale front limbs.

But forget the markings: this bizarre creature is all about shape. At the front end is a head that looks more weevil than mammal, with an absurdly long, tube-like muzzle, and tiny eyes and ears stuck like an afterthought at the back. Bringing up the rear is the shaggy wedge of a tail, which accounts for about half the animal's length and resembles nothing so much as the roller brushes from a car wash.

Then there's the way it moves. The whole curious package ambles along with a peculiar shuffling gait, head down and tail sweeping behind. Look closer and you'll see that the animal is walking on its knuckles – and with good reason: each front foot ends in four fearsome claws, which it must curl up and out of the way in order to make any progress.

Little and often

A giant anteater (surprise, surprise!) eats ants: the adults, eggs and larvae. It is equally partial to termites. An animal this big needs serious quantities of such tiny prey in order to sustain itself and indeed a giant anteater can get through 30,000 insects a day.

This diet explains many of the bizarre adaptations. Inside that long muzzle is an even longer tongue: 60cm of sticky ribbon, rooted deep down at the

sternum, that can shoot in and out of the small oval mouth 150 times per minute in order to trap prey. An anteater has no teeth, but it flexes its jaws to grind the insects against its hard palate and ingests grit to help break down the food in its stomach.

Giant anteaters are solitary animals that feed by day where undisturbed but by night where people are around. They wander their territory – about 1–2 km² of grassland or woodland – with nose to the ground, using a sense of smell 40 times more powerful than our own to sniff out anthills and termite mounds. Once the food store is located then it's just a matter of hacking in with those massive claws and licking up the goodies.

An anteater never exhausts an anthill, however, and feeds for just a few minutes before moving onto the next. In this way it maintains a circuit of local snack bars, where food is always readily available. It also avoids the worst of the biting worker ants, which swarm out when under attack in order to defend their home.

There is plenty of time to recover from these feeding exertions, as giant anteaters sleep for about 15 hours a day. They curl up in a small hollow in the ground and cover themselves with their tails for camouflage and protection. This general lack of activity means they can maintain an average body temperature that, at just 32.7°C, is the lowest of any mammal.

Piggy back

A female giant anteater mates while lying on her side and gives birth standing up on her hind legs, using her tail as a prop. Her single infant, weighing about 1.3kg, is born after a gestation of 190 days and immediately climbs up onto her back. There it stays for about a year, until it is half her size, climbing down

At a glance

Size: head and body 1.8–2.4m (including 90–120cm tail)
Weight: 220–340g
Food: ants, termites and their larvae; other insect larvae
Reproduction: 1 young, born after 190-day gestation
Habitat: grassland and savanna to woodland and tropical forest
Distribution: Central and South America east of the Andes, from southern Mexico to northern Argentina
Status: Vulnerable

periodically to feed and explore, then clambering back up to continue the ride.

Giant anteaters may live up to 26 years in captivity. In the wild they occasionally fall prey to jaguars or pumas, though they will defend themselves vigorously, rearing up on their hind legs to strike lethal blows with their front claws. In 2007 a Buenos Aires zookeeper died of injuries inflicted by an anteater in this way.

Mankind, as ever, poses a greater threat than any natural predator. This species is listed as Vulnerable by the IUCN, with only an estimated 5,000 or so remaining in the wild. Illegal hunting and habitat destruction continue to play a part in their decline, while road traffic also takes a significant toll.

21. Star-nosed mole

Condylura cristata

Small and black, with thick velvety fur and big, burrowing feet: so far, so mole. But then you notice *that* nose: an outrageous pink sea anemone, with tiny fleshy tentacles wriggling like a hydra's head of maggots. Could this be some kind of joke?

Touchy-feely

It's no joke: this extraordinary facial fungus is deadly serious. The 22 mobile tentacles that make up the mole's 'star' are, collectively, the most sensitive tactile equipment in the mammalian world. Each is covered with tiny receptors called Eimer's organs – named after the German zoologist Theodor Eimer – of which a staggering 25,000 are crammed into a single square centimetre of skin. With the help of its star, the mole can touch, identify and consume up to 12 objects per second, making it the fastest feeder of all mammals. There is even evidence that the star, like the bill of a platypus (see page 118), enables the animal to detect electrical currents.

Like most moles, this one is functionally blind. It finds its prey by patrolling the network of shallow tunnels that it digs beneath the ground with its big, shovel-like front feet, snapping up worms and other juicy morsels that stumble into its path. The burrow network of one individual mole may extend for 270m.

You can't miss the telltale molehills in the meadows and marshes where this animal lives. What you won't spot, however, are the burrows that exit underwater. The star-nosed mole, you see, is equally at home rooting about on the bottom of a pond, where its spade-like feet become paddles, powering it along with alternating strokes in a distinct zigzag motion. It will even forage beneath the ice in the middle of winter.

When immersed, the star-nosed mole reveals yet another extraordinary talent: it is one of just a handful of mammals that can smell underwater. It does so by breathing out a continuous stream of bubbles and then breathing them back in once they have captured telltale odour molecules. A swimming star-nosed mole will snort out and sniff in ten times per second.

A star is born

Female star-nosed moles gives birth to an average litter of four or five young in a spherical nest that they make in a tunnel above the waterline. The hairless infants, which weigh just 1.5g each, are born with tentacles folded inwards. After a few days, these begin to emerge and, along with the eyes and ears, are fully functional after two weeks. The youngsters become independent at 30 days.

Star-nosed moles mature at ten months and may live for three to four years. They are active all year round and in winter subsist largely on the fat supply in their long tail, which may swell to five times its usual diameter.

Being more exposed to predators than many moles, this species falls prey to everything from hawks to mink. Rampant predation has little effect on its numbers, however, and it remains common in suitable habitat throughout its range. The only serious threat is, as usual, a human one – namely the destruction of its favoured wetland habitats.

At a glance

Size: head and body 17–20cm (6–7cm tail)
Weight: 35–75g
Food: worms; other small underground and aquatic invertebrates
Reproduction: bears a litter of 2–7 young (typically 4–5)
Habitat: wet lowlands with poor drainage, including marshes, peatlands, forests and meadows
Distribution: eastern North America, north to Quebec and Newfoundland and south to Georgia
Status: Least Concern

22. Aardvark

Orycteropus afer

Truly there is nothing like an aardvark. As if its alphabet-opening name wasn't weird enough – derived from Afrikaans, it literally means 'earth pig' – the animal itself defines oddness. Yes, its humped and mostly hairless body does vaguely recall a pig, but add the ears of a rabbit, the tail of a kangaroo and the snout of an anteater and you have a creature straight out of *Alice in Wonderland*.

One of a kind

Appearances, in this case, are not deceptive: in taxonomic terms, at least, this animal is indeed unique. Known locally as 'antbear', it is neither pig nor bear – nor, for that matter, rabbit, kangaroo or anteater – but, in fact, the sole remaining species of the order Tubulidentata, whose lineage pre-dates that of most modern mammals. This gives the aardvark a loose affinity to several groups that evolved in Africa around the same time, including elephant shrews, elephants, manatees, tenrecs and hyraxes. But with no direct relatives around today it is, genetically speaking, a living fossil.

The Tubulidentata get their name from their teeth: the 'tubes' in question are clustered inside each tooth in the space where other mammals have a pulp cavity. An aardvark's teeth also lack an enamel coating, and they grow continuously throughout its life to compensate for the continual abrasion of a soil-filled diet.

Digging deep

Inspecting an aardvark's teeth might prove tricky. Every glimpse of this shy, nocturnal animal is notoriously rare. It ventures out only well after dark on its solitary quest for ants and termites, swinging its long nose from side to side to scent its prey then breaking into the ground using the massive, spade-like nails on its powerful front limbs. The aardvark is the JCB of African animals, reputedly able to dig a hole quicker than a team of road-builders with shovels. And once it has broken in, its sticky, 30cm-long tongue can lick up insect prey at the rate of an astonishing 50,000 per night.

This heavy-duty digging gear also enables an aardvark to excavate its breeding quarters: a labyrinth of passages with as many as 20 different entrances (or exits, depending on where you're standing), which it tends to occupy for a

At a glance

Size: head and body
100–158cm; tail 44–63cm
Weight: 40–82kg
Food: ants, termites and
their larvae; beetle larvae
Reproduction: 1 (rarely 2) young after
7-month gestation
Habitat: open country with year-round
supply of ants and termites; avoids hard or
stony soils and regularly flooded areas
Distribution: across sub-Saharan Africa in
suitable habitat
Status: Least Concern

month or so before moving on. Only a mother and her single offspring will share a burrow. The youngster first ventures outside after two weeks. By six months it can dig for itself, but stays with its mother until the next breeding season.

Aardvarks inhabit open country all over sub-Saharan Africa. They are among the few mammals to benefit from ranching, since overgrazing clears the way for termites. Many other creatures, from wild cats and warthogs to porcupines and pythons, find welcome refuges in abandoned aardvark burrows (though not all at the same time). Farmers, whose land is often riddled with excavations, tend to be less grateful.

23. Narwhal
Monodon monoceros

The unicorn – sadly – is about as real as the Tooth Fairy. So in its absence this amazing creature will have to do. Granted, it's a blubbery sea mammal, not a dashing white charger. But the enormous spiral javelin projecting from its face is as impressive as anything dreamed up by storytellers of old. Indeed, it may well explain where the unicorn myth originated.

Tusk force

Forget the face for a moment and the narwhal is easily described. A medium-sized toothed whale, it is white below and dark brown above with pale mottling. It lacks a dorsal fin – an adaptation to swimming beneath the pack ice – but has two front flippers and a deeply notched tail. Its rounded forehead houses the echolocation apparatus, and a thick layer of blubber insulates its stocky body from the freezing Arctic waters.

But it is the male's spectacular tusk that grabs the attention. This is not a horn – despite the name *monoceros*, which translates as 'one horn' – but is the left of two incisor teeth that has erupted through the upper jaw and kept going. It grows straight, in an anticlockwise spiral, and may reach nearly 3m. The right incisor occasionally forms a second, parallel tusk. Females are generally tuskless, their incisors remaining embedded in their gums.

The function of this tusk has puzzled scientists for centuries. The traditional – and not unreasonable – explanation was that it served as a weapon.

But narwhals have never been seen defending themselves with their tusks nor, despite fanciful early stories, jousting with rivals. Neither has anyone witnessed narwhals using their tusks to carve out ice holes, dig in the seabed or spear fish.

Today it is generally assumed that a narwhal's tusk is a secondary sexual characteristic, like a peacock's plumes, with which males establish breeding status. But recent research suggests that it may also serve as a sophisticated sensory organ. Microscopic analysis has revealed millions of tiny nerve cells that extend from the pulpy core to the surface. This enables the whale to detect changes in the water temperature, salinity and pressure, which may assist in navigation and feeding. It also suggests something tactile is going on when males rub tusks together.

People have long ascribed magical powers to the narwhal's tusk. According to Innuit legend, it was created from the spiralling hair of a woman who became a narwhal after being dragged into the water by one she had harpooned. Medieval Europeans used the powdered tusk as a cure for everything from epilepsy to poisoning, and traders from the north sold narwhal tusk for many times its weight in gold. Queen Elizabeth I received a carved and bejewelled narwhal tusk worth £10,000 – the equivalent of millions today.

Deeper and down

The narwhal goes to great lengths – or at least depths – to obtain the various fish, squid and crustaceans on which it feeds. It is the only large predator able fully to exploit the bottom of the Arctic Ocean and does this by diving deep. Indeed a narwhal may exceptionally descend to 1,500m and stay down for 25 minutes. In the pitch darkness it uses echolocation to find its prey, listening to the returning echoes from its continuous stream of clicks and whistles.

Most such feeding occurs during winter, when the narwhals' inshore summering grounds ice over and they move to deeper water off the edge of the continental slope. Here they hang out in holes and 'leads' among the pack ice, where prey such as Greenland halibut concentrates in the small areas of open water.

In summer, as the ice breaks up, the narwhals migrate back to the shallower inshore bays where they breed. Though they usually travel in mixed groups of 20–30, larger groups of 1,000 or more may gather. Back on the breeding grounds, a female gives birth to her single 1.5m calf. The infant, born a uniform blue-grey, stays with its mother for about 20 months.

Trapped

One hazard of life in the Arctic Ocean is becoming trapped by the pack ice. This phenomenon, known as a *sassvat* in Innuit, occasionally proves disastrous for narwhals: 1,000 died in one incident in 1915. It also leaves them at the mercy of predators, which include polar bears, orcas and – significantly – people.

The Innuit people have hunted narwhals for centuries, using their bones for tools and carvings and their skin and blubber as a vitamin C-rich food called *muktuk*. Today traditional hunting has given way to more advanced technology. A subsistence quota of about 1,000 narwhals is hunted every year, but there is some debate over whether this remains sustainable. Like all Arctic species, the narwhal is highly vulnerable to climate change, and recent studies have found high concentrations of pollutants in narwhal tissue.

At a glance

Length: 4.5m (male); 4m (female)
Weight: 1,500kg (male); 900kg (female)
Food: fish (including Arctic cod, Greenland halibut and flatfish); squid, crustaceans and other benthic organisms
Reproduction: single calf born every 3 years in July, after 15-month gestation
Habitat: deep inlets and bays in summer; edge of the pack ice in winter
Distribution: Arctic Ocean, including Canadian High Arctic, Greenland Sea and Russian Arctic
Statust: Vulnerable; estimated worldwide population of ±75,000

24. Amazon river dolphin

Inia geoffrensis

A grinning, flamingo-pink dolphin wielding an underwater stun gun? Sounds like a recipe for a bad cartoon. But this is no fictitious aquatic superhero with mutant ninja tendencies; rather it is a real-life cetacean with some ingenious ways of grabbing a meal in the murky waters of a South American river.

Minesweeper

The Amazon river dolphin – known locally as *boutu*, *boto* or *bufeo* – is the largest of five river dolphin species worldwide. Like all its family, it has a long, toothy beak, a bulging forehead 'melon' and a ridge along its spine in place of a dorsal fin. But the first thing you'll notice is its colour, which varies from soft rose to lurid flamingo. Occasionally it may also be pale blue or even white. Whatever the hue, it is never less than conspicuous as it breaks the murky brown river waters.

Small parties of these aquatic mammals scour turbid rivers and flooded forests for fish and crustaceans, using their large flippers to manoeuvre among the drowned vegetation. They have reasonable eyesight, unlike some river dolphins, but this counts for little when visibility is so poor. Thus they depend upon echolocation to catch their prey, sending out a stream of clicks and whistles, and orientating themselves by the returning echoes. This is standard practice among dolphins, but the Amazon river dolphin takes it to extremes, emitting such violent and concentrated bursts of sound that it is able to knock some prey effectively senseless.

Furthermore this dolphin's neck vertebrae are not fused, which means it can bend its head by 90° sideways or downwards in order to sweep a greater arc of its surroundings – working like a minesweeper before it drops its depth charges. Once located, the prey is snapped up in that toothy grin, gripped by the peg-like teeth at the front then crushed by the flattened, molar-like teeth further back.

Flood baby

Amazon river dolphins give birth to a single calf in May to July, after a nine to 12-month gestation, when the floodwaters are at their peak. The 80cm-long, 7kg infant is dark grey when it emerges. As it matures the pink flush gradually spreads from its underside up its flanks and onto its back. Females reach sexual maturity once they have reached a length of about 1.5m.

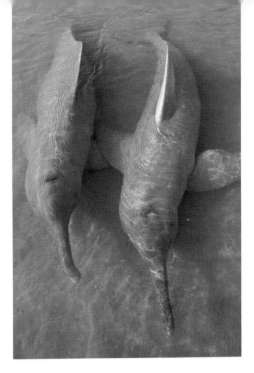

Many communities hold a tradition of respect for the Amazon river dolphin; indeed killing one was long considered taboo. In more recent times, however, it has been heavily hunted for its skin and fat, and this – combined with the even greater threats posed by habitat destruction and pollution – has left it an endangered species. Ironically this dolphin is a confiding creature, whose natural curiosity often leads it to approach small boats. Left alone, it may live to 30 years.

At a glance

Length: 2.5–2.9m (male); 1.8–2.4m (female)
Weight: 85–160kg
Food: river fish, including catfish and piranhas; bottom-dwelling crustaceans
Reproduction: single calf born May–July after 9–12-month gestation
Habitat: brown, slow-moving rivers and flooded forests
Distribution: the river systems of the Amazon, Orinoco and Araguaia/Tocantins
Status: Data Deficient

25. Aye-aye
Daubentonia madagascariensis

Just one glimpse of this bizarre creature leaves no doubt about why it is feared across Madagascar as a harbinger of evil. That gremlin combination of big eyes, bat's ears and witch's fingers certainly looks sinister. It is also sufficiently odd to have left generations of scientists arguing about the animal's true identity.

Finger of blame

The aye-aye, we now know, is a lemur. And that makes it a primate. But it doesn't look remotely like any other lemur. Its lithe body, the dark fur dusted with straggly white guard hairs, looks half monkey and half cat. Its racoon-shaped face sports bulging orange eyes and naked bat-like ears. And its rodent-like chisel incisors convinced early zoologists that the aye-aye was some kind of squirrel.

But it's those long, skinny fingers that really inspire the heebie-jeebies; in particular the middle finger, which is almost skeletally skinny. This digit has evolved for a very specific purpose. As the aye-aye clambers around the forest canopy it uses its long finger to tap on old bark. When a hollow ring reveals a cavity, it listens for the sound of grubs and then – if it hears movement – rips off the bark with its teeth and winkles out the prize with its finger. This lifestyle means that aye-ayes effectively occupy the ecological niche that is taken by woodpeckers in other parts of the world.

The aye-aye's diet also extends to seeds, nuts, fruit and nectar, and that probing finger comes in just as useful for winkling the flesh from a coconut. It feeds by night and generally up in the branches, which it negotiates with great agility. By day it roosts in a nest that it constructs in a tree fork.

Love battles

A male aye-aye occupies a territory of up to 30ha which overlaps with that of other males. He marks out his boundaries with urine and glandular secretions, but can be more sociable with other males than was once thought. Courtship, however, is a time of aggressive competition, as many males may gather in response to the call of a single female. One jealous male may even pull a mating couple apart.

The fear inspired by aye-ayes has proved a double-edged sword for the primate. In many parts of Madagascar it is killed on sight, as its mere presence around a village is thought to herald a death. Elsewhere, for similar reasons, it is left well alone. Either way, the taboo means that at least nobody hunts aye-ayes for food.

Unfortunately Madagascar's rampant deforestation has spelt trouble for aye-ayes, as their fondness for raiding coconut plantations has brought increasing conflict with people. The good news, however, is that the species is now known to be more widespread than scientists once feared. Healthy new populations have recently been discovered across Madagascar and several reserves are now set up specifically for the primate's protection.

At a glance

Size: head and body length 30–37cm; tail 44–53cm
Weight: 2.5–3kg
Food: insect larvae; fruits, seeds, nectar
Reproduction: 1 baby every 3 years, born after 160-day gestation; weaned after 7–10 months and able to climb after one month
Habitat: tropical rainforest and tropical dry forest
Distribution: Madagascar; most numerous in eastern rainforests.
Status: Near Threatened

26. American long-eared bats

Corynorhinus spp

'Big ears' is an understatement. These lengthy lugholes account for nearly a quarter of their owner's entire length. Indeed, so long are they that the bat sometimes has to curl them up to prevent itself from getting chilly. But, like all nature's most preposterous appendages, these ears are there for a reason.

Insect interceptors

American long-eared bats are medium-sized insectivorous bats found in scattered locations across North America. They are greyish above, with the colour of the underparts differing between the three otherwise very similar species. As well as the enormous, naked, rabbit-like ears, all have two large facial glands that resemble a pair of mittens on either side of the nose.

These bats roost by day in cave entrances, hollow trees or abandoned buildings. They emerge after dark to hunt flying insects – especially moths, but also mosquitoes, flies and beetles. And this is where those enormous ears earn their keep. Like most insectivorous species, long-eared bats catch their prey by echolocation; in other words, they emit a continuous stream of high-frequency sound waves, inaudible to us, that bounce off their prey and reveal its location. The ears are the radar dishes that pick up the returning signals. The bigger the ears, the better they work, so these bats have moth-catching down to a fine art.

American long-eared bats do not migrate. When winter brings an end to the insect supply they are obliged to hibernate, which they do in tight clusters in traditional roost sites. This is when they must curl up those ears, winding them tightly into the shape of ram's horns to reduce their surface area and so prevent the leaking of too much precious body heat.

Night nurseries

Long-eared bats mate during autumn, attracting partners with ritualised calls and cementing bonds with much affectionate head nuzzling. Females store the males' sperm over winter, and ovulation and fertilisation occur in early spring, just before they emerge from hibernation. In late spring the pregnant females leave the males to establish separate nursery colonies, where each gives birth to her single youngster, or pup.

There are three species of American long-eared bats: Rafinesque's big-eared bat (*Corynorhinus rafinesquii*), Mexican big-eared bat (*C. mexicanus*) and Townsend's big-eared bat (*C. townsendii*). Little is known about any of them. But all are struggling, primarily due to the loss of their traditional roost sites – especially large, hollow trees. They are also vulnerable to disturbance during migration, which causes them to exhaust vital winter fat reserves. Ongoing research into the provision of artificial roost sites aims to arrest their decline.

At a glance

Size: head and body length 12cm (ears 2.5–3.5cm); wingspan 30–34cm
Weight: 85–160kg
Food: moths, beetles, mosquitoes and other flying insects
Reproduction: single 'pup' born late spring
Habitat: feeds in forests; roosts in cave entrances, hollow trees and old buildings
Distribution: southeastern USA (*Corynorhinus rafinesquii*); western North America, from British Columbia to Mexico (*C. townsendii*); Mexico (*C. mexicanus*)
Status: Vulnerable; 2 subspecies of Townsend's big-eared bat (*C. t. virginianus* and *C. t. ingens*) are federally endangered

27. Shoebill

Balaeniceps rex

'King whale-head', the translation of this bird's scientific name, hardly suggests small or discreet. And indeed the shoebill sports a quite outrageous conk. Its common name is derived from the Arabic *Abu markub* – literally 'father of the shoe'. Imagine a size-ten clog on the face of an outsized heron and you'll get the picture.

Fitting the bill

The shoebill is steely blue-grey in colour, stands an imposing 1.5m tall and measures 2.5m across its broad wings. But these were not the qualities to which naturalist John Gould was referring in 1851 when, describing the species for the first time, he called it 'The most extraordinary bird I have seen for many years.'

What struck Gould, of course, was that beak. Measuring 23cm long by 10cm wide it is, indeed, as capacious as your average shoe. What's more, it comes equipped with a wicked hook on the end, and sharp slicing edges to the lower mandible that tuck neatly into the upper.

This appendage makes the shoebill Africa's ultimate ambush fisherman. Lurking in the shallows, it lunges forward at any suitable victim within range – showing alarming speed for such a big bird – and uses its bill to scoop, stab and crush all in one. Prey includes the African lungfish, along with turtles, lizards, snakes, waterbirds and even young crocodiles. In short, anything that fits the bill.

Swamp thing

You might wonder how such a distinctive bird eluded Western science until 1851. But the shoebill lives only in Africa's deepest swamps – hardly the

planet's most accessible habitat – favouring papyrus stands in particular, and often frequenting the narrow channels between larger water bodies where fish tend to concentrate. Furthermore it is a solitary species, with each pair requiring at least 2km². You try finding one.

Breeding takes place at the onset of the dry season as the floods are receding. A female lays two to three eggs in a ground nest that the pair constructs in an open area of swamp grass. Parents carry beakfuls of water to cool the exposed nestlings, but inter-sibling rivalry means that generally only one youngster fledges. The hatchling reaches independence 140 days after the egg is laid and must wait another three to four years to mature fully.

The shoebill's taxonomy has puzzled scientists ever since Gould examined that first specimen. His initial theory that it was related to pelicans was soon dismissed, with some scientists subsequently placing it among the herons and others among the storks. But DNA evidence has now returned it to the Pelecaniformes. It seems Gould was right.

Today the shoebill occurs from Sudan in the north, whose southern swamps are the species' stronghold, to Zambia in the south. It is more numerous than was once thought, with an estimated population of 5,000–10,000. Nonetheless it remains vulnerable to swamp drainage and disturbance, and is still one of the global birder's most sought-after ticks.

At a glance

Size: 115–150cm; wingspan 230–260cm
Weight: 5–7kg
Food: fish (especially African lungfish); aquatic reptiles; small aquatic mammals and waterbirds
Reproduction: 2–3 eggs; generally only 1 chick fledges
Habitat: papyrus and other swamps, with floating vegetation and large reed beds
Distribution: sub-Saharan Africa, from Sudan to Zambia, also including Uganda, Kenya and Tanzania
Status: Vulnerable

28. Black heron
Egretta ardesiaca

It is a bird? Is it an umbrella? What *is* that strange black mound shuffling across the water? A black heron out fishing looks like nothing that belongs to the animal kingdom. But watch carefully: it knows exactly what it is doing.

Check canopy

At rest, the black heron looks like a small dark version of any other heron. Its dark slate-grey plumage, combined with its slim neck, fine crest, dagger-like bill and long legs, creates a distinct and elegant profile. And, like all herons, it is an expert hunter, wading stealthily through the shallows and using patience and lightning speed to capture small fish, frogs and aquatic invertebrates.

This heron, however, has stolen a march on the competition by using a unique strategy called 'canopying' with which to snare its prey. First it finds a promising fishing spot. Then it stretches out its wings to form an umbrella-like canopy that reaches to the water's surface and completely encloses its body – rather like a Victorian melodrama villain flourishing his black cape. The effect is to cast a shadow on the water that offers a tempting refuge to unsuspecting prey. With the glare taken off the water's surface, the heron gets a

perfect view as the fish swim right up to its feet. It strikes with its bill and – before they know what's hit them – gulps them down. Then it finds a new spot and starts all over again.

With such an ingenious technique, the question is not so much why the black heron does it – but why all the other species of heron don't.

Colonial ties

Black herons sometimes fish alone. At other times they may form loose groups of up to 50; as many as 200 have been recorded fishing together where prey is especially rich. Such gatherings are a strange sight, resembling a collection of discarded black umbrellas bobbing around the shallows.

Whether solitary or sociable on its feeding grounds, however, the black heron definitely prefers a crowd when it comes to roosting and nesting. Indeed it forms large colonies for these purposes – often with other heron species. Each female lays her clutch of two to four dark blue

eggs in a twig nest that a pair builds together in a tree or reed bed overhanging the water. As soon as the young herons have fledged, they set out to master the fine art of canopying.

Black herons are widespread across sub-Saharan Africa and also on Madagascar, feeding around the edges of lakes, lagoons and other wetland habitats. The species is not currently of any conservation concern – though, like all wetland birds, the draining or destruction of its habitat is an ever-present threat.

At a glance

Size: 65cm; wingspan 90–100cm
Weight: 5–7kg
Food: small fish, frogs, aquatic invertebrates
Reproduction: nests in tree or reed bed; 2–4 eggs
Habitat: the edges of shallow open waters, including lakes, marshes and coastal lagoons; also rice fields and tidal rivers
Distribution: sub-Saharan Africa, from Senegal and Sudan to South Africa
Status: Least Concern

29. Sword-billed hummingbird

Ensifera ensifera

This bill is more medieval jousting lance than sword. At up to 12cm it takes up around half the owner's total length and is, proportionally, the longest bill of any bird in the world.

Probing investigation

There are more than 325 species of hummingbird, all of which have bills adapted to probing flowers for nectar. The shape of each has evolved to suit the blooms of particular plants: some are short and sharp; some are long and curved. The sword-billed hummingbird has by far the longest, adapted to probe deep into flowers with long corollas, such as those of *Passiflora mixta*.

Like all hummingbirds, this one feeds while hovering in mid-air in front of its food plants, its iridescent emerald and bronze plumage glittering as it zips from one bloom to another. It beats its wings at around 25 times per second to hold itself

stationary while the bill reaches up into the hanging petals. The protrusible, grooved tongue flickers in and out beyond the tip to lap up nectar that no other hummer can reach.

Handy as this appendage may be when feeding, it is a serious inconvenience at all other times. At rest, the bird must perch with its bill held up at an almost vertical angle to relieve the strain on its neck. And when preening, it must resort to using its feet.

Sugar rush

Hummingbirds of all species live a high-octane life and this one is no exception. Their metabolism runs higher than that of all other vertebrates in order to generate the energy necessary to beat their wings, while the heart rate of some species has been measured at more than 1,200 beats per minute. Just to survive they must consume more than their own weight in

nectar daily. This entails visiting hundreds of flowers. At any moment they are just hours away from starvation, and can only just store enough energy to survive overnight (when they enter a torpid state in which their heart rate and breathing slow dramatically).

Nesting, as with all hummingbirds, is the responsibility of the female. She builds her neat, cup-shaped nest from moss and foliage, using spider silk to bind it together – which also allows it to expand as the young grow – and help secure it to the branch. She incubates her two white eggs for 15–19 days, then feeds her nestlings on small arthropods and nectar by inserting her bill into their open gapes and regurgitating the food.

Sword-billed hummingbirds are found in the South American Andes, in Bolivia, Colombia, Ecuador, Peru and Venezuela. They are locally distributed in humid forest areas at altitudes of 1,700–3,500m.

At a glance

Size: 23–25cm (including 10–12cm bill)
Weight: 12g
Food: nectar from *Passiflora brugmansia* and other blooms with long corollas; also spiders and other small arthropods
Reproduction: 2 eggs; chicks hatch after 15–19 days
Habitat: montane, cloud and elfin forest at 1,700–3,500m; borders and bushy slopes where preferred nectar plants grow in abundance
Distribution: northern Andes: Bolivia, Colombia, Ecuador, Peru and Venezuela
Status: Least Concern

30. Black skimmer
Rynchops niger

Evolution has fashioned a veritable toolbox of variations on the basic design of a bird's bill: there are tongs, saws, sieves, hooks, spatulas, nutcrackers – something for every ecological challenge. But a skimmer's bill is that awkward tool left at the bottom of the box to flummox the DIY novice: you have no idea what it does or even which way up to hold it. Clearly it belongs to a specialist.

Fish slice

The black skimmer is one of three very similar skimmer species around the world, the other two being the Indian skimmer and African skimmer. All have a dark cap and upperparts, white underparts and short red legs. Together they comprise the family Rynchopidae, which is closely related to the gulls and terns. And, putting aside the bill for one moment, you can see the resemblance: these medium-sized, long-winged waterbirds nest on the shore and fly around squawking very much like their better-known cousins.

But it's the bill that sets them apart – and it's what they do with it that gives them their name. Skimmers are unique among birds in that the lower mandible of their big bill is substantially longer than the upper. And the whole bill is flattened laterally, making it knife thin. They feed by flying low over the water with their bill held open and the lower mandible 'skimming' the surface. When it encounters a prey item, such as a small fish or crustacean, the bill snaps shut in a lightning-fast reflex response, scooping up the titbit into the bird's mouth. The food goes straight down and the skimmer continues on its way.

Skimmers do not skim at random. Once a bird has found a promising feeding patch – often a small pool or backwater – it will trawl it systematically, repeating the same flight path in a series of runs and slicing a characteristic V-shaped wake each time with that blade-like bill. The long wings allow a typically elastic, buoyant flight, so it can manoeuvre low over the water with great agility.

Sharp, bark-like 'yip yip' calls herald the arrival of a feeding party of black skimmers, which often work the water in large flocks. Prime feeding time is sunset – but they will happily continue feeding after dark, being reliant on touch rather than sight to capture their food.

Life's a beach

Black skimmers frequent fresh and coastal waters, including lakes, lagoons and slow-flowing rivers, wherever there are sandy beaches and sandbanks. They spend their downtime simply loafing on the sand – all facing the same direction – and it is here that they also breed, forming loose colonies set back from the water's edge.

The nest is simply a small scrape in the sand. Here the female lays three to seven buff or pale blueish eggs that are decorated with a blotchy camouflage pattern. Both parents incubate the clutch. After hatching, the chicks hunker down in the scrape, where their patterning continues to provide excellent camouflage. Chicks hatch with mandibles the same length, but by four weeks the lower mandible is already 1cm longer. Parents feed their brood by day then set out on longer communal fishing trips by night. Immature birds can be identified by the pale speckling on their plumage.

There are three distinct subspecies of the black skimmer: *R. n. niger* breeds along the southern Atlantic coast of North America and from southern California to Ecuador along the Pacific coast; *R. n. cinerescens* is found in north and northeastern South America and the Amazon Basin; *R. n. intercedens* occurs from the Atlantic coast of South America south to central Argentina. Birds from the North American race migrate south for winter to the Caribbean and the tropical Pacific coasts, whereas the two South American races move more in response to flood patterns than seasonal changes.

The black skimmer is not currently a threatened species. Nonetheless it is vulnerable to disturbance and damage to its wetland habitats. A serious threat to all skimmer species worldwide is the wash of powerboats, which can swamp their sandbank nests.

At a glance

Size: 40–50cm; wingspan 107–127cm

Weight: 212–447g (males larger)

Food: small fish; crustaceans and other aquatic invertebrates

Reproduction: 3–7 eggs; chicks fledge after 40 days

Habitat: lakes, coastal lagoons and slow-flowing rivers

Distribution: coastal North America, as far north as Massachusetts and California; Central and South America south to Argentina, including the Caribbean, Amazon Basin and Atlantic coast

Status: Least Concern

31. Gharial
Gavialis gangeticus

From the neck down this appears to be a perfectly normal crocodile – if such a thing exists. Big tail, scaly body, knobbly back: the works. But then you see those preposterously skinny jaws, looking as though some joker has replaced the head with a long pair of pliers. And that great bulbous lump on the end of the snout – like a comedy bee sting. Can evolution have made a mistake?

Slim-line snout

The name gharial is derived from the Hindi word *gharra*, which means 'mud pot' and refers to the bizarre bulge on the male's snout. Various explanations – all related to sex – have been advanced for this: a visual come-on for females,

a vocal resonator to amplify its buzzing courtship calls, or perhaps an aid in its bubble-blowing display. Whatever the truth, the bulge certainly grows bigger as its owner becomes more sexually mature.

The long, thin jaws – which grow longer and thinner in mature males – are lined with 106–110 needle-like teeth that slot neatly together when they close. These jaws are less robust than those of other crocodilians, and lack the strength required to rip chunks off a carcass or haul an animal from the bank. But their slimline design minimises water resistance, which means that the gharial can turn its head and snap its jaws underwater much more dextrously than can other crocodiles – a vital skill when it comes to catching fish.

Other than the jaws, what first strikes you about the gharial is its sheer size. This is one of the three largest crocodilians on the planet, with measurements of over 6m reliably recorded. Indeed today's

gharial may be descended from an ancient group, the Gavioloidea, which dates back to the Cretaceous (over 65 million years ago) and included one species, *Rhamphosuchus crassidens*, that may have reached a colossal 15m. The tail is particularly impressive: long and more laterally flattened than in other crocodiles, it can power a gharial through the water with great speed.

Water world

Gharials are the most aquatic of all crocodilians. And it is their exceptional speed and agility in the water – combined with the lightweight jaws – that enables them to subsist almost entirely on small fish. They capture this elusive prey with a rapid sideways slashing and snapping, pinioning it with those needle teeth and swallowing it whole.

their life feeding on aquatic invertebrates and small vertebrates, but graduate to fish as their jaws begin to develop their adult shape.

Sadly, this remarkable reptile is today the most endangered crocodilian on the planet. Its population across the northern Indian subcontinent has declined inexorably over recent decades. This reflects a combination of direct persecution – mostly to supply the trade in medicinal products and aphrodisiacs that thrives in China and the Far East – and the destruction and exploitation of its riverine habitats. In the 1970s the gharial reached the verge of extinction. An intensive conservation programme – including the establishment of nine special protection zones in India, and a captive breeding and release programme – has since achieved some success. Nonetheless this is the first crocodilian to have received the dubious distinction of IUCN Critically Endangered status. Just 1,500 are thought to remain in India, with up to 200 scattered across neighbouring territories.

Larger prey is off the menu; gharials simply don't have the equipment. But they do sometimes scavenge – and this may explain their undeserved reputation for man-eating in some parts of India. Human remains occasionally found inside gharials have almost certainly come from corpses cast into rivers during Hindu burial rites, while the jewellery that has also turned up in their stomachs has probably been snapped up from the riverbed as a buoyancy aid – just as many crocodilians will do with pebbles.

On land gharials are less comfortable. They live beside large, fast-moving rivers and seldom move further from the water than the sandbanks on which they haul out to rest and breed. Their limbs lack the musculature that enables other crocodiles to perform the 'high walk'; instead they simply slither on their bellies.

Sandbank survival

Female gharials reach breeding maturity at ten years (or at roughly 3m in length). Each male establishes a territory along a length of river bank, which he defends vigorously against rivals, and gathers a harem of females. Mating takes place in a two-month window between November and January, and the females build their nests in March–May. Each buries her clutch of 30–50 eggs in a sandbank. The 160g eggs are the largest of any crocodilian.

The clutch hatches after 83–94 days, whereupon the hatchlings make their way down to the water. The parents don't offer any help at this stage – their teeth are too sharp to carry their brood in the manner of some other crocodiles – but they do guard the youngsters until they grow large enough to strike out on their own. Young gharials start

At a glance

Size: 4–6m, exceptionally 7m
Weight: up to 1,000kg (males larger than females)
Food: small to medium-sized fish; occasionally carrion
Reproduction: 30–50 eggs (average clutch 37) laid March–May; incubation 83–94 days
Habitat: large, deep, fast-flowing rivers, with sandbanks
Distribution: northern India; small populations in Nepal, Bangladesh and possibly Pakistan, Bhutan and Myanmar
Status: Critically Endangered

32. Mata mata
Chelus fimbrialis

That's no animal, surely. It's just a load of old rubbish: waterlogged bark and debris, overgrown with weed and rotting slowly into the sediment. A perfect hiding place for a passing fish. Or perhaps not.

Under cover

The mata mata is a large freshwater turtle – a member of the Chelidae family of snake-necked

At a glance

Size: 45cm
Weight: 15kg
Food: small fish and aquatic invertebrates
Reproduction: 12–18 eggs laid October–December; incubation 200 days
Habitat: shallow, turbid streams; swamps, marshes and ponds
Distribution: northern South America: Amazon and Orinoco river basins, south to Bolivia, east to Ecuador and north to Trinidad
Status: Least Concern

turtles, to be precise. But you'd be hard-pressed to tell this at first glance, or indeed any subsequent glance, so spectacularly has it evolved to meet the challenge of underwater camouflage.

The algae-encrusted carapace is coloured in the faded browns and yellows of rotting leaves, and surmounted with three knobbly ridges, like old bark. At the end of the wizened neck is a triangular, leaf-shaped head, flat on top and sprouting flaps of skin, feelers and tubercles below – like some fungal infestation. And on the tip of the snout is a nozzle that sticks up like a leaf stalk: its celebrated snorkel.

Sucked in

Mata matas are not given to dashing about. They lurk on the muddy bottom of shallow, turbid water bodies waiting for life to come to them. In fact, they can hardly even swim, their weak legs being good just for a few steps along the bottom when taking up a new position. The only time they come onto land is when females leave the water in search of a nest site.

The idea behind that killer camouflage is to blend into the bottom so that prey suspects nothing. And indeed unsuspecting fish and invertebrates may even make for a lurking mata mata as a refuge or feeding place. Thus it hardly needs move. Its snorkel snout pokes just above the surface, allowing

it to breathe while it waits. And the flaps of skin and other facial protrusions are endowed with sensory organs that alert it to the motion of approaching prey.

The next stage seems predictable enough: the reptile lunges out and seizes the prey in its vice-like jaws, right? Not quite. In fact the jaws are quite weak, so the mata mata waits until the prey is close enough then opens them wide – wide enough to create a low-pressure vacuum that sucks the victim inside. It then spits out the excess water and swallows the prey whole. Nice.

Eggs exit

Mata matas become almost animated during courtship, males moving their heads, legs and face flaps seductively. Females haul out to excavate a nest in the waterside vegetation, where they lay 12–18 spherical eggs. The hatchlings emerge after 200 days, with not a parent in sight, and make their way to the water. Youngsters are more colourful than adults: salmon pink, with rufous markings.

Mata matas are widespread in suitable habitat. Threats include the destruction of their wetlands – and also the depredations of the pet trade, which has long coveted this bizarre-looking creature. Escaped captive mata matas have established a feral population in Florida, which may not bode well for the native fauna.

33. Leaf-horned frog

Megophrys nasuta

Another death trap decked out as foliage. This southeast Asian amphibian sports an elaborate disguise that leaves it indistinguishable from the forest floor where it lurks. But distinguish it you must: especially if you're any passing animal that might fit in that massive maw.

Leaf well alone

The 'horns' that give this frog its name are actually supracilliary projections – flaps of skin, in other words, that stick out from above its eyes and nose and look just like the curled edges of a dead leaf. Further skin flaps run like seams along the angular contours of its smooth back and flanks, perfectly mimicking the ribbing of a leaf. Patterned in variegated shades of russet, tan and grey, with darker tones on the flanks to reproduce the effect of shadow, this frog is undetectable among the leaf-litter until it moves.

But of course it doesn't move. At least not often. Rather, it sits tight until prey comes within range. Then it springs up, engulfs the victim and gulps it down alive in an explosive attack. Prey includes anything from insects, crabs and scorpions to small lizards and even rodents.

You won't locate it by its call, either. This frog utters a soft, metallic 'ching' to stake out its territory and attract females. But it shuts up at the slightest disturbance.

Hatching a plan

The upland forests where this frog makes its home are damp and cool, and it seldom moves far from the banks of a stream. Like all amphibians, water is vital for its reproduction, and a female – twice the weight of a male – attaches her clusters of eggs to the underside of rocks and logs that are partly or wholly submerged. The eggs of this species are large and relatively few in number.

If the eggs are laid in the water, the tadpoles hatch directly and swim free. If they are laid above the waterline, however, they slide down towards the surface on gelatinous filaments and hatch when they get there. Either way, the tadpoles suspend themselves by their mouths from the water's surface, feeding on the micro-organisms that accumulate there.

At a glance

Size: 7–10cm (male); 9–12.5cm (female)
Food: large invertebrates, including crabs and scorpions; small vertebrates, including lizards, rodents and other frogs
Reproduction: eggs laid in clusters on submerged rocks and logs
Habitat: damp leaf-litter of forest floor, up to 1,600m
Distribution: southeast Asia, including Borneo, Sumatra and peninsular Malaysia
Status: Least Concern

The leaf-horned frog is widespread in suitable forest habitat across southeast Asia. It has acquired quite a collection of common names across its range, from Malaysian leaf frog to Asiatic horned toad. The species is not currently considered threatened, though deforestation continues to erode its habitat. Like many of the more bizarre-looking reptiles and amphibians, it is a prize quarry for the exotic pet trade.

34. African egg-eating snake

Dasypeltis scabra

So you're feeling peckish. But could you swallow something three times the size of your own head? A microwave, perhaps, or a Jack Russell? It's a good trick if you know how – and there's a snake in Africa that doesn't think twice about such feats of gluttony. It has only one meal in mind.

Egg-ceptional

The African egg-eater, also known as the common or rhombic egg-eater, is the best known of five species in the genus *Dasypeltis*, all of which feed exclusively on eggs. They are the only snakes in the world to do this, except for the Indian egg-eating snake (*Elachistodon westermanni*), which belongs to a different genus.

from grey to brown, with a geometric pattern of black squares or zigzags along its spine.

Look inside the mouth, however, and you'll find a couple of oddities that hint at an unusual lifestyle. First, there are no teeth to speak of. Second – and you'll have to look really deep to see this – there are a series of knobs along the roof of the throat. These, known as 'gular teeth', are modified projections of the vertebrae, and they have a job to do.

Down in one

The African egg-eater feeds on eggs from a variety of birds. In particular it is the nemesis of weavers, small African members of the finch family that tend to construct their neat, woven nests in conspicuous colonies. The snake infiltrates a colony at night, looking for an unguarded or abandoned clutch. When it finds one, it uses the sense organ on its tongue to check out the eggs – rejecting any that are either too rotten or too far developed – until it alights upon the prime candidate.

At a glance

Size: 60–95cm (females larger)
Food: birds' eggs
Reproduction: 6–25 eggs laid in summer; hatch after 80–90 days
Habitat: woodland and savanna
Distribution: sub-Saharan Africa, from South Africa to Sudan in the north and Gambia in the west
Status: Least Concern

Once it has passed beyond the head, the snake bends its neck sharply, puncturing the shell with those projecting gular teeth. The egg collapses, and the snake squeezes out and swallows the contents. It then regurgitates the flattened and empty shell in one piece. The whole process is remarkably

Under normal circumstances – at least, when it's not eating – there's nothing special about the African egg-eater. It is a small, nervous and non-venomous snake that moves fast, climbs trees and is most active after dark. Its background colour varies

Then the party trick begins. The snake opens its mouth wide – unhinging its jaws in the process – and wraps it around the egg. As the lips work their way forward, with no teeth to get in the way, the egg is drawn further down the extremely flexible throat.

efficient: very little that is edible remains in the regurgitated shell. In this way, the snake will consume a whole clutch of six or seven eggs one after the other.

Bluffing it

In sacrificing its teeth, this snake has also sacrificed its self-defence. But there are more tricks to come. That pattern down its back looks remarkably like the pattern of the African night adder, an aggressive snake with a venomous bite – at least it looks *enough* like it to give any predator pause for thought, thus buying the egg-eater time to escape. This is no coincidence: it is the perfect example of a principle known as Batesian mimicry, whereby harmless creatures have evolved to resemble harmful ones as a survival strategy. (Think of the inoffensive hoverfly that looks just like a stinging wasp.)

In arid western areas, where the night adder is absent, the egg-eater's pattern has adapted to resemble the equally unpleasant horned adder.

If a predator calls its bluff, the egg-eater backs up the deception by rubbing its coils together to produce a rasping sound, just like the hissing of an adder. And if this is still not enough, it will coil and uncoil rapidly and strike out – albeit toothlessly – at its assailant. Either way, it's enough to make you think twice.

Snakes alive

African egg-eaters breed in the spring. A female lays a clutch of six to 25 eggs after a gestation period of 80–90 days, scattered in a number of locations. Hatchlings learn the egg-eating habit fast, starting with those of small birds such as finches.

This species is widespread across sub-Saharan Africa, especially in savanna and woodland areas. Its behaviour is sufficiently well known to feature in the mythology and folklore of several African societies. What better explanation for an eclipse, for example, than a giant snake in the sky that swallows the disc of the sun and then spits it back out in the morning?

35. Banded archerfish

Toxotes jaculatrix

Question: when is a water pistol a deadly weapon? Answer: when you're an insect and an archerfish is the marksman. Splat! One blast and down you go – straight into the jaws of this sharpshooting predator.

Water cannon

This small fish is one of seven similar species that frequent the mangroves and tidal waters of tropical southeast Asia and Australasia. It is nothing special to look at: just a flattened, black-and-white body with fins towards the back and eyes at the front. But look closer. That narrow shape and two-tone pattern are hard to spot beneath the dappled light of the surface. And those big eyes, set close to the mouth, give it fine binocular vision – perfect for judging distance. Both features are adaptations for a remarkable way of grabbing a bite.

Archerfish, you see, are the only fish on the planet that capture their prey out of the water. They do this, amazingly, by shooting it down. Any creepy-crawly that perches on a leaf within a metre or so of the surface is fair game. The fish sticks out its snout and fires a pinpoint accurate jet of water at its prey, either knocking it down directly or drenching it so it topples off under the weight of water. It then reacts with astonishing speed – calculating the landing spot within one forty-thousandth of a second – to snap up the prey before it knows what has hit it.

Baffling ballistics

The mechanics are ingenious. The fish holds its tongue against a groove in the roof of its mouth to form a tube – the gun barrel – then snaps its gills shut to force out the water through its mouth. It can do this at least seven times in quick succession and is deadly accurate at a range of up to 1.5m. It can even compensate for the effects of refraction: it positions itself directly below the prey, where possible, to negate any distortion, but its aim is no less accurate at angles of up to 40° from the perpendicular. It seems that this is a skill that a young archerfish learns – just as it also learns to modify the force of the jet according to the size and distance of the target.

Sharpshooting is not the only feeding method. If prey is no more than 30cm above the water, the archerfish may leap out and grab it. This prevents competition with rivals who might get there first when tumbling prey hits the surface. Mature fish may also go the more conventional route and snap up swimming prey underwater.

Small fry

Banded archerfish lay their copious spawn on reefs. From the thousands of eggs only a few juveniles reach maturity, and these settle in the brackish water around mangroves and estuaries, where yellow fluorescent markings help them school together for protection. These markings fade as they mature.

Archerfish are widespread in the tropical waters of the Indo-Pacific, from India to Australia and Polynesia. Among the threats they face are the widespread destruction of mangroves and collection for the pet trade.

At a glance

Size: 15–25cm
Food: insects, arachnids and occasionally small vertebrates
Reproduction: spawn laid on reefs: 20,000–150,000 eggs
Habitat: mangroves and estuaries on tropical shorelines
Distribution: Indo-Pacific oceans, from India to Australia and Polynesia
Status: Least Concern

36. Frogfish
Antennariidae spp

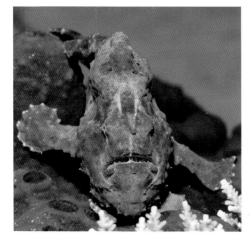

Any angler will tell you that rewards come to those who wait. These peculiar fish belong to the anglerfish order (Lophiiformes), so they should know all about this. Indeed, they are masters of the art of sitting, waiting and reeling in the catch. They even have their own rod and line.

Blending in

It must be the squat body and lugubrious expression that give frogfish their name. Certainly it can't be related to any frog-like leaping about, as these fish do very little but sit in one place. That place varies from a coral reef to – in one species – the floating seaweed of the Sargasso Sea.

Whatever the setting, however, a frogfish is an indistinguishable part of it. Its camouflage has evolved to mimic the background perfectly, with tones that replicate the colour of the surface – for instance, a purple frogfish sitting on a purple sponge – to warts, spots, stripes and skin flaps that reproduce the pattern and texture. And it can change colour with precision as it moves from one surface to another. In other words – at least from a victim's point of view – by the time you know what you're looking at it's generally too late.

But how to bring the victim close enough? Simple: just dangle the right bait. Frogfish, in common with all angler fish, have a long spine called an illicium – the first of three modified dorsal spines – projecting from their snout. On the end is a fleshy lure, called an esca, which they wiggle like a worm to entice curious prey closer.

This prey includes smaller fish and crustaceans. And once it is lured within reach of that cavernous maw the frogfish strikes at lightning speed, engulfing the victim within six milliseconds. The mouth can expand to 12 times its usual size in the process, allowing the frogfish to swallow prey 25% bigger than itself. If the lure gets bitten off in the struggle it will quickly grow again.

Getting around

Frogfish do not have a gas-filled swim bladder to keep them buoyant, like many fish. Instead they move around on the bottom using their modified pectoral fins as legs. They can get up quite a gallop, if required, but for an extra speedy burst they resort to jet propulsion – expelling water from the opercular opening behind the pectoral fins.

Male frogfish are virtually indistinguishable from females, except during spawning, when the female swells up with eggs. After spawning, a ribbon-like veil of spawn drifts for few days through the water before settling on the bottom.

There are 43 recognised species of frogfish in 12 different genera. They are widespread across the world's oceans – though the majority are confined to the Indo-Australian archipelago.

At a glance

Size:
10–20cm
Food:
small marine fish and crustaceans
Reproduction: female lays copious spawn in open water, fertilised externally by male
Habitat: coral reefs and other seabed environments, to depths of 100m; the Sargassum fish *Histrio histrio* lives entirely among floating *Sargassum* weed
Distribution: tropical and temperate seas and oceans, except for Mediterranean
Status: varies by species

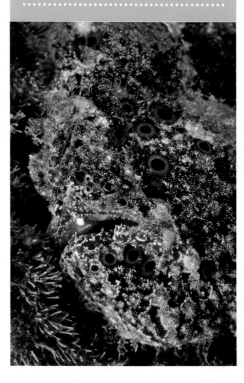

37. Scalloped hammerhead shark

Sphyrna lewini

Here is yet another animal where, to our ignorant eyes, it seems someone up high has been having a laugh. From the head down, this predatory fish has all the sleek elegance of any shark. So why, you wonder, spoil that celebrated lean-and-mean look by replacing the perfectly streamlined head that seems to work so well on other species with a great flat hammer? As ever, of course, there is method to evolution's madness.

Head case

Hammerhead sharks collectively make up the genus *Sphyrna*, which translates literally as 'hammer'. They are closely related to other Carcharhiniid sharks, and the fossil record suggests they can be traced back to the late Eocene or Oligocene, 30–40 million years ago.

The scalloped hammerhead is the best known and most widespread of ten species. It is a medium-sized shark, reaching a maximum length of 4m, and has the slim build, long tail and high dorsal fin characteristic of all hammerheads. Its white underside contrasts with its grey-brown to olive-green upperparts, which – in common only with pigs and humans – will tan a deeper shade if the shark spends much time close to the sunlit surface.

But there's no escaping that head. Known scientifically as a 'cephalofoil', it slices through the water as incongruously as a snowplough on the front of a Ferrari. The distinct wavy profile on the leading edge, caused by an indentation at the centre and one along each side, is what gives this species the 'scalloped' part of its name and identifies it from others in the genus. Like all its kind, the eyes and nostrils are placed far apart: one on each end of the cephalofoil.

Sensitive shark

Scientists have offered various explanations for the hammerhead's hammer. Some have suggested that it provides extra balance to help the shark manoeuvre after prey at close quarters. Others, noting that hammerheads are more negatively buoyant than other sharks, have suggested it acts as

a wing to boost lift under water. Many have also noted how a hammerhead uses its cephalofoil to pinion prey – such as stingrays – to the bottom, while delivering the killer bite.

These factors may all come into play. Most intriguing, however, is the discovery that a hammerhead's cephalofoil is covered with tiny sensory pores, known as ampullae of Lorenzini. All sharks have these sensors – they allow them to detect electrical signals emitted by prey – but in hammerheads they are especially abundant due to the extra surface area of the cephalofoil. This, coupled with the wide arc of perception that comes from having eyes and nostrils spaced so far apart, means that these fish are super-sensory machines, able to sniff out the merest hint of prey, like a minesweeper, and track it to its source.

Hammerheads feed on fish, both large and small, as well as octopus, squid and crustaceans. Their electro-sensitivity makes them expert at detecting flatfish hiding in the sand of the seabed; indeed, the stingray spines often found embedded in the mouths of hammerheads suggest that these are favourite prey.

Going without

Scalloped hammerheads reproduce once a year. A female gives birth to a litter of 12–38 'pups' after a gestation of nine to ten months. The youngsters develop inside a placenta – like mammals – and are born alive, emerging headfirst with their hammer folded back. Mating can be a violent affair, with the male biting the female as they spiral together in courtship. However, hammerheads are also capable of giving birth through parthenogenesis – with no sperm required from the male – meaning that the two sexes can live completely separate lives.

Young scalloped hammerheads are gregarious, forming schools of 100 of more by day, often around underwater seamounts. They migrate *en masse* to cooler waters during summer, heading away from the tropics towards the poles, for reasons that may have to do with reproduction or feeding. However, scalloped hammerheads may also feed alone, and older individuals tend to be more solitary. This species lives for 20–30 years.

Like most sharks, the scalloped hammerhead has often been tarred with the brush of 'killer'. In reality very few attacks on humans have even been recorded from any species of hammerhead. It will defend itself if threatened, however, so should always be treated with respect.

Sadly, our treatment of hammerheads has been far more brutal. This fish has long been heavily persecuted, both as a game fish and for the highly destructive trade in shark's fin soup. Many also meet a sorry end as part of the 'by-catch' waste of drift-net fishing. Today this species has been declared Endangered by the IUCN.

At a glance

Size: 3–4m

Food: fish, including rays and small sharks; crustaceans, squid, lobster

Reproduction: viviparous – female bears 12–38 pups after 9–10-month gestation; may also reproduce asexually, through parthenogenesis

Habitat: temperate and tropical waters, offshore and inshore; migrates to cooler waters in summer

Distribution: tropical and temperate seas and oceans worldwide

Status: Endangered

38. Large-tooth sawfish

Pristis perotteti

We humans may pride ourselves on our ingenious tools. Yet evolution had already honed most of the basic designs long before we could so much as shake a stick. This fish is a prime example: it carries on the end of its nose a fearsome implement that belongs somewhere between lumberyard and torture chamber. And it wields it to deadly effect.

Saw point

Sawfish are elasmobranches, along with sharks and rays, and thus have a skeleton made of cartilage, rather than bone. Their flattened body, with gills on the underside, shows that they are more closely related to rays.

No prizes for guessing how they got their name. The implement in question is an extension of the snout, known as the rostrum, and takes up about one-fifth of the fish's total length. It is lined on either side by 16–20 evenly spaced 'teeth', which are actually modified versions of the denticles that cover its rough skin.

Other distinctive features include the broad, flattened fins – like any ray's – and the golden to ochre-brown colouring of the upperparts, with which it can blend into the muddy or sandy bottom. Its sheer size is also impressive: this species, the largest of seven, can measure 6m long and weigh over half a tonne.

Slasher attack

The large-tooth sawfish lives in coastal shallows, including estuaries and lagoons, where it feeds on fish, crustaceans and other bottom-dwellers. It has even been found as far as 750km up the Amazon. Like all sawfish, it is fairly lethargic, mostly lying on the bottom or hovering just above it.

But this lethargy is not permanent. The sawfish finds its prey by rooting in the bottom with its motion-sensitive rostrum. Then – and this is the scary bit – it erupts into a frenzy of violence, slashing about it like something from *The Texas Chainsaw Massacre* and leaving its prey stunned, mutilated or even impaled. Victims are then scraped off the teeth and swallowed whole.

A sawfish's gills are ineffective while it is lying on the bottom, so it breathes through large holes behind its eyes, called spiracles. The eyes themselves are little use in the murky conditions, and the sawfish gets nearly all its sensory information via electro-sensory pores on the rostrum.

At a glance

Size: up to 6m
Weight: maximum recorded 591kg
Food: fish, especially bottom-dwelling species; crustaceans
Reproduction: ovoviviparous; ±8 young born live
Habitat: shallow coastal waters, including lagoons, estuaries, tidal rivers
Distribution: tropical northwest Atlantic and central eastern Pacific, between latitudes 32°N and 19°S
Status: Endangered

Sawfish struggles

Sawfish reproduce slowly. They are ovoviviparous, which means that the young develop in a weak eggshell inside the mother, nourished by a yolk sac, and are born live. Each of the eight 'pups' emerges with a rubbery sheath around its rostrum to protect the mother during birth. This falls away shortly after it is born. Sawfish can live for 25–30 years and reach breeding maturity at 10–12 years – about 3.5m.

Natural predators of the large-tooth sawfish include bull sharks and the American crocodile. But humans are a much greater threat. Today all sawfish species are endangered. Overfishing – both for meat and for the rostrum as a trophy – has drastically depleted the population of this species and this, combined with the degradation of coastal wetlands, has seen it disappear from much of its former range. Once common in Lake Nicaragua, it has not been seen there for years.

39. Splitfin flashlight fish

Anomalops kaptotron

Turn it off! This small fish has an extraordinary ability to illuminate the inky darkness of an underwater cave by flashing bright lights beneath its eyes. The trick is enough to confuse prey and predator alike.

Living lights

The lights in question are actually organs called photophores, one located beneath each eye. They contain bioluminescent red bacteria, which produce the light, and can be turned on and off – as it were – by covering them with a thin membrane of skin or rotating the organ in its socket. With the fish's body being a velvety blue-black, these lights are all that is visible in the darkness of the depths.

By turning its lights suddenly on and then off, a flashlight fish can dazzle a passing predator and make good its escape. Alternatively, by leaving them on, it can attract a cloud of the tiny shrimps and other zooplankton on which it feeds – like moths to a flame. Flashlight fish can probably also communicate with each other by blinking their lights. Their huge eyes enable them to pick up reflected light from their own signals.

The splitfin flashlight fish is one of eight species in the family Anomalopidae and inhabits the tropical waters of the western Pacific. It is a deep-water fish, found in small shoals in caves and other darkened places, and ascends to shallow waters to feed at night. Unsurprisingly, it is popular in the aquarium trade.

At a glance

Size: up to 35cm (in deep water form)
Food: zooplankton; small crustaceans
Habitat: caves and trenches near drop-offs; moves to surface at night
Distribution: western Pacific – Indonesia to Japan and Australia
Status: Least Concern

---

40. Sloane's viperfish

Chauliodus sloani

Abandon hope all ye who enter here. The front end of this fish is the stuff of nightmares, with a grotesque battery of fangs protruding from its cavernous mouth like the spikes of an iron maiden.

All mouth

It's hard to see beyond that mouth: the rest of the slim body seems to taper away to insignificance. But close inspection reveals other strange features, such as a long spine for a dorsal fin and a row of light-producing photophores along its flanks.

The explanation for these features lies in the fish's habitat. This is a deep-sea, or bathypelagic, species, which lives 1,000–2,000m down. It uses the bioluminescent lights to attract a mate and dangles the dorsal spine over its head to lure victims. The large light-sensitive eyes help it to see what it's doing.

Prey, which includes crustaceans and other fishes, has little chance of escape from that mantrap of a mouth. The viperfish has an elongated stomach that can accommodate prey up to 63% of its own body length. It also has a unique hinge between backbone and skull to help get big mouthfuls down.

Like many deep-sea dwellers, this one moves closer to the surface at night when it can more easily avoid predators. This is when it often ends up in fishing nets – our only opportunity to get a close look at such a bizarre fish.

At a glance

Size: up to 35cm
Food: bony fish and crustaceans
Reproduction: oviparous; reproduces by external spawning
Habitat: bathypelagic zone of ocean (1,000–2,000m deep); moving to mesopelagic zone (200–1,000) at night
Distribution: temperate and tropical seas and oceans, from 63°N to 50°S
Status: Least Concern

41. Fog-basking beetle

Onymacris unguicularis

The towering dunes of the Namib Desert appear, at first glance, to be as hostile as the surface of the moon. Rain here is a fleeting luxury and may not fall for years at a stretch. Yet the dunes harbour a secret: a thick blanket of coastal fog rolls inland at night, bringing life-giving moisture to those who can capture it. And this extraordinary insect has evolved an ingenious means of doing just that.

Desert gymnast

The fog-basking beetle lives on west-facing dune slipfaces – the sheltered side, where windblown detritus accumulates. After a day spent foraging over the scorching desert surface, it buries itself beneath the sand. Then, in the early hours, as the fog begins to roll in from the sea, it emerges and makes its way up a dune. On top, it turns to face the wind, and – by straightening its long back legs and lowering its head – performs a headstand.

Why the gymnastics? The beetle is simply harnessing, intuitively, the laws of physics. The fog condenses on its upturned body in tiny droplets of

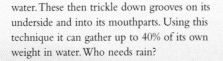

At a glance

Length: 1.5–2cm
Food: wind-blown detritus on desert surface
Habitat: the west-facing slip-faces of desert sand dunes
Distribution: Namib Desert, Namibia
Status: Least Concern

water. These then trickle down grooves on its underside and into its mouthparts. Using this technique it can gather up to 40% of its own weight in water. Who needs rain?

Family ties

The fog-basking beetle is not the only species to have perfected a trick or two for capturing water. One related species, *Lepidochora discoidalis*, also buries itself in the sand at night, but returns to the surface when the fog rolls in to excavate a narrow trench in the sand across its path. The ridges that line this trench absorb all the drinking moisture it needs. Not surprisingly, this species is known as the 'fog-trapping' beetle.

Fog-baskers and fog-trappers are among an estimated 20,000 species around the globe that belong to the Tenebrionid family, also known as darkling beetles. Southern Africa is particularly rich in tenebrionids, and even those without a water-capturing party trick are still remarkably well adapted to the arid conditions of the region.

Unlike most other beetles, they are flightless. Beneath their fused wing cases, in place of folded wings, is a humid cavity into which their spiracles (respiratory pores) open. This means they lose much less water to evaporation than if those pores were exposed to the dry air outside, as they are on other beetles.

To compensate for being earthbound, many tenebrionid species have also evolved exceptionally long legs, which allows them both to sprint away from danger and to dash from one patch of shade to another. Many also use their long legs to tap out a tattoo with which to attract a mate – hence their local name of tok-tokkies.

42. Malaysian orchid mantis

Hymenopus coronatus

When is a flower not a flower? Answer: when it's an insect pretending. With this mantis the deception is so complete that most prey never spot the difference – until it's too late.

Blooming deadly

The Malaysian orchid mantis, as its name suggests, lives among tropical blooms in the rainforests of southeast Asia. Not only does its colouration match this background to a tee, but its four 'standing' legs also sport petal-shaped projections.

This disguise renders the mantis invisible to moths, insects and other prey drawn to the flowers' nectar.

And this is when the front two legs shoot out to grab the unsuspecting victim so the deadly mandibles can get stuck in. Large individuals can even take small lizards.

The disguise also helps the mantis hide from birds and other potential predators. When danger threatens it will enhance the petal look by arching up its thorax. But if its cover is blown it will bite viciously at any would-be predator.

Female mantises are twice the size of males. They deposit their eggs in a foam capsule called an ootheca. The nymphs are bright orange and black when they emerge. They feed on tiny insects, and become paler at each shedding of the exoskeleton as they progress towards adulthood. Adult females may become entirely white.

At a glance

Length: 6cm (female); 3cm (male)
Food: mostly flying insects, including moths and butterflies
Habitat: flowering plants in tropical rainforest
Distribution: Malaysia and Sumatra (Indonesia)
Status: Least Concern

43. Cone snails

Conidae spp

What could be more harmless than one of these pretty seashells? Just pick it up and admire the gorgeous colours and patterns, right? Wrong! Inside is a predatory snail that fires poison harpoons. Mess with it at your peril.

Murderous mollusc

There are around 500 species in the family Conidae. Most live on coral reefs; a few inhabit subtropical coasts. All have an ornate conical shell – though, while alive, this may be obscured by an outer skin called the periostracum. The largest are as big as a small shoe.

Some cone snails hunt molluscs, some worms and some even fish, and all use an ingenious means of capturing prey. The snail extends a long tubular proboscis towards its target, down which it fires a venom-laden 'harpoon' – actually a modified tooth

At a glance

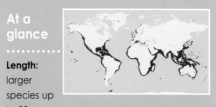

Length: larger species up to 23cm
Food: worms, fish, molluscs (according to species)
Habitat: coral reefs; intertidal areas
Distribution: tropical seas and oceans worldwide; some subtropical coasts, including California and South Africa
Status: varies by species

formed in a structure called the radula. This paralyses the victim and is then reeled back in – complete with prey – on a cord. Once the meal is digested, the snail retracts its proboscis and reloads with another harpoon.

A cone snail's venom is a complex neurotoxin that packs a powerful punch; powerful enough, in a few species, to kill a human – though fatalities are rare. It has also important pharmacological applications, being a powerful painkiller and offering potential use in the treatment of Alzheimer's and Parkinson's diseases.

3 STAYING ALIVE

Self-defence has produced some of the most ingenious adaptations in the animal kingdom. Just as predators have evolved an arsenal of weaponry and strategy with which to capture their prey, so prey animals have evolved just as many means of escaping their clutches. In this perpetual arms race, natural selection ensures that neither side gains the upper hand for long.

Low profile

Some animals rely on vigilance to avoid predators, keeping a constant lookout for trouble on the horizon and clearing off when it appears – often using alarm calls to alert their companions. But both sentry duty and running away take precious energy and there is an inevitable trade-off with feeding time.

An alternative way to avoid being eaten is to avoid being spotted in the first place. Crypsis is the scientific term for the many and varied strategies of disguise – including straightforward camouflage, in which an animal's shape or colouration allows it to blend unnoticed into its background. Among the more extreme masters of the camouflage art are the leaf-tailed geckos of Madagascar (page 77), which are not only the exact colour and texture of bark, but also press down a fringe of skin onto the surface to avoid casting any telltale shadow. Other top exponents include the tawny frogmouth (page 76), whose cryptically patterned plumage almost

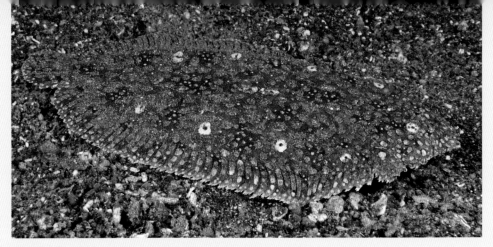

▲ Flatfish, such as this peacock sole, are the masters of lying low.

▼ The sunbittern has both cryptic plumage for camouflage and bold wing markings to startle a predator.

exactly replicates the surface against which it hides by day, and the leafy seadragon (page 84), whose ornate embellishments render it indistinguishable from the weedy tangle in which it lurks.

A slight variation on camouflage is mimesis, whereby an animal does not exactly avoid detection but is disguised to resemble a part of its background that is of no interest to the predator. Thus the treehopper (page 89) looks just like a thorn, while the leaf-nosed snake (page 83), is a dead ringer for a vine, complete with a bizarre bud-like protrusion on the end of its nose.

The best form of defence

But what to do if you're spotted and there's no time to run away? One technique is to fight back. Many prey species can use hooves, horns, quills, stings and other armaments to lethal effect – enough to make any predator think again. Often the threat alone is enough, thus the lowland streaked tenrec of Madagascar (page 74) erects its bristling battery of spines to unnerve an assailant, just as a rattlesnake shakes its rattle.

Seizing on this principle, some animals use bluff to exaggerate the threat they pose – puffing up fur or feathers to increase their apparent size, and hissing, gnashing or baring fangs. The frilled lizard (page 80) inflates an umbrella-like ruff of skin around its neck that makes it appear a far more intimidating creature than the rather skinny reptile it really is. The caterpillar of the puss moth (page 88), rears up its body to reveal two rather alarming false eyes at the front and a double-pronged 'sting' at the back. It's completely harmless, but many birds don't hang around long enough to find out.

Other threats are less empty. The animal kingdom does a fine line in noxious sprays, from the pungent aroma of a skunk to the hot, toxic jet of a bombardier beetle. A spitting cobra (page 81), having already spread a warning hood, will spray an eyeful of blinding venom at any attacker that fails to heed the sign. A desert horned lizard (page 82), more bizarrely, will squirt blood out of its eyes – not deadly, but both shocking and foul-tasting enough to be a highly effective deterrent.

Colour coding

Many of nature's most noxious animals use bold warning colours to advertise their identity. This is called aposematism. It explains, for example, the stripy livery of a wasp or the garish bands of a coral snake. The idea is that predators, through experience, learn to heed the signal and keep clear. Natural selection has taken this principle an intriguing step further by endowing many perfectly harmless creatures with colour schemes exactly like those of their harmful relatives. This is known as Batesian mimicry and has produced a wide spectrum of creatures that, like sheep in wolves' clothing, closely resemble their much more dangerous relatives. Hence the wasp stripes of the humble hoverfly or the coral snake bands of the non-venomous milk snake.

Master among these impersonators is surely the mimic octopus of Indonesia (page 86). By changing colour and rearranging its limbs it can mimic not only the appearance, but also the movements of a whole range of its aquatic neighbours, from lionfish to sea snake. It even tailors each disguise to the specific threat it faces, choosing the one that is most likely to intimidate the approaching predator.

When the game's up

Occasionally, however, no amount of bluff, disguise, threat or concealment will do the trick. The predator has seen through your tactics and, undeterred, is moving in for the kill. Time, then, for a final roll of the dice – and nature still has a few of these up its sleeve. An armadillo lizard (page 82) will seize its tail in its mouth and roll itself up

into an unswallowable bracelet of spiky scales; a short-beaked echidna (page 72) will dig itself into the ground, leaving only its spines protruding; and a ground pangolin (page 70) will curl itself into a seemingly impregnable ball of scales, its tail sawing wickedly back and forth if an inquisitive paw or muzzle intrudes. Only the most determined predator will brave such defences.

But what if the predator does persist and makes a grab? Well, just don't try this with an electric eel (page 85), which can generate enough electric current to knock you senseless, or a hagfish (page 85), that will cover you in glutinous slime while writhing in knots to make good its escape.

In short, every animal, however vulnerable and defenceless it may appear, knows how to take care of itself. But still there are some that take the hands-off message to extremes. Chameleons (page 78) not only change colour – both for disguise and warning – but also shake like a swaying leaf, hiss, bite and inflate themselves. Despite being utterly harmless, these animals are feared by people across Africa as evil spirits – and, as far as they're concerned, that's job done.

▲ *Deadly coral snake or harmless milk snake? In fact it's the latter, but who's to know?*

44. Ground pangolin
Manis temminckii

A 15kg walking artichoke? A metre-long ant-eating pinecone? It's hard to describe a pangolin in animal terms. This bizarre mammal is the only warm-blooded creature on the planet that is completely covered in scales. And its peculiarities do not end there.

Scale model

The ground pangolin, also known as the Cape or common pangolin, is the most widespread of Africa's four pangolin species, and the only one found in the eastern and southern parts of the continent. Its broad range, however, does not make it any easier to see. Indeed the elusiveness of this animal is legendary in African safari circles; even game rangers can spend a lifetime in the bush and never set eyes on one.

A pangolin's scales, like our fingernails, are made of keratin. They form a suit of armour that completely covers the animal's upperparts and accounts for nearly 20% of its total weight. A threatened pangolin curls up to protect its vulnerable belly, wrapping its tail tightly over its head to form a virtually impregnable ball. And this strategy is not only a passive one: while curled up it will scythe its tail back and forth, using the blade-like edges of the scales to slice viciously into any unwelcome paw or muzzle. It will even dowse an assailant, skunk-style, with a foul-smelling spray from its anal glands. With a pangolin, you know when you're not welcome.

Uncurled, a pangolin looks more reptile than mammal. At one end is a long, broad, almost crocodile-like tail. At the other is a tiny pointed head. Each front leg bears three formidable, curved claws, which are held curled up to make walking easier. In fact, pangolins often walk on their back legs only, holding their front legs off the ground and using the tail as a counter-balance.

Ant extraction

If you're familiar with the giant anteater (page 38) or aardvark (page 41), you'll have guessed what those claws are for. Pangolins eat ants and, just like the other devotees of this special diet, they have special gear for the job. Indeed, their daily routine is very similar to an aardvark's: they are solitary, nocturnal foragers that hole up in a burrow or thicket by day, then emerge at night to sniff out ant and termite mounds with their powerful sense of smell. Once the prize is located, they use those claws to hack their way in and a long, sticky tongue to extract the goodies.

A pangolin's tongue, like that of a giant anteater, is not attached to the hyoid bone but rooted deep in its thorax, down towards the sternum. This flickering ribbon can measure 50cm in length and is coated in sticky spittle, produced from an enlarged salivary gland. Pangolins have no teeth so can't chew their food. Instead, a gizzard-like muscular adaptation allows them to grind it down in the stomach, aided by the grit and small stones that they ingest while feeding.

A female ground pangolin gives birth in a burrow – either one she has dug herself, or the old residence of an aardvark or warthog. Her single youngster, weighing just 200–300g, emerges after a gestation of 120–150 days. It stays underground for the first three or four weeks then begins to accompany her on excursions above ground, hitching a ride on the base of her tail.

A common plan

Pangolins belong to a unique order (Pholotida) that is confined to Africa and Asia. They are entirely unrelated to the armadillos and anteaters (Xenarthra) of the New World, with which they are often confused. The fact that these groups have so many unusual traits in common – the body armour, extensible tongue, digging claws and lack of teeth – is down to convergent evolution. The adaptations that each has evolved separately for a lifestyle based on eating ants have 'converged', through natural selection, towards a common form. What works on one continent, it seems, works just as well on another.

Ground pangolins inhabit savanna and woodland habitats, preferably with sandy soil. They are vulnerable to bush fires, and occasionally fall prey to predators such as hyenas and leopards. A more serious threat, however, comes from people, who have long ascribed mystical properties to pangolins. In parts of Africa these animals are sacrificed for rain-making ceremonies and their scales used in charms to ward off witchcraft. Today there is a thriving market for pangolins in China and the Far East – both as food, and for the medicinal products derived from their scales, which are thought to help with everything from blood circulation to fertility.

At a glance

Length: head and body 34–61cm; tail 31–50cm
Weight: 7–18kg
Food: ants, termites, other insect larvae
Reproduction: one young, born after gestation of 120–150 days
Habitat: lowland woodland and savanna
Distribution: southern and eastern Africa, from Lake Chad to northern South Africa
Status: Near Threatened

This species is classified as Near Threatened by the IUCN. In truth, however, its secretive nature makes populations very hard to assess. Nobody really knows how many there are.

45. Short-beaked echidna

Tachyglossus aculeatus

This outlandish mammal, also known as spiny anteater, would surely make any bizarre animal top ten. Not only does it look extremely odd, combining a hedgehog's spines with an anteater's snout; it also has several surprising party tricks – not least of which is the ability to lay an egg.

Sinking ship

'Spiny anteater' is not strictly correct. Echidnas are not, taxonomically speaking, anteaters. In fact they and the platypus (see page 118) make up the monotremes: the only order of mammals to lay eggs. In fairness, however, they most certainly do eat ants and are unquestionably very spiny.

The spines in question are modified hairs, which cover the entire upperparts and offer an almost impregnable defence. A cornered echidna will dig rapidly down, disappearing like a sinking ship into soft soil until only its spines protrude. Alternatively it will roll into a ball or wedge itself into a crevice, either strategy presenting a thorny dilemma for any would-be assailant.

Once an echidna reveals itself you'll notice further peculiarities. Its short legs stick out sideways, more like a lizard's than a mammal's, and give it a distinct rolling gait. Its hind feet bear long claws adapted for grooming between the spines, which helps it deal with its personal parasite *Bradiopsylla echidnae*, the world's largest flea. (Males also have a spur on their hind feet, although – unlike in the platypus – this evolutionary relic no longer delivers venom.) The small head has barely visible eyes and no external ears, but the long snout powers a keen sense of smell that is especially attuned to ants.

Lapping it up

Echidnas forage in dry, open country – by night in warmer areas but also by day in cooler southern locations. They move slowly but travel widely, and will even swim, using their long snout as a snorkel. Once they have located ants or termites in the ground or an old log, they dig in quickly, using the long claws on their front feet to reach the prize.

An echidna's tongue is like that of all ant-eating mammals: long, thin and sticky. It darts rapidly in and out to capture prey (*Tachyglossus* means fast tongue), protruding up to 18cm beyond the snout, and is sharp enough to penetrate soil and rotten wood. Echidnas have no teeth and can open their jaws only 5mm, but hard pads on their palate and tongue crush prey inside the mouth. Larger prey, such as beetle grubs, is first squashed so they can lap up the juices.

It is not only echidnas' legs that seem reptilian. These animals have a normal body temperature of just 31–33°C – among the lowest of any mammal – and allow their temperature to fall in cold weather, sometimes entering a state of torpor. Unusually among mammals, they also have a cloaca: a single orifice for both their urinary and excretory tract.

From egg to puggle

Echidna courtship is a curious business. A female leaves a scent trail for males, which follow her in a kind of conga line of up to ten individuals. A successful suitor pushes the female onto her side so that the pair can mate without fear of spines. Gestation lasts 21–28 days, during which the female digs a nursery burrow. Here she lays a single rubbery egg, from which a tiny 1.5cm-long baby, known as a puggle, breaks out after ten days. The youngster immediately climbs up into its mother's small, backward-facing pouch. Here it is nourished on her milk, which – having no nipples – she secretes onto her under-fur from glands known as milk patches. The puggle leaves the pouch after two to three months, having grown too spiny for further confinement. It is weaned at six months.

The short-beaked echidna is the most common of three species, and is Australia's most widespread native mammal – found in almost any suitable habitat with ants and termites. It has few natural enemies, though eagles, Tasmanian devils and introduced dogs and foxes have all been known to try their luck. A worse threat is traffic, and road signs in some areas warn drivers to look out. The two species of long-beaked echidna (*Zaglossus* spp) are much rarer, and confined to rainforest habitats in New Guinea.

Echidnas have long been celebrated in Aboriginal culture: one Noongar myth explains that the animal came into being after hunters threw spears into a wombat, which then returned, bristling with spines – and indignation – to turn the tables on its attackers.

At a glance

Size: 30–45cm (larger in Tasmania)

Weight: 2–5kg

Food: ants, termites, grubs

Reproduction: lays 1 egg; hatches after 10 days

Habitat: dry, open country, from savanna to woodland; adapts well to cleared land

Distribution: widespread across Australia and New Guinea

Status: Least Concern

46. Lowland streaked tenrec

Hemicentetes semispinosus

Attack is the best form of defence – or so contends the lowland streaked tenrec. This spiky, hedgehog-like creature rushes at any would-be assailant, bucking and bristling as it attempts to drive home its lethal quills. Bizarrely, in less perilous situations, those same quills give it a language all its own.

Island isolation

To connoisseurs of the weird it will come as no surprise that tenrecs (Tenrecidae) hail from Madagascar, home to a true gallery of oddballs. These insectivorous creatures were among the island's earliest colonisers after it broke away from the super-continent of Gondwana about 120 million years ago. With no competition from other small mammals, they evolved a great variety of forms. Today the lowland streaked tenrec is among the more striking of 16 very different species.

Like all tenrecs, this one exhibits various primitive features that are rare among modern mammals, including a cloaca (a single orifice for urinary and excretory tracts) and a variable body temperature. These aren't likely to grab your attention when you first clap eyes on one. What you *will* see, however, is a pointy-nosed, rat-sized animal, bristling with quills and boldly decked out in yellow and dark-brown stripes.

The quills are modified hairs – the most lethal being the barbed, detachable ones around the nape. The patterns provide camouflage on the forest floor but may also be warning colouration, suggesting to an aggressor that it is more prudent to back off.

Quill talk

Streaked tenrecs forage in small groups on the forest floor, using their long snout and sensitive whiskers to detect worms and other invertebrates among the leaf-litter. They keep in constant contact by vibrating the stiff quills on their mid-back to produce a chirping sound. This technique, known as stridulation, is similar in principle to the noise made by grasshoppers rubbing legs against wings. Tenrecs can also hiss and grunt by more conventional vocal means.

Breeding takes place during the rains, when food is most abundant. This species is not as fecund as some (the common tenrec can bear an amazing 32 young, suckling them on up to 29 nipples). A female, nonetheless, produces a litter of up to 11 babies after a gestation of 55–63 days. These young, in turn, can breed after just 35 days. This leads to quite a complex social grouping, at least by insectivore standards, with up to 20 animals of different generations sharing a burrow and each group producing several litters per season.

Natural enemies of the streaked tenrec include any mongoose or fossa brave or canny enough to take on those quills. A more serious threat is deforestation – and, worryingly, recent studies have suggested that tourism may also be having a negative impact on populations. Nonetheless this species is not currently threatened.

At a glance

Size: 13–19cm
Weight: 90–220g (average 130g)
Food: worms and other invertebrates
Reproduction: 2–11 young (average 6); mature at 35 days
Habitat: lowland and mid-altitude rainforest
Distribution: eastern Madagascar
Status: Least Concern

47. Common wombat

Vombatus ursinus

It's an ignominious fate for any predator: crushed to death by your prey's backside. But that's the risk of pursuing a wombat into its burrow. This thickset marsupial has a reinforced rump, and it's not afraid to use it.

Stocky-in-trade

Wombats have a stocky frame, blunt head and bristly fur that suggests a cross between a bear and a guinea pig. They waddle about on short limbs, cropping the grass and periodically disappearing down a burrow.

This species is the most widespread of three. It is distinguished from its two 'hairy-nosed' cousins by its naked, black nose. All are marsupials, like most Australian mammals, and thus boast both a pouch and an ancient evolutionary heritage. Indeed wombats are thought to have diverged from other marsupials more than 40 million years ago.

Slow burn

Common wombats inhabit the cooler, temperate regions of southeastern Australia, frequenting woodland and heathland from coast to mountain. They prefer sloping ground, for burrow drainage, and are perfectly at home in winter snow. Their diet consists mostly of fibrous grasses, which they grind down with powerful jaws, their teeth growing continuously to counteract the effects of wear.

Food takes a long time to pass through a wombat. Indeed a wombat's extremely slow metabolic rate helps explain why it is that anomaly among mammals: a large herbivore that burrows. Its low energy requirement means it needs to feed only a few hours each day, leaving plenty of time for the digging.

Pouch protection

Wombats may excavate burrows up to 30m long, using the long claws on their powerful forepaws and bulldozing the earth out behind them with their backside. Inside, a female gives birth to a single tiny offspring, known as a joey, once every two years. As in all marsupials, the youngster crawls up immediately into its mother's pouch, which faces backwards to keep the soil out of the joey's face while she is digging. Here it stays for up to ten months, by which time it weighs 3.5–6.5kg. It is not independent until 18 months.

A wombat confronted by a predator will generally then make headfirst for its burrow. Below ground the specially toughened skin on its behind defends it against attacks from the rear and it will reverse into an attacker – which cannot easily manoeuvre in the narrow tunnel – and use its great strength to drive it out or, worse, crush it against the sides.

The common wombat once ranged throughout Australia but has declined due to persecution and habitat loss. The Bass Strait subspecies (*V. u. ursinus*) is now confined to Flinders Island and classed as Vulnerable. In some places people regard this animal as a pest for its habit of burrowing under rabbit-proof fences.

At a glance

Size: head and body length 90–130cm; tail 2.5cm

Weight: 22–45kg; southern races larger

Food: High-fibre grasses

Reproduction: one young, carried in pouch and weaned at 12–15 months

Habitat: temperate woodland, heaths and coast; rocky slopes and sandy soils

Distribution: Southern and eastern Australia, from Tasmania to southern Queensland

Status: Vulnerable

48. Tawny frogmouth

Podargus strigoides

It's the stuff of fairy-tale nightmares: a gnarled old stump on a dead, twisted tree suddenly reveals blazing yellow eyes and a huge gaping mouth. But it's not a haunted forest: it's just a nocturnal bird from Australia. And the dead-stump act is a vital strategy in its self-preservation.

Owl illusions

The general appearance and nocturnal ways of the tawny frogmouth have led to the popular misconception that it is some kind of owl. It certainly has the eyes – and also a wicked hooked bill. But one look at those short legs and rather feeble feet reveal that this is no bird of prey that kills with its talons. In fact this crow-sized bird belongs in the same order as the nightjars (Caprimulgiformes). The fine feathers around its bill, known as rictal bristles, are characteristic of this group, giving them added sensitivity when capturing small insect prey.

You might easily get a good look at a tawny frogmouth without actually seeing it, so effective is its camouflage. The cryptic patterning of fine dark bars and streaks on a mottled silver-grey background perfectly mimics a dead branch. Some individuals have the same pattern in rufous, which is just as hard to make out. Either way, the bird often

enhances the deception by perching in the middle of a dead branch with its bill tilted upwards and its eyes narrowed to slits, as though part of the tree.

Night shift

Tawny frogmouths live in open woodland and savanna. They roost by day, using their camouflage to avoid the attention of predators. By night they feed on a variety of ground-living prey, from large invertebrates, such as beetles and cicadas, to small frogs or even mice. They generally adopt the sit-and-wait approach of the camouflage hunter, waiting until prey passes beneath their perch then swooping down to snatch it up in their huge gape. Sometimes they may also flutter out to capture moths or other flying insects on the wing.

A pair sticks together until one bird dies. They use the same nest each year, patching it up with a few running repairs. This generally consists of a shallow stick platform on a horizontal branch, often camouflaged with mosses, lichens or spiders' webs and lined with green leaves. The breeding season is August to December (though in arid areas it will depend upon the rains). The female lays two to three eggs, which the pair take turns to incubate: the male by day; both by night. The chicks hatch after 30 days and fledge after another 25 days, not leaving the nest until they can fly.

The tawny frogmouth is the most common and widespread of three frogmouth species in Australia. It is not considered threatened – though sadly it often falls victim to traffic when pursuing prey in front of car headlights after dark.

At a glance

Size: length 35–50cm (larger in the south of its range)
Weight: 300–600g (males heavier)
Food: large invertebrates, including spiders, beetles and centipedes; occasionally small vertebrates
Reproduction: 2–3 eggs; young fledge after 55 days
Habitat: open woodland and savanna (not rainforest or desert)
Distribution: throughout Australia, including Tasmania
Status: Least Concern

49. Leaf-tailed geckos

Uroplatus spp

Many animals use camouflage to blend in with tree trunks. But few have taken this strategy to the extremes of Madagascar's leaf-tailed geckos, whose deception is almost literally seamless. Colour, shape, texture and posture all combine to make this elusive reptile the master of rainforest disguise.

Barking up the right tree

There are at least 12 species of *Uroplatus* gecko – though the count has steadily risen since they were first discovered, and their sheer elusiveness suggests that more could be waiting in the wings. They fall into two main categories.

The larger species, such as the common leaf-tailed gecko (*U. fimbriatus*), are adapted to hide on tree trunks, which they do head-downwards. Not only is their flattened body the colour and pattern of the bark, right down to the faux moss and lichen; it also sports fringing flaps of skin (called dermal flaps) that overlay its contours, sealing the join between reptile and tree and obliterating any telltale shadow. Some species, such as the mossy leaf-tailed gecko (*U. sikorae*), have pimpled skin that mimics the bark's texture. Most can change colour to match their background as they move from one tree to another.

The smaller leaf-tailed gecko species feed in bushes and so are adapted to mimic foliage. The whole body of the satanic leaf-tailed gecko (*U. phantasticus*) looks like a curled-up leaf, and its tail even has tiny notches as though the leaf has decayed at the edges. The prominent eye ridges and red eyes of this species give it a diabolical expression, hence the name.

Night wanderers

Leaf-tailed geckos are nocturnal, foraging after dark through the tangled greenery of Madagascar's rainforest. Their huge eyes are an adaptation to night vision, and their large mouths can engulf any prey they are able to subdue – mostly large insects such as beetles and cicadas. These geckos actually have the most teeth of any lizard: all the better for dealing with awkward, crunchy prey.

By day leaf-tailed geckos remain still, glued in position and trusting to their camouflage. Indeed they often return to the exact same spot day after day – a fact revealed by the bare patches they leave on a tree trunk. If disturbed, however, they can put on an alarming show by suddenly raising the head and gaping wide to reveal the bright pink or orange lining of the mouth. This, accompanied in some species by a malevolant hiss, can be enough to give any predator second thoughts and has cast these lizards as evil in local folklore.

Female leaf-tailed geckos lay two to four eggs (depending on the species and the local conditions), which hatch after 60–70 days. All species are vulnerable to deforestation, especially those with highly localised distributions. They are also threatened by the illegal pet trade – indeed the WWF places them in its top ten 'most wanted' species, and CITES has given them special protection.

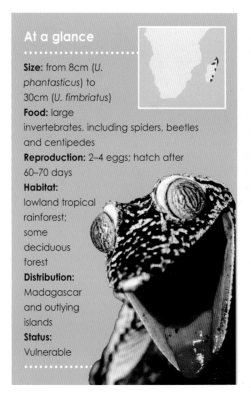

At a glance

Size: from 8cm (*U. phantasticus*) to 30cm (*U. fimbriatus*)
Food: large invertebrates, including spiders, beetles and centipedes
Reproduction: 2–4 eggs; hatch after 60–70 days
Habitat: lowland tropical rainforest; some deciduous forest
Distribution: Madagascar and outlying islands
Status: Vulnerable

50. Chameleons
Chamaeleonidae spp

How much weirdness can you handle in one animal? Chameleons have the lot: skin that changes colour on demand; eyes that swivel every which way; an outrageously extendable tongue; and the horned, crested head of a dinosaur. Small wonder that these perfectly harmless lizards excite fear and superstition right across rural Africa.

What's in a name?
The word chameleon is the Latinised form of the ancient Greek *khamaileon*, which derives from *khamai* ('on the ground') and *leon* ('lion') and translates loosely as 'ground lion'. This refers to the reptile's intimidating defensive display, in which it inflates its body, gapes wide, hisses and lunges at its assailant.

Treeline trickery
The unusual traits of chameleons have not evolved merely to give credulous people the jitters: they are ingenious adaptations to a life in the trees. Most chameleons live in low trees and shrubs, and their hunched, flattened body shape closely resembles the leaves among which they clamber. The horns, crests, flaps and other projections further serve to break up their telltale animal outline, helping render the retiring reptile invisible to predator and prey alike.

Similarly, the slow-motion progress of chameleons – they do not dash about like other lizards but take one deliberate step at a time – reflects the premium they put upon stealth and concealment among the branches. In the arboreal ambush game, a good grip is more important than speed and agility. Each long leg ends in tong-like feet, with opposable, sharp-clawed toes fused into one set of three and one of two. Back-up comes from the prehensile tail, with which a chameleon can anchor itself while plotting its course through the flimsy foliage.

Point and shoot
Typical chameleon prey comprises jumpy, fast-moving insects such as crickets and mantids – which is where the extraordinary optics come in. The conical eyes have permanently fused eyelids, leaving just a pinhole through which to see, and revolve independently of one another, like turrets. This allows the chameleon a 360° arc of vision with which to scan for prey. Once a target is sighted, both eyes swing round to focus on it together, providing the stereoscopic depth perception required for an accurate tongue strike.

And this strike is perhaps the most alarming trick in the whole repertoire. A chameleon can shoot out its tongue further than its own body length to capture prey – and at a frightening speed of around three hundredths of a second. The sticky ball of muscle on the tip forms a suction cup upon impact, trapping the unsuspecting victim, which is then whipped back into the chameleon's maw.

All change

The famous colour changing – now, rather unjustly for chameleons, a metaphor for fickleness in humans – is not, contrary to popular belief, all about camouflage. A chameleon's general colour does indeed match its surroundings and will adapt as these change – from green to brown, for example, as it descends from tree to ground. But the vivid flashes of brighter hues, including reds, yellows and blues in some species, are more to do with communication, such as when a chameleon feels threatened (usually a dark colour) or aroused (a more intense flush). Males, who perform sexual displays to females, have the brighter colours – and also sport the more extravagant horns, crests and other embellishments.

The mechanism of colour change involves specialised cells called chromatophores that lie in layers under the chameleon's transparent skin. These layers comprise a mixture of pigmented, light-reflecting and melanin cells, which the reptile can use like an artist's palette in order to achieve the required effect.

Theme and variations

A few chameleons give birth to live young, but most are egg-layers. The female digs a hole in the ground and deposits her clutch at the bottom. This clutch varies from just two to four eggs in some species to nearly 100 in others. The hatching time is similarly variable: generally from four to 12 months, but in some species up to two years.

One Madagsacar species, Labord's chameleon, has a life cycle that is more akin to that of insects than other reptiles: its young spend eight to nine months in the egg before hatching in November. They then rush through a four-to-five-month burst of eating and reproduction, after which they all die simultaneously. This makes this species the shortest-lived of all four-limbed vertebrates.

True chameleons belong to the family Chamaeleonidae and are confined to the Old World. Nearly half of the 160 or so species are endemic to Madagsacar. Most of the rest are found in Africa, with a handful in Europe and southern Asia. Species vary in size from the miniscule Madagascar dwarf chameleon (*Brookesis minima*), at just 2.8cm, to the impressive Oustalet's chameleon (*Furcifer oustaleti*), also of Madagascar, which may reach 70cm.

Although the greatest density of species occurs in tropical forest, others have adapted to arid or mountainous terrain. The Namaqua chameleon (*Chamaeleo namaquensis*), for instance, is a desert species of southwest Africa that has evolved for a life on the stony ground, losing its prehensile tail in the process.

At a glance

Size: varies with species, from 2.8cm (*Brookesis minima*) to 70cm (*Furcifer oustaleti*)

Food: typically arboreal insects; a few species also eat small vertebrates and some take plant matter

Reproduction: most species are oviparous, laying from 2–100 eggs (depending upon species); a few bear live young

Habitat: tropical and mountain forest to savanna and steppe.

Distribution: Africa, Madagascar, India, Sri Lanka and Mediterranean

Status: varies by species; a number are severely threatened, especially those endemic to shrinking forest patches

51. Frilled lizard

Chlamydosaurus kingii

It's a shocking experience for any predator: one minute you're casually investigating an old stick; the next you're being rushed by a hissing, gaping lunatic brandishing a bright yellow umbrella. Before you can recover, the madman is off again, bounding for the horizon then veering off suddenly up a tree trunk. Time for a stiff drink, perhaps.

Dragon down under

The frilled lizard, also known as the frill-necked lizard, is an Australasian member of the Agamidae family. Its slim, rat-sized body is coloured to match its background, from grey to ochre according to habitat. It has long legs – especially the back ones – and an extremely long, whip-like tail.

The pleated cape of skin from which the lizard gets its name normally hangs loose around its shoulders. But by means of cartilaginous rods attached to the muscles of the tongue and jaws – like umbrella spokes – the lizard can erect the frill by simply gaping wide.

This sudden apparent doubling of its size can bamboozle an assailant long enough to allow a speedy getaway. The frill may also play a role in thermoregulation, allowing the lizard to gain or shed heat by raising or lowering it accordingly.

Lunge out then leg it

Frilled lizards inhabit open woodland and savanna in tropical and warm temperate areas, especially with tussocky grass. They forage on tree trunks for cicadas, caterpillars and other large invertebrates, but will also descend to feed on ants. Occasionally they may even snap up a small lizard or rodent.

When approached by a predator, the lizard's first line of defence is to freeze – or edge away around a tree trunk. It is only when it feels cornered that it erects the frill, standing tall to enhance the effect. If pressed further it may hiss, jump, lash its tail and even lunge out, before turning and sprinting straight to the nearest tree without so much as a backwards glance. This comical, upright run on two splayed legs has earned it the local nickname 'bicycle lizard'.

Frilled lizards breed during the early wet season. A female buries her clutch of 8–23 eggs up to 20cm below the ground, and may sometimes lay two clutches per season. The hatchlings emerge in February, weighing just 3–5g, but fully independent and able to use their frill.

Incubation temperature determines the sex of the hatchlings; extreme temperatures produce only females; intermediate temperatures (29–35°C) produce either females or males.

Despite their theatrics, frilled lizards fall victim to a number of predators, including birds of prey, snakes, larger lizards and feral cats – though they are not thought threatened. They have long featured prominently in Australian culture, and were chosen as mascot for the 2000 Paralympics and as the emblem for the Norforce, the Australian Army's Regional Force Surveillance Unit.

At a glance

Size: 70–90cm, of which head/body 28cm
Weight: 500g
Food: cicadas and other large invertebrates; occasionally small vertebrates
Reproduction: 8–23 soft-shelled eggs; 2–3-month incubation
Habitat: tropical/warm temperate dry forest, woodland and savanna
Distribution: northern Australia; southern New Guinea
Status: Least Concern

52. Spitting cobras
Naja spp

It's a cobra. That much is obvious as it rears and spreads a hood. You take a couple of steps back to be on the safe side. But this cobra can reach you without moving.

Not a dry eye …

Among the 22 or so species of 'true cobra' found in Africa and Asia, there are about 11 'spitters'. These vary from the relatively small red spitting cobra (*N. pallida*), to the large brown spitting cobra (*N. ashei*), which can reach a whopping 2.7m. All will spread a hood when threatened, though this is not a prerequisite for spitting.

In fact, 'spitting' is a misnomer. These snakes expel their venom through a tiny forward-facing hole at the tip of each fang using a muscular contraction of the venom glands. Larger species have a range of up to 3m. The action is purely in self-defence: the venom is directed at an attacker's eyes and the resulting agony and temporary blindness allows the snake to escape. Left untreated, that blindness can become permanent.

Recent experiments have revealed why the spray is so unerringly accurate. It seems that the snake tracks the movement of its target's face and then, as it starts to release the venom, uses tiny, rapid movements of its head and neck to direct it in geometrical patterns. The idea is to maximise the spread. Movement is critical: the snake will not spit at a face that remains still.

Reality bites

The prime purpose of a spitting cobra's venom is – like that of all venomous snakes – to kill its prey. This it does not by spitting but with a bite. Prey depends on the snake's size, ranging from large insects to frogs, nestlings, rodents and other reptiles. Some species are largely nocturnal while others also hunt by day.

Spitting cobra venom combines paralysing neurotoxins, found in all cobras, and haemotoxins, which are what damage the eye. It is more dilute than that of other cobras, for easier spitting. And there is plenty of it: a black-necked spitting cobra (*N. nigricollis*) may produce 200–350mg, of which just 40–50mg could kill you.

Spitting cobras lay their eggs in a hidden location such as a termite mound. The tiny hatchlings emerge ready to go, already loaded with venom and able to spit it with the lethal accuracy of their parents.

Like all venomous snakes, spitting cobras inspire fear throughout their range. However, their threat to people has been greatly exaggerated. In general they will avoid humans and spitting is a last resort. If venom enters the eye, however, it should be rinsed out immediately with clean water. Bites occasionally occur with more common species, such as the Mozambique spitting cobra (*N. mossambicus*) in southern Africa, but fatalities are very rare.

Meanwhile these snakes play a vital ecological role and are very useful in controlling rodents. Accidents often result from somebody attempting to batter one to death. Best to admire from a safe distance and leave well alone.

At a glance

Length: from 50–100cm (*N. katiensis*) to 180–270cm (*N. ashei*)
Food: large invertebrates, frogs, reptiles, small mammals, eggs and nestlings
Reproduction: typically 10–22 eggs, depending on species
Habitat: from semi-desert to woodland, savanna and coastal forest
Distribution: sub-Saharan Africa and southeast Asia
Status: varies by species

53. Armadillo girdled lizard
Cordylus cataphractus

Swallow me if you dare! An armadillo girdled lizard defies predators by gripping its tail in its mouth and rolling into a spiky ball. Most take one look at this biker's bracelet of a reptile and head elsewhere for dinner.

Armour-plated

This creature gets its name from the armadillo-like plating of spiky scales that covers its thickset, flattened body. Small colonies live among rocky outcrops in South Africa's Namaqualand, an arid region famed for its prolific floral display. The lizards venture out from the crevices to feed on insects lured to the blooms, especially harvester termites.

When danger threatens, the lizard's first reaction is to dash back and wedge itself into a crevice, where it is unassailable. If caught out in the open, however, it will perform its defensive display, becoming an unswallowable ball of spikes. Only the hungriest predator will persist.

Armadillo lizards give birth to one or two live young in late summer, just before the winter rains bring the flowers out in bloom. Unusually among lizards, a female may help feed her offspring. This species is threatened by the illegal pet trade.

At a glance

Length: 16–21cm
Food: insects, especially harvester termite (*Michrohodotermes viator*)
Reproduction: 1–2 live young
Habitat: succulent Karoo (semi-desert)
Distribution: Namaqualand, South Africa
Status: Vulnerable

---

54. Desert horned lizard
Phrysonoma platyrhinus

Your enemy has seen through your camouflage, dug you out of the ground and – unimpressed by your armour – is about to chew you up. What do you do? Squirt it with blood from your eyes, of course!

Blood simple

The desert horned lizard, one of 14 similar *Phrysonoma* species, inhabits the arid west of North America. It has a flattened, toad-like body – hence its nickname 'horned toad' – adorned with rows of spines on the head and upperparts, and camouflaged in mottled greys and tans against the sandy ground.

This lizard feeds on ants, licking them up from their trails and retreating into the shade when the sun gets too hot. When ambushed by a predator, its first strategy is to sprint away then stop suddenly, making its camouflaged body hard to relocate. If this doesn't work, it will inflate itself, erecting its spines into a thorny deterrent. Only when all else fails does it deploy its grisly party trick, restricting the blood flow from its head until the pressure bursts blood vessels around the eyes. The resulting jet may reach 1m and tastes foul to most predators.

Desert horned lizards lay 2–16 eggs in July and the young hatch after 50–60 days. They are threatened in areas where native harvester ants, their staple diet, have been displaced by invasive ant species from South America.

At a glance

Length: 7.6–13cm
Food: insects, especially harvester ants
Reproduction: 2–16 eggs
Habitat: arid, stony semi-desert
Distribution: western North America, southern Idaho to northern Mexico
Status: Vulnerable

55. Leaf-nosed snake
Langaha alluaudi

This snake takes arboreal camouflage a step further than others by sprouting a plant on the end of its nose. OK, so it's not a real plant, but this is hard to tell until you get really close – which, if you're a small lizard, could be a big mistake.

By a nose
The outlandish bud-like protrusion on the snout of this leaf-nosed snake shows it to be a female. The male sports a bayonet-like projection that more resembles a fine leaf. In either case, the head perfectly mimics a part of the tree or bush in which the snake lurks. The deception is completed by the thin body, which is coloured just like the branches – lichen grey in the female, olive in the male – and renders it virtually invisible to predator and prey alike.

Four similar species make up the genus *Langaha*, which is endemic to Madagascar. All make their living among the transitional forest in the southwest, where they hunt geckos and other small vertebrates among the lianas and undergrowth. Little is known about their biology or status, so seldom are they seen. They are thought to be relatively secure from habitat loss, as the soils of their native forest are unsuitable for agriculture. But collecting remains a threat, with this species highly prized in the lucrative reptile trade.

At a glance
Length: 75–100cm
Food: lizards, including geckos, and other small vertebrates
Reproduction: 13 eggs (average)
Habitat: transitional forest
Distribution: southwestern Madagascar, especially Mikea Forest
Status: Data Deficient

---

56. Water-holding frog
Litoria platycephala

Lost in the Outback? Feeling thirsty? No problem: just dig up a frog and give it a squeeze. Hey presto! A refreshing drink of cool, fresh water.

Skin deep
At first glance the water-holding frog seems just like your average frog: dull grey to olive brown, with a flat head and a pale stripe down the spine. You might hear its repetitive croaking after rain, as males seize this brief window of opportunity to attract females to their puddles. Breeding is quick, with tadpoles developing into froglets before the water dries up.

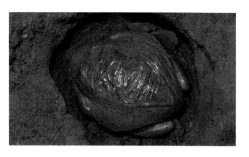

This frog's real party trick, however, comes during the long droughts. First, it fills up with water – enough to add 50% more body weight – which it absorbs through its skin and stores in pockets and a specially adapted bladder. It then digs itself into a burrow, where it cocoons itself in layers of dead skin, slows down its metabolic rate and sits out the drought, sometimes for many years. When the rains finally arrive, the sleepers break out of their cocoons and dig their way to the surface to begin another frantic breeding season.

Aboriginal peoples in Australia have traditionally excavated the water-holding frog as a source of life-sustaining liquid. While this is a disaster for the individual amphibian, habitat loss is a much more serious threat to the species as a whole.

At a glance
Length: 7cm (female); 5cm (male)
Food: small fish, insects, small frogs and tadpoles
Reproduction: up to 500 eggs
Habitat: temporary ditches, pools and clay-pans in arid regions
Distribution: Australia
Status: Least Concern

57. Leafy seadragon
Phycodurus eques

It's just seaweed, surely: a delicate sprig, embellished with tiny leaves, swaying gently like an underwater spray of mistletoe. And yet this 'seaweed' appears to be moving away as you approach. Could your eyes be playing tricks on you?

Leaf well alone

Camouflage does not come more extravagant – or more effective – than that of the leafy seadragon. This extraordinary fish has its entire body adorned with leaf-shaped, gossamer appendages that perfectly mimic the seaweed tangle of the temperate Australian coastal waters where it lives. To enhance the deception it tumbles and drifts in slow motion, as though at the mercy of the current.

Peer through the fake foliage, though, and you'll spot a long body with a thin tail at one end and a pipe-like snout at the other. The leafy adornments are for camouflage only; they help the dragon to ambush tiny crustaceans, shrimp, sea lice and other marine prey. Look closer and you'll see the translucent, whirring dorsal fins on the spine, which propel it forward, and the similar tiny pectoral fins on the side of the head that serve for steering. Movement is slow, graceful and almost imperceptible – though a seadragon may stay put for a long time; up to 68 hours has been recorded.

Dad duties

Seadragons belong, along with seahorses, to the Syngnathidae family. At up to 45cm they are rather larger than any seahorse, and lack their smaller relative's prehensile tail. Like seahorses, however, they assign all parental care to the male. A female deposits her eggs – up to 250 of them – on a brood patch on his tail, where they receive a supply of oxygen. The eggs hatch after eight weeks or so, the male pumping his tail and rubbing it against seaweed and rocks to help the infants emerge. Once out, the tiddlers are fully independent, and feed on tiny zooplankton until they can graduate to larger prey. Only about 5% make it to maturity.

This spectacular creature is the official marine emblem of the state of South Australia, where the District Council of Yankalilla holds a biennial Leafy Sea Dragon festival to celebrate the arts and environment. Unfortunately the species' popularity has also contributed to its downfall, with seadragons often targeted by collectors – either as pets or for use in alternative medicine. Other threats include pollution and industrial run-off, and the species is now protected under Australian law, with its export strictly regulated.

At a glance

Length: up to 45cm
Food: plankton, small crustaceans (especially mysids), and other marine life
Reproduction: up to 250 eggs, incubated by male; hatch after 8 weeks
Habitat: kelp forests and sea grass in coastal waters up to 50m deep
Distribution: temperate waters off southern Australia
Status: Near Threatened

58. Electric eel
Electrophorus electricus

This is a stunning creature – literally. One wrong step in the murky shallows of a South American river and you'll find out why.

Current affairs

The electric eel is more closely related to catfishes than true eels, but there is no doubting the 'electric' part of its name. When defending itself or attacking prey it can emit a current of up to 600 volts, enough to knock a horse off its feet. The power is stored in about 6,000 specialised cells, called electrocytes, packed like tiny batteries into three unique abdominal organs that together take up four-fifths of its body. It generates the current by sending a signal that momentarily reverses the charge.

Electric eels can top 2m in length. Although their eyesight is poor, they can navigate by emitting a low-voltage charge that functions like radar. This also helps them to locate fish and other prey. Breeding takes place in the dry season; a male makes a bubble nest from his saliva, into which the female lays copious eggs.

Human fatalities from electric eels are exceptionally rare, though multiple shocks can cause heart failure and victims knocked unconscious have drowned. On a more positive note, researchers believe that artificial cells modelled on those of the electric eel could be developed as medical implants.

At a glance

Length: up to 2.5m and 20kg
Food: freshwater fish, amphibians, some small aquatic birds and mammals
Reproduction: female lays eggs in nest made from male's saliva; up to 17,000 young may hatch
Habitat: shallow murky waters in river floodplains, swamps and creeks
Distribution: Amazon and Orinoco river basins, northern South America
Status: Least Concern

59. Hagfish
Myxine glutinosa

'Revolting' is the term most often applied to these primitive sea creatures, which have changed little in over 300 million years. This owes as much to their bizarre defence strategy as to their unprepossessing appearance.

Spineless slimeball

With its serpentine body and paddle-like tail, a hagfish resembles an eel. But it differs from eels and other true fish in its lack of jaws, bones and fins. Other unusual features include four hearts, two brains, only a partial cranium and no vertebrae – meaning that it is not even a true vertebrate.

Hagfish lurk in clusters at the muddy bottom of cold oceanic waters, where they sense food using the four pairs of tentacles (barbels) around their

mouth. Prey includes worms and dead or disabled fish. Using tooth-like projections on their tongue, they latch onto and burrow inside larger prey, consuming it from the inside out. Fishermen sometimes haul up their nets only to find that hagfish have plundered the catch.

And it gets worse. When grabbed by the tail, hagfish secrete copious quantities of slime, which expands into sticky goo, making them impossible to handle. One hagfish can fill a 20-litre bucket in minutes.

To clean themselves, they form a 'travelling knot' scraping off the slime as it unties from head to tail.

At a glance

Length: ±50cm; *Eptatretus goliath* reaches 127cm
Food: dead and disabled fish; marine worms
Reproduction: spawns year round; 2–30 eggs laid on seabed; no larval stage.
Habitat: the seabed, in waters colder than 50°F at depths of several 100m
Distribution: all oceans, in temperate and polar regions
Status: Least Concern

60. Mimic octopus
Thaumoctopus mimicus

**Is it a fish? Is it snake? Is it a crab? No, it is –
believe it or not – an octopus! Scientists
diving in a river mouth off northern
Sulawesi in 1998 were astonished to discover
this spectacular new species: an eight-legged
impersonator that takes the art of disguise to
levels previously unknown in the animal
kingdom.**

The great pretender
We already knew that octopuses are impressive and
intelligent molluscs. They change the colour and
texture of their skin at will in order to blend into
the rocks, weed or corals of their undersea
background, and can squeeze their flexible,
muscular bodies into all manner of improbable
hiding places. We also knew, of course, that
evolution has equipped some animals to imitate
others in order to gain an advantage in the struggle
for survival.

What scientists had never previously observed,
however, was an animal with the capacity to
impersonate a whole range of others. This small,
60cm octopus is just such an animal. Careful
observation over two years revealed that it was able
to mimic at least 15 of its neighbours, ranging from
lion fish and flat fish, to sea snakes, anemonies,
stingrays, mantis shrimps, jellyfish, giant crabs and
brittle stars. Small wonder, then, that it remained
undetected for so long.

Eight-legged oscars
The mimic octopus lives in tunnels and burrows
on the estuarine seabed. Often it lurks beneath the
mud with just its eyes protruding. But when it
ventures out into exposed water – either in search

of prey or simply to get from A to B – it
must run the gauntlet of predators such
as sharks and barracuda. And this is
when the show begins.

When confronted with a threat,
the octopus contorts its
body ingeniously
and controls its
movements in order
to impersonate each
model. For a
flounder or sole, for
example, it draws up
all eight legs into a
flattened leaf shape and –
powered by jet propulsion
from its funnel – undulates
across the seabed in the manner of
a flatfish. For a lionfish, it hovers just
above the sand with its arms trailing
below the body in the form of a lionfish's

poisonous fins. For a jellyfish, it swims to the surface, then spreads out its arms around its body and sinks slowly downwards. And for a sea anemone, it stations itself on the seabed and waves its arms upwards, each crimped into the telltale zigzags of stinging tentacles.

Colour also plays a part. When impersonating a venomous banded sea snake, for instance, the octopus's usual mottled brown and white transforms into the bold black and yellow bands of the reptile. It then buries six of its legs in the sand and waves the remaining two in opposite directions in an uncanny imitation of two venomous serpents.

As though this remarkable repertoire wasn't enough, the mimic octopus can shift from one impersonation to another as it crosses the seabed, and will tailor its disguise to each threat.

It produces the sea snake act, for instance, when attacked by territorial damselfish, which fear the reptile as one of their chief predators.

Armed for life

The mimic octopus feeds on small crustaceans, worms and fish, using its long arms to probe deep into burrows and flush out small prey, and its tough beak to kill and crunch up its catch. Its disguises do a job here too: it will, for instance, wave an arm to mimic the courtship display of a crab then grab and devour the unsuspecting would-be suitor when it comes within range.

Like all octopuses, a male mimic octopus deposits his packets of sperm directly into the female's mantle cavity using a specialised arm called a hectocylus. Shortly afterwards, this falls off and in the months following he dies. After fertilisation, the female lays her eggs, which she arranges into strings and carries in her arms. The female dies around the time that the larvae hatch. They then join the ocean's plankton cloud and, when mature, return to take up their place on the seabed.

At a glance

Length: up to 60cm
Food: small crustaceans and fish
Reproduction: female carries eggs in strings
Habitat: nutrient-rich river estuaries
Distribution: Sulawesi and Bali (Indonesia); discovered in the Lenbeh Strait, northern Sulawesi
Status: Data Deficient

61. Puss moth

Cerura vinula

The hideous face rears up at you like a miniature dragon, ringed in fiery orange, with two black eyes that fix you in their malevolent glare. At the other end, two striped, whiplash tails flail at the air like devils' bullwhips. 'Back off!' comes the unambiguous message – and you're happy to oblige, grateful that this unnerving beast is only 6cm long.

At a glance

Size: adult, 65–80mm wingspan; larva, up to 65mm
Food: food plants include sallow, willow, aspen and poplar
Reproduction: eggs laid on leaves of food plants; pupa overwinters in cocoon
Habitat: woods, parks and gardens
Distribution: Europe and Asia, east to China
Status: Least Concern

Bluffer

In fact this nightmare apparition is only a caterpillar – the larva of the puss moth, to be precise, a species that belongs to the Notodontidae family. In its adult form the moth varies from creamy-white to greyish in colour, with a delicately marbled patterning on its wings and black-and-white stripes on its abdomen. It gets its name from the soft cat-like fur that covers its chunky body.

The caterpillar's alarming appearance is a defensive strategy aimed at intimidating predators into leaving it alone. The 'eyes' are simply markings, while the 'whips' are modified back legs. The rest of the body is a striking bright green, with a dark purple saddle outlined in white. When approached by a predator the caterpillar arches its back to form a U shape, rearing its head and lashing its tails. And it's not all bluff. If this display doesn't do the trick, then it resorts to its secret weapon: a burst of eye-watering formic acid that its sprays at its assailant.

The use of false eye markings of this kind, known as ocelli, is a widespread defence strategy in the animal kingdom – especially among butterflies and moths, but also seen in everything from mantids (on the wings) to pygmy-owls (on the back of the head). These markings are thought to exploit the fact that many predators are intimidated by what they imagine to be the eyes of an even larger predator looking back.

Toughing it out

Puss moths are found across Europe and much of Asia. The adult lays its eggs on top of the leaves of its host plants, which include sallow, willow, polar and aspen. The caterpillar munches through the foliage, growing rapidly bigger, until – just prior to pupating – it turns purple. It then makes a camouflaged cocoon, by chewing bits of wood that it mixes with silk. This material hardens into a tough casing, which is attached, limpet-like, to a tree or post and almost exactly matches its background. Here the pupa survives the winter, ready to emerge as an adult in spring.

62. Treehoppers
Membracidae spp

Watch out – that branch is covered in thorns! Wait a minute, though: there don't appear to be any on the other branches. Take a closer look. Those wicked spikes aren't part of the plant at all. In fact, you could almost swear that one of them just moved.

Plant impersonator

Typical treehoppers belong to the Membracidae family, of which there are 3,200 known species in over 600 genera. They are bugs – part of the Hemiptera order of insects – and in common with cicadas and others of their kind, have piercing mouthparts with which they suck the vital juices from plants.

The mouthparts, however, are not the first thing you will notice about these insects. That is, if you notice them at all. Treehoppers – also, for obvious reasons, known as thorn bugs – are prime exponents of mimesis: the art of disguising yourself as a part of your environment. It is not so much that you don't see them but that what you see does not register as an insect.

The secret is in an enlarged pronotum, a kind of saddle over the thorax, which almost exactly replicates a thorn, both in shape and colour. The insect enhances the deception by squatting flat. Many species are gregarious and, when clustered in position, their resemblance to part of the plant is uncanny. Thorns are not the only shape they can manage; some species have a more ornate, horn-like pronotum that resembles a dead leaf. Either way, if the disguise is rumbled, they spring away on powerful hind legs.

Mutual interests

Treehoppers feed on sap from plant stems, which they pierce with their beaks, and a few are considered a minor pest to gardeners. The by-product of this diet is honeydew, which ants are mad for. Many species, particularly the more gregarious ones, have evolved a mutual relationship with ants: the ants 'farm' the honeydew from the treehoppers and, in return, offer protection from predators, such as parasitic wasps.

Female treehoppers use their ovipositor to cut a slit in a plant stem, in which they lay their eggs. They may sit over their clutch to protect it, buzzing their wings at any intruder – and the females of some gregarious species will work together in order to protect one another's eggs. The nymphs, when they hatch, also feed on plant sap, and use an extensible anal tube to deposit the honeydew away from their body. This is important to their health, as honeydew can become infected with moulds.

At a glance

Size: largest species up to 2cm
Food: plant sap; immatures generally on shrubs and grasses, adults on hardwood trees
Reproduction: females lay eggs in slit of plant stem; nymphs tended by ants
Habitat: woodland and forest, both temperate and tropical
Distribution: worldwide, except polar regions
Status: varies by species

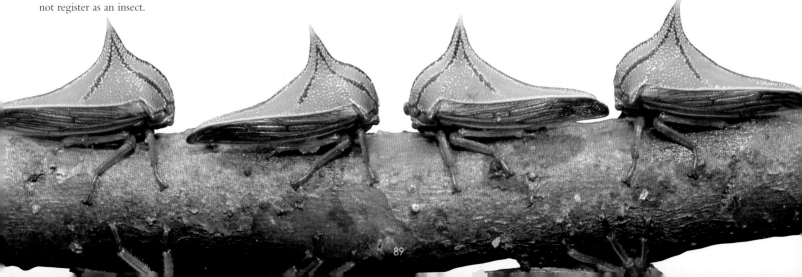

4 SHOWING OFF

If you've got it, flaunt it. This is the maxim behind animal displays where, caution thrown to the wind, the performers do everything they can to advertise their presence. Voice, colour, posture, movement and outrageous ornamentation all help get the message across. And that message is twofold. First, territorial: 'Keep out, this is my patch!' Second, sexual: 'Why don't you try me?'

Dress to impress

Colour is central to display in the animal kingdom, and few animals do colour better than birds. From the glorious livery of a pheasant to the wispy plumes of an egret, all this finery serves either to seduce a partner or scare off a rival. In most species it is the male that sports the showier plumage, since he is the one charged with courtship and territorial duties. After the breeding season, he exchanges the flashy gear for a dowdier outfit that leaves him less conspicuous – and so less vulnerable to predators.

Feathers are not the only way to carry off colour, though. Many birds flaunt lurid skin tones around their faces during the breeding season and, in the case of the magnificent frigatebird (page 109) and Temminck's tragopan (page 108), can inflate that skin to alarming effect during their display.

Skin also makes a perfect palette for lizards, such as the anoles of the Caribbean (page 112), which unfurl a prominent dewlap flushed with garish colours, and wave this in the direction of both rivals and suitors. There are many very similar species of anole, each of which waves its dewlap like a flag of identity. This demonstrates another vital role of colour: the unique insignia of each species ensures that it mates only with its own kind, forestalling any embarrassing courtship *faux pas*.

▲ *Japanese cranes, like all their kind, put on perfectly choreographed courtship displays.*

Mammals are less colourful than birds or reptiles, fur being a rather less effective palette. But colour can nonetheless enhance communication – especially among social species, such as the mandrill (page 94), in which the bright red nose and blue cheeks of a dominant male both emphasise his rank and enable him better to get his message across to uppity rivals or recalcitrant females.

Mandrill males, as in many primates, are markedly bigger than females – and size plays an important part in both their sexual allure and territorial authority. The proboscis monkey (page 96), lacking much in the way of colour, has a very prominent accessory that does a similar job: his huge pendulous nose. Needless to say, individuals with the biggest conks enjoy the most successful love life.

◀ *A male rock agama in breeding colours nods his head with all the swagger of a peacock's strut.*

Putting on a show

It's not just what you wear, of course, but how you wear it. On this premise, many animals use ritualised posture and movement in order to maximise the impact of their breeding finery. And none combine costume and choreography to more spectacular effect than New Guinea's dazzling birds-of-paradise (page 102). Male greater birds-of-paradise, to take just one of the 43 species, exhibit all the principles of display in a single bird: their rich emerald-and-chestnut plumage is adorned with golden plumes that cascade over the back and tail; they perform together in a treetop arena, even pruning the branches for greater visibility; and their hopping, bowing display, in which the golden plumes quiver like flickering flames, is irresistible to the audience of waiting females.

Such ritualised performance is not restricted to birds. Crocodiles blow a fountain of bubbles from beneath the surface, nyala antelope perform a slow-motion high-step, and male fiddler crabs (page 113) wave their single outsized claw from the entrance to their burrows as an unambiguous come-on to females.

Performers also need a stage. The satin bowerbird (page 107) builds his own out of sticks, constructing an elaborate avenue-like bower, which he decorates with colourful objects in order to entice female spectators to watch his exuberant song-and-dance routine. In a number of species, from sage-grouse to hammerhead bats (page 97), males get together to strut their stuff before assembled females in a carefully chosen arena. Such a group performance is known as a lek; it enables the females – the true decision makers – to select the most promising suitor.

Loud and proud

At a hammerhead bat lek the males do not rely upon their appearance to attract females – good thing too, you might think, once you've seen the beasts – but bellow out a loud, honking call that is amplified by the resonating chamber in their outsized nose. They are among countless animals, from tree frogs to humpback whales, for whom voice is the key to breeding success.

Again it is birds that have taken this approach to the most elaborate lengths, with the voices of nightingales, skylarks and other songsters celebrated for their beauty and lyricism by poets down the ages. Somehow, in our rapture, we contrive to overlook the rather earthy message behind these performances.

Not all songs are melodic, however. At least not to our ears. The male superb lyrebird (page 106), which also erects a fabulous train of tail feathers in display, has perhaps the bird world's most versatile voice, being able to imitate not only the sounds of countless other species, but also mechanical noises

such as car alarms and camera shutters. No such virtuosity for the kakapo (page 104), a bird that qualifies as bizarre on multiple grounds. But this lumbering, flightless New Zealand parrot digs out its own resonating chamber – a shallow depression in the ground – into which it broadcasts its loud, low 'booming' call, sending it echoing for kilometres around the surrounding hills to enthrall waiting females.

Battling it out

One of the purposes of ritualised display between rival males is to avoid fights, which can do serious damage. Thus antelope flaunt their antlers and hippos their huge teeth in order to intimidate a rival into retreat. Among the weirder weaponry in this respect are the canines of the Chinese water deer (page 100), which protrude like a vampire's fangs and look most inappropriate on a humble herbivore, and the tusks of a babirusa (page 101), which grow straight through the face of this combative Indonesian pig.

But when contestants are evenly matched and neither is prepared to back down, fisticuffs can become unavoidable. Territorial skirmishes don't come more thunderous than those of bull southern elephant seals (page 98), which square up to one another on the beaches of the Antarctic, inflicting slashing blows with their canines as they battle out the role of beachmaster. Females and young head for cover.

▲ 'Back off!' is the message behind a hippo's yawn.

63. Mandrill

Mandrillus sphinx

Come to a fancy dress party as a male mandrill and the room will soon empty. That monstrous voodoo mask of a face – all flaming lips, yellow fangs, scarlet nose and vivid blue snarl – is the stuff of lurid nightmares. And when you beat a retreat, expect another gasp or two at the sight of your rear end.

Colour co-ordinated

A male mandrill becomes progressively more outrageous-looking as he gains in age and status. The colours on his face intensify and the nasal ridges that frame his long, dog-like muzzle become more swollen, as though locked in a permanent snarl. Meanwhile the golden mane around his throat grows more luxuriant and his tufted topknot more prominent. At the rear end, his massive, muscular buttocks flush an ever-deeper pink and blue, framing a scarlet penis and anus that are not for the prudish.

As if all this were not intimidating enough, the mandrill is the largest and most powerful monkey on the planet, weighing up to 30kg or more and endowed with the physique of a prizefighter. Add 5cm canines – as long as a lion's – and you have a primate to reckon with.

The female is rather less alarming. Only about half the male's weight and lacking his colourful face, her olive fur and slimmer build resemble those of a baboon. Indeed mandrills were once classified along with baboons in the genus *Papio*.

Face values

Unlike baboons, which inhabit open country, mandrills are jungle monkeys, confined to a small area of tropical rainforest in the Congo Basin of central Africa. This habitat helps explain their bold colours. In the low-light environment, it is important for mandrills to be able to see and recognise one another's faces.

Mandrills are highly sociable and hierarchical primates that live in troops of around 20, with a mature male presiding over his harem of females and young. This Mr Big is responsible both for the troop's security and for siring the next generation. His bright face – instantly visible in the forest gloom – sends a sexual signal to females and a message of authority to subordinates. Lower-ranking males have duller faces, so troop members can quickly identify rank and behave accordingly; conflict is best avoided in an enclosed forest environment, where escape can be harder.

The bold face also amplifies the facial expressions with which mandrills communicate. These highly expressive monkeys use ritualised yawns and grimaces to convey or dispel tension and other emotions. They're noisy, too, filling the forest with their barks, grunts and squeals, and sometimes beating the ground in excitement.

As for the rear end, this provides a convenient flag by which members can follow one another through the dense understorey. The colours also intensify when females enter oestrus.

Super-troopers

A mandrill troop forages over an average of 50km² per year. Its members travel entirely on the ground, covering 5–15km per day, but take to the trees to sleep. Their diet ranges from seeds, nuts and fruits to small animals, and they have even been known to hunt duikers (small antelope). Food is often stored in secret locations, and they can stuff a fair amount into their capacious cheek pouches.

When fruits are scarce mandrills will turn to herbaceous growth, and where this food source is abundant troops may come together in 'super troops', hundreds-strong. One such gathering in Lopé National Park, Gabon, numbered over 1,300 animals and – with the exception of humans – is the largest gathering of primates ever recorded. In such densities mandrills can do serious damage to crops.

A female mandrill gives birth to her dark-furred baby after a 6½-month gestation. The infant clings to its mother's belly immediately and forms a bond with her that, with daughters, will last into adulthood. Females mature after 3½ years; males after seven to eight.

Captive mandrills have lived to over 30 years, although life expectancy is less in the wild. Natural predators include leopards, pythons and – for subadults – the formidable crowned eagle. A greater threat comes from humans, in the form of deforestation and, especially, the bushmeat trade. Hunters pursue mandrills with guns, dogs and nets, their meat fetching more than beef in parts of central Africa.

At a glance

Length: 81cm (male); 56cm (female); plus 8cm tail

Weight: male 25–30kg, exceptionally 50kg; female 11.5–13.6kg

Food: plant matter, including seeds, nuts, fruits; small animals

Reproduction: one young (occasionally two); 6½-month gestation

Habitat: tropical rainforest and adjacent woodland

Distribution: southern Cameroon, Gabon, Equatorial Guinea and Congo; range bounded by Sanaga River to north and Ogooué and Ivindo rivers to east; nowhere more than 300km from Atlantic coast

Status: Vulnerable

64. Proboscis monkey

Nasalis larvatus

The Malay word for this primate is *orang belanda*, **or 'Dutchman', its potbelly and big nose having reminded locals of Borneo's first European settlers. Regardless of stereotypes, this monkey certainly boasts one of the most comical faces in the animal kingdom.**

Nose surprises

Proboscis monkeys belong to the leaf-eating Colobinae subfamily of Old World monkeys. Their diet explains their belly, which has multiple chambers and fizzes with bacteria for breaking down cellulose and neutralising toxins. An individual's stomach contents can account for one-quarter of its body weight.

The male's dangling, sausage-like nose is harder to explain. Its most likely role is in sexual selection: females prefer males with bigger noses, who consequently produce more offspring than smaller-nosed rivals and so pass the trait on. It may also help amplify sound: when a male is agitated his nose fills with blood and his call becomes louder. Certainly it is only males that have the all-conquering conks; those of females and young are snub-shaped and much smaller.

The nose isn't the only difference between the sexes. Males are twice as big as females – the biggest disparity in any primate. Both share the same basic colouration, however, with reddish-brown upperparts, greyish underparts and a white rump and tail. Adult males have red faces; those of infants are bright blue.

Arboreal amphibians

Proboscis monkeys inhabit coastal mangroves and riverine forest. They form breeding groups of up to 30, each comprising a dominant male with females of all ages and younger males. Adolescent males form separate bachelor gangs.

Groups set out early each morning in search of food, foraging for young leaves and, in season, fruits, flowers and other plant goodies. With webbed hind feet, they are also surprisingly comfortable in water, belly-flopping down from the treetops, wading upright across rivers and even swimming to islands a mile from shore. By evening, however, they have returned to their riverside roost. Different groups may get together in noisy gatherings at this time, rival males displaying and crashing through the branches.

Females initiate sexual behaviour, signalling their readiness with pursed lips and a shake of the head. They may compete within a group over top males, and both sexes sometimes switch harems. Mating takes place at any time. A single baby is born six or so months later.

Proboscis monkeys are endemic to Borneo, where their population has been drastically depleted in recent years by habitat loss – including the clearing of swamps for palm oil plantations. Illegal hunting for the pot also remains a problem. Fewer than 5,000 remain.

At a glance

Length: head/body 55–75cm; tail 50–75cm
Weight: 12–23kg, average 20kg (males); 7–12kg, average 10kg (females)
Food: leaves, fruits, flowers, seeds, aquatic vegetation
Reproduction: 1 young (occasionally 2); 6½-month gestation
Habitat: mangrove, riverine and swamp forest, mostly along the coast
Distribution: Borneo (Sabah, Sarawak and Kalimantan), largely restricted to about a dozen protected areas
Status: Endangered

65. Hammerhead bat

Hypsignathus monstrosus

This most outlandish of bats has a megaphone of a muzzle, built for broadcasting its message of love (alright, sex) around the forests of the tropical African night. But it doesn't have the airwaves to itself; the competition is lining up – literally.

Loud and proud

The hammerhead is Africa's biggest bat, with a wingspan of nearly a metre. But its size pales beside the male's extraordinary face. His swollen, hammer-shaped head sports a grotesque combination of bulging cheeks, boggle eyes, warty snout and huge fluted lips. Small wonder that scientists named the species *monstrosus*.

These bizarre adaptations are not for show: the animal is a flying loudspeaker. The trumpet-like mouth and resonating chambers help amplify a honking call that can be heard kilometres away. The huge larynx that generates this noise fills its chest cavity. Females, by contrast, have the smaller, fox-like snout of a standard fruit-bat and are much smaller than males.

Honk to bonk

Hammerhead bats are among very few mammals that practise the 'lek' system of courtship, in which males assemble at a traditional arena to advertise themselves to females, who take their pick of the performers.

In this case, the arena is a riverbed, where the males gather at dusk to hang from low branches at 10m intervals. The assemblage may number anything from 25–130 bats. Once in position they start their

loud honking, while flapping their wings frantically. Females fly up and down the line to check out the talent. When a male takes their fancy, they perch beside him, whereupon he gives a staccato buzzing call – presumably of triumph. Mating takes less than a minute. The two partners then go their separate ways, the female making her own post-coital 'release' call.

During peak courtship season performances can be twice nightly. Females are very picky, however, and only about 10–20% of males get lucky. Success for males comes down both to quality of performance and position in the lek, with those bagging prime

central sites enjoying more success. Battles over top spots tend to be fought early in the season, before mating gets under way in earnest.

The female, as with all fruit-bats, is entirely responsible for looking after her single 40g infant. Females mature at six months and can produce two young per year. Males develop their facial features after a year and are sexually mature at 18 months. This species can live up to 30 years.

Fruits of the forage

Hammerhead bats feed mostly on figs, but annoy farmers by also taking soft fruits such as mangos. Females forage close to home but males travel up to 10km per night, searching for higher-quality food to fuel their energy-draining displays.

By day these bats roost close together in the canopy to escape the detection of predators. Their greatest threat is parasites, however, which can severely weaken the exhausted males.

At a glance

Length: average 25cm (male), 21cm (female); wingspan 68–97cm
Weight: average 377g (male), 275g (female)
Food: figs – also mangos, guavas, bananas and other soft fruit
Reproduction: 1 young (occasionally 2) of 40g; gestation unknown
Habitat: riverine forest, swamp, mangroves; at elevations less than 1,800m
Distribution: central Africa, from Senegal to northern Angola to western Uganda
Status: Least Concern

66. Southern elephant seal

Mirounga leonina

Not all seals are cute and cuddly. The grotesque face and immense bulk of this lumbering behemoth make it one of the more alarming characters you could meet on a beach. Its hidden life beneath the waves, however, is as extraordinary as its appearance on land is unnerving.

Big boys

The southern elephant seal owes its name to the inflatable, trunk-like proboscis that amplifies its bellows. But 'elephant' could equally describe its size: this is not only the world's biggest seal but also the largest mammalian carnivore ever to have lived. Large bulls can top four tonnes – that's jumbo-sized – and measure 5m. One monster shot on South Georgia in 1913 was a staggering 6.9m.

There are two species of elephant seal, the other being the slightly smaller northern elephant seal (*Mirounga angustirostris*), found along the Pacific coast of North America. Both exhibit extreme sexual dimorphism, with bulls weighing up to five times more than females. Adults have a silvery sheen to their grey-brown coat, and the wrinkled, leathery hide of mature males is scarred by years of fighting.

Like all 'earless' seals (Phocidae), elephant seals haul themselves around using their strong front flippers. Their hind limbs are next to useless on land, unlike those of the 'eared' sealions (Otariidae), and serve primarily as a back fin to power them through the water. They have excellent underwater hearing, despite lacking earflaps, and their large black eyes are adapted to dealing with extremes of light intensity, tolerating levels of UV radiation that would frazzle the human cornea.

Deeper and down

Elephant seals divide their year between feeding and breeding. The former they do out in the open ocean, alone, males staying around the Antarctic shelf, females wandering more widely. Unsurprisingly, we know little about what elephant seals get up to in the depths. We do know, however, that they eat fish and squid, and dive deeper that any other seal. Indeed, their ability to descend to a staggering 1,400m and stay down for over two hours rivals even that of most whales.

When feeding, the seals make repeated dives and spend little time at the surface. Deep down they may be able to detect prey using their hypersensitive vibrissae (whiskers), and also from its bioluminescence. Their body tackles the extreme demands of these depths by maximising the storage of oxygen and minimising its consumption. The heart rate can drop to just one beat per minute.

Life's a beach

Adult males arrive at the breeding beaches in August, a few weeks before females, and set about establishing territories. This involves noisy bellowing, back-arching displays of size and, when all else fails, thunderous battles. Rivals rear up and slash at one another with their canines. Despite the apparent carnage, however, their thick blubber generally protects them from serious injury.

Hierarchies are rigid. An alpha male – the 'beachmaster' – will round up a harem of up to 50 females. Lower-ranking males acquire far fewer; indeed some studies suggest at least 80% get none at all. Mating takes place on land and is a brutal affair. A bull forces himself on females without preliminaries: he simply slaps a flipper over her back, bites her on the neck and gets down to business. If she protests, he uses more weight and bites harder. In this testosterone-fuelled frenzy females may be separated from their young, and up to 10% of pups on any breeding beach may be crushed beneath lumbering males.

Females give birth to a single pup in September or early October, about a week after arriving on the breeding beaches. The black-coated infant weighs 40kg at birth but quadruples its weight to around 120kg after 23 days' intensive suckling on its mother's fat-rich milk. Weaned pups form nurseries, where they stay until they have moulted their birth coat. As they grow they practise swimming – usually in shallow estuaries or ponds. Males acquire their trunk at eight years old.

Elephant seals spend longer on land than any other seal. During the breeding season and moult males can fast for up to three months, living off their blubber.

Cold waters

Southern elephant seals inhabit the Southern Ocean, breeding on sub-Antarctic islands and coasts, and occasionally wandering as far north as Australia or South Africa. The largest breeding populations are in the south Atlantic, with smaller colonies in the southern Pacific and southern Indian oceans.

The species' only natural predator is the orca, which takes mostly pups. Humans, however, have taken a heavy toll. Numbers plummeted during the 19th and early 20th centuries when elephant seals were heavily hunted for oil. Protection since the 1950s has seen a dramatic recovery, and today's population is an estimated 650,000 worldwide.

At a glance

Length: female 2.6–3m; male 4.2–5m (max 6.9m)

Weight: female 400–900kg; male 2,200–4,000kg (max 5,000kg)

Food: fish and squid

Reproduction: 1 40kg pup born after 19-month gestation; weaned at 23 days

Habitat: feeds in Southern Ocean; breeds on sub-Antarctic coasts and islands

Distribution: 3 breeding subpopulations: south Atlantic (South Georgia, plus Falklands, Valdes); south Indian Ocean; south Pacific (Macquarie Island)

Status: Least Concern

67. Chinese water deer

Hydropotes inermis

A deer with fangs? Sounds more Hammer Horror than *Bambi*. But fear not: this is no cloven-hoofed bloodsucker, simply an ungulate that evolution forgot.

Fangs very much

The impressive canines of this primitive deer – protruding like those of some cervine sabre-toothed tiger – are found in the buck only and compensate for his lack of antlers. They represent a throwback to an age before antlers, when all deer used tusks to defend themselves and contest territorial claims. Growing up to 8cm long, and reaching their full length at 18 months, these weapons are drawn back out of the way while feeding but thrust forward during combat.

Otherwise there is little remarkable about this deer's appearance. It has a long neck, teddy-bear ears, and a profile that slopes up towards the high haunches. Its russet-brown coat is unrelieved by markings (no white rump like that of the similar-sized roe deer) and turns a thicker grey-brown in winter.

Middle Englanders

Chinese water deer are – as you'd expect – indigenous to China, where they frequent reed beds, woodlands and fields on alluvial plains. They are declining in their native land, threatened by habitat loss, and classified as Vulnerable by the IUCN. However, a fair number now also roam central England. Founded on escapees from Whipsnade Zoo in 1929, this population has spread to East Anglia – where the Fens and Broads provide ideal habitat – and today accounts for around 10% of the world's total.

Males are largely solitary and aggressively territorial. They demarcate their territory using urine, faeces and scent. Females, by contrast, may get along in small groups. Both are active around the clock, though may lie up to ruminate for long periods after feeding. They are selective grazers, nibbling from various nutritious plants but also turning to grasses and sedges in harder times.

Rut trap

The rut takes place in November and December. Males kick off hostilities with a ritualised 'parallel walk', in which two rivals parade stiffly side by side, checking each other out as they try to establish dominance. Only if this fails do they come to blows, slashing with their canines. The loser ends the fight by laying his head along the ground in an act of submission, or by turning tail and scarpering. Injuries are common but fatalities are rarer than among antlered deer.

A dominant male mates with most females in his territory. These give birth from May–July after a gestation of six to seven months. They are exceptionally prolific for deer, producing an average of two to three fawns but exceptionally up to seven. The young are born with a spotted coat, which camouflages them among the dense vegetation where they lie hidden for their first month.

Water deer are unusually vocal. In addition to a gruff alarm bark, the males emit a strange clicking noise while chasing rivals, and squeak when following a doe.

At a glance

Length: 75–100cm (body); 6–7.5cm (tail); 45–55cm (at shoulder)
Weight: 9–14kg
Food: herbaceous and woody plants, selecting the most nutritious parts
Reproduction: 2–3 fawns (max 7) born after 6–7 month gestation
Habitat: reed beds, woodlands and fields on alluvial soils
Distribution: China – lower reaches of the Yangtze, coastal Jiangsu province, islands of Zhejiang; feral population in east and central England
Status: Vulnerable

68. Babirusas
Babyrousa spp

It's one thing being a pig with tusks – nothing unusual there – but tusks that grow through your own face? Small wonder that the bizarre headgear of the babirusa is the stuff of legend on Sulawesi, inspiring tall tales and demonic masks among the islanders who share its home.

Face fights

Babirusa means 'pig-deer', and certainly the slender legs and almost antler-like tusk arrangement of these animals do have a deer-like quality. But the rounded body, upturned snout and bristly, naked hide leave little doubt that they are really pigs – albeit weird ones.

The male's tusks are two pairs of elongated canine teeth. The upper ones, which can reach 31cm, grow vertically up through his snout and curl back towards the forehead. The lower ones grow out of the mouth and above the upper lip. Scientists have long been unsure about their precise role but it seems probable that rivals can size one another up from their tusks. Should it come to blows, they will also rear up on their hind feet and box with them. The stabbing lower canines make lethal weapons and are regularly sharpened against trees.

Babirusas are endemic to Sulawesi and its neighbouring islands. Until recently there was thought to be just one species, with several different races. Recent studies based on size, hair, skull and teeth, however, suggest that there are four full species: the Sulawesi babirusa (*Babyrousa celebensis*) on mainland Sulawesi; the Buru or 'golden' babirusa (*B. babyrussa*) on Buru and Sula; the Togian babirusa (*B. togeanensis*) on the Togian Islands; and the Bola Batu babirusa (*B. bolabatuensis*) on the islands of Bola and Batu.

Forest foragers

Babirusas naturally frequent rainforest and deciduous forest near water, although persecution has largely driven them away to higher, less accessible ground. They forage by day along time-worn trails, searching for fruits, fungi, leaves, nuts and insect larvae. Like all pigs, they enjoy a good mud wallow, which helps them offload skin parasites. Unlike others, however, they seldom root around with their snouts. They are swift runners and good swimmers, capable of reaching offshore islands. Adult males are mostly solitary, while females form small groups.

A litter of two to three young is born after a gestation of 150–157 days. Youngsters lack the stripes of other piglets and are plain brown, like adults. They are weaned at six to eight months and reach sexual maturity after one to two years, going on to live for up to 24 years.

Illegal poaching and habitat loss through logging take a continued toll on babirusa numbers. Scientists estimate that no more than 5,000 animals – of all species – remain.

At a glance

Length: 110cm; 65–80cm at shoulder
Weight: 45–100kg
Food: fruits, fungi, leaves, nuts and insect larvae
Reproduction: 2–3 young born after 150–157-day gestation
Habitat: rainforest and deciduous forest along the banks of rivers and lakes
Distribution: Indonesia: Sulawesi and outlying islands, including Sula, Togian Island and Buru (Moluccas)
Status: Vulnerable

69. Birds-of-paradise
Paradisaeidae spp

They have no legs so never land. Instead they float around the heavens, living on dew, until eventually they fall to earth. Or at least that's what Mollucan islanders told the first Europeans to clap eyes on a bunch of bird-of-paradise skins. *Bolong diuata*, they called them: 'Birds of the gods'. And for more than 150 years the Europeans believed them. After all, such extraordinary feathers must surely belong to something seriously weird.

Fancy crows

The more prosaic truth is that birds-of-paradise, of which there are some 42 species spread across at least 13 genera, are a perfectly mortal, flesh-and-blood family of birds that are loosely related to crows. Strip away the fancy breeding plumage and you'll see they range in size from starling to pigeon, and have bills that vary – according to diet – from short and thick to long and curved.

But it is the males' breeding plumage, of course, that causes all the fuss. Not only are most species dazzlingly colourful, but many also sport extravagant ornamental plumes. Best known are the cascading golden flank plumes of *Paradiseae* species, such as the greater bird-of-paradise. But other even more bizarre embellishments include shining emerald disks on long wires (king bird-of-paradise); violet, spiral-coiled outer-tail feathers (Wilson's bird-of-paradise); a triangular, iridescent-green breast-shield (magnificent riflebird); and two 50cm-long erectile brow-plumes (King of Saxony bird-of-paradise). Vivienne Westwood could hardly have dreamed up a more outlandish collection.

Females have less to flaunt, in most species being much more drab than their suitors. Indeed, birds-of-paradise are among the most sexually dimorphic of all passerines, with many also showing major differences in size.

Show time

The point of the males' finery is, of course, to impress females. And the way in which they flaunt it can be just as startling. Thirty-two species are polygynous, each male mating with several females. Of these, 22 display in an individual and specially prepared 'court'. The other 12 (notably the *Paradisaea*) use a lek system, in which several males display together so females can take their pick.

Displays involve various choreographed routines, including wing clapping, head shaking, jumping, swinging upside down and puffing into a feather ball. Most species sing loudly, while many prepare their stage by clearing debris or pruning leaves. The overall effect can be truly bizarre. The male superb bird-of-paradise (*Lophorina superba*), for instance, erects a black cape and blue-green breast-shield that meet to form an oval fan around his head, while hopping in circles and rhythmically snapping his tail against the ground. Even then, the average female rejects 15–20 suitors before choosing Mr Right.

In most species the female performs all parenting duties. Nests are typically made of soft materials, such as leaves, ferns and vine tendrils. Some species nest in a tree fork, while others choose dense foliage or a rocky cleft. Large species lay one to two eggs, smaller ones may lay three. The young depend on their parents for food until they fledge. Males can take up to five years to develop their display plumage, though females can breed after two.

At a glance

Length: varies from king bird-of-paradise (50g/15cm) to curl-crested manucode (430g/44cm); longest is black sicklebill, at 110cm (including tail)

Food: fruits and arthropods; ratio varies by species

Reproduction: large species lay 1–2 eggs; smaller ones 2–3. Eggs hatch after 14–26 days (average 18–19); young fledge after 17–30 days (average 20–22)

Habitat: tropical forest, including mangrove and swamp forest (from sea level to 3,000m, according to species); wet temperate forest in eastern Australia

Distribution: New Guinea; Moluccas; eastern Australia

Status: Vulnerable to Least Concern (varies by species)

Birds-of-paradise are more given to hybridisation than any other bird family. This most often occurs between similar species with overlapping ranges and has led in the past to some hybrids being erroneously described as new species.

Island forests

Most birds-of-paradise are restricted to New Guinea and its satellite islands, with a few on the Mollucas and in eastern Australia. They are primarily birds of tropical forest, with at least 30 species found between 1,000–2,000m in altitude, and many have highly restricted ranges. The southernmost, Australia's paradise riflebird, also occurs in subtropical forest.

Both fruit and arthropods are on the menu, the ratio varying between species. Those that eat primarily fruit tend to feed higher in the tree canopy and to be more sociable. Some species have bills adapted to a specific feeding strategy, such as riflebirds, which dig insects out of logs woodpecker-style.

Feather frenzy

Birds-of-paradise plumes and skins have featured in New Guinea dress and ritual for millennia, and have been traded in Asia for at least 2,000 years. The first seen in the West were a gift to the Portuguese explorer Magellan from the Sultan of Batchian in the 16th century. The wings and feet had been removed, which explains the 'birds of the gods' myth. The plumes became fashionable during the 19th century, with 155,000 skins sold in London alone from 1904–08. In 1922 the feather trade was banned and today hunting is illegal, excepting for a sustainable quota used in traditional culture. Habitat destruction poses a more serious threat.

70. Kakapo
Strigops habroptila

This unique bird is a parrot all right, but hardly one that Long John Silver would have recognised. It can't fly, comes out only at night and in place of a cheerful squawk offers an eerie 'boom'. What's more, it's far too heavy to perch on your shoulder.

Pretty peculiar polly

The kakapo is one of three parrot species in the genus *Nestor*, endemic to New Zealand. It lives on the ground, where its soft greenish plumage blends into the vegetation. Owl-like facial disks, bristling with whiskery feathers, give it a rather pompous expression, while its wings are as short as you'd expect from a bird that never takes off. The chunky bill is adapted for grinding seeds and the solid feet for trotting about on terra firma. Females are lighter and slimmer than males, with a longer tail and smaller head.

The kakapo owes its oddness to plate tectonics. When New Zealand broke away from Gondwana 82 million years ago it left mammals behind, making ground level a much safer place for birds. Many evolved to do without flight. Thus the kakapo lacks the strong pectoral muscles, keeled sternum and fused clavicals of flying birds. Also, its exceptionally soft plumage – which lacks feather-stiffening barbs – is adapted for insulation rather than aerodynamics. Furthermore the large fat reserves it accumulates during lean times make it far too heavy to get airborne. In fact this is the world's heaviest parrot, with males weighing up to a whopping 4kg.

Baby boomers

Kakapos evolved to fill an ecological niche occupied by mammals on other continents. They roost by day in dense cover and come out at night to feed on the seeds, fruits and pollens of various native plants, notably the rimu. They will grip foliage in their foot while stripping out the nutritious parts, leaving behind a telltale ball of fibre.

Unlike most parrots, Kakapos do not form pair bonds. Instead, males perform at special locations to attract the favours of females. Each breeding season they trek up to a favourite 'mating court' in the hills, sometimes more than 5km from their home range. Here, having fought off rivals, each scrapes a number of 10cm-deep, saucer-shaped depressions in the ground. These 'bowls' are amplifiers for their mating calls, and are usually sited near a rock or tree trunk for added resonance.

A calling male settles into a bowl, lowers his head, inflates an air sac in his chest and launches into a series of low throbbing 'booms', finally ending with a metallic 'ching'. He moves from one bowl to another to project his call in different directions, calling for eight hours a night over a period of up to three months, losing nearly half his body weight in the process. On a still night the sound can carry for up to 5km, drawing females from afar. When one shows up, the male rocks from side to side, clicks his beak then shuffles backwards towards her. After mating, the female heads back to lay her eggs and raise the chicks. The male just keeps booming to attract the next in line. He plays no part in the parenting process.

Kakapos breed, on average, only once every three years, notably when rimu trees fruit. A female lays her three eggs in a hidden ground nest. The fluffy, helpless chicks hatch after 30 days and leave the nest at 10–12 weeks. Conditions can determine the sex of offspring: protein-rich foods produce more males, which will grow to be 30–40% heavier than females, so lean years produce more females.

Kakapos are slow to mature: males start booming at five to six years but females don't seek mates until nine to 11 years. Life expectancy is an astonishing 60 years or more, with some individuals reaching 90.

Pining for the fjords?

Sadly the kakapo is now critically endangered, undone by its terrestrial lifestyle the moment people appeared on the scene. The Polynesians who arrived 1,000 years ago hunted kakapos for food and feathers, and the birds were a sitting target for their rats and dogs. By the 1840s the Europeans had brought cats, stoats and other lethal new predators, plus a wave of deforestation that desecrated the bird's habitat.

Conservation got under way in the 1890s, but alien predators ransacked every safe haven and individuals removed to captivity seldom survived. The species clung on in the remote forests of Fjordland but by the 1970s was feared extinct – until a small population was discovered on Stewart Island. In 1989, under the Kakapo Recovery Plan, all remaining birds were relocated to a handful of offshore islands, where invasive mammals had been eradicated and native vegetation restored. By early 2010 there were 125 kakapos, each individual known to researchers. More islands are now being prepared in Fjordland in order to establish self-sustaining populations, but progress is slow.

At a glance

Length: 60cm

Weight: 2–4kg

Food: roots, seeds, fruits, bulbs, flowers, leaves and other parts of many different plants, notably rimu

Reproduction: 3 eggs per breeding cycle; chicks hatch after 30 days and leave nest at 10–12 weeks

Habitat: formerly wide ranging, from lowland forests to mountain grasslands

Distribution: New Zealand, on a handful of protected, predator-free islands

Status: Critically Endangered

71. Superb lyrebird

Menura novaehollandiae

A shimmering fountain of feathers and a voice that mingles sweet melodies with the growl of a chainsaw: this bird appears to have landed from another planet.

Tail of the unexpected

The superb lyrebird is technically a songbird, belonging – like sparrows – to the order Passeriformes. But the first impression of its long-tailed form on the ground recalls a pheasant. Indeed, at 1m in length, the male is the longest of all the world's 5,000 or so songbirds.

The celebrated tail comprises a train of 12 wispy 'filamentary rays', with two wire-like plumes projecting from the centre and two broad outer tail feathers in the elegant curving form of an ancient Greek lyre. The female's tail is long but lacks the plumes. Both sexes are largely rufous above and grey below.

This species is one of two in the Menuridae family, endemic to Australia, and inhabits woodland in eastern areas, often favouring inaccessible gullies. It uses powerful feet to rake through the leaf-litter for invertebrates and other food. Shy and wary, it is most often seen dashing across the forest floor, uttering its alarm shriek, and occasionally using its short wings to flit between branches or rocks.

Show time

The male's extravagant tail comes into its own during the May–August courtship season. Perching on top of a special display mound he fans the plumes forward over his head in a fountain of silver. It's hard to believe, as he prances, revolves and shivers, that what you're seeing is a bird.

And that's not all: the performance comes with an amazing soundtrack. The bird's uncanny vocal powers enable it to mimic everything from local birds and other forest creatures to mechanical noises, including chainsaws, car alarms and even camera shutters. It weaves all these sounds into a complex torrent of song that may last up to 20 minutes.

Once a male has secured the attention of a female the show comes to a close and he reverts to a soft clicking sound of encouragement. The pair then mate, but no bond is formed. Once the female goes off to lay her eggs the male simply carries on with the show, trying to pull in further suitors.

A female builds her domed nest of leaves, twigs and sticks in the undergrowth or among rocks. The single egg takes around 50 days to hatch – exceptionally long for any bird, let alone a passerine. This is because, with no help from a male, she must regularly break off incubation to feed herself, so the egg periodically cools and thus develops more slowly. The nestling remains in the nest for six to ten weeks, during which time the female brings it food and carries away droppings.

Lyrebirds grow their tail at three to four years. Until then they are known as 'plain-tails', and stay together, practising their calls. Youngsters learn the secrets of song from their elders, so birds in a particular area tend to share a similar repertoire.

At a glance

Length: male 100cm (including 70cm tail)
Weight: up to 1kg
Food: invertebrates, including insects, spiders and worms; occasionally seeds
Reproduction: 1 egg; 50-day incubation; chick fledges at 6–10 weeks
Habitat: eucalypt forest, rainforest or wet woodland
Distribution: endemic to Australia: east of Great Dividing Range to coast, from southern Queensland to Dandenong Range, Victoria; introduced to Tasmania
Status: Least Concern

72. Satin bowerbird

Ptilonorhynchus violaceus

Many birds build amazing nests. But only male bowerbirds turn their hand – or at least their bill – to constructing stage sets. Of course every stage needs a performance, and that's exactly what happens next.

Rhapsody in blue

The thrush-sized satin bowerbird is one of 20 species in the Ptilonorhynchidae family, confined to Australia and New Guinea. The male's glossy blue-black plumage is set off by a silvery bill and blue-violet iris. Females and young are largely olive-green above and pale below.

But bowerbirds do not owe their fame to their looks. Their 'bowers' are among nature's most unusual feats of architecture. There are two main designs: maypole bowers, in which sticks are arranged around a sapling; and avenue blowers, in which they are arranged in two parallel lines. This species is a master of the latter.

It is also an accomplished interior designer, decorating its bowers with various colourful objects. Must-have accessories include feathers, snail shells and flowers, while bowerbirds living near town will use clothes pegs, drinking straws, bottle tops, pen tops and other litter. Blue is the colour of choice; a preference that strengthens as the bird matures. It also uses its bill to 'paint' the inside of its bower with a paste of chewed plant matter and saliva.

Stage craft

The idea behind the male's bower is – of course – to impress the opposite sex. When a female arrives, the bower becomes his stage. He launches straight into an elaborate song-and-dance routine, leaping, strutting and bowing, with wings outstretched and quivering, while pouring out his strange song of mechanical-sounding buzzing and rattles.

The female doesn't leap to a decision. She first checks out all the males in the neighbourhood, assessing the quality of both bowers and performance, and then goes off to build a nest. Once she's ready to get serious, she makes another tour of the talent and finally settles on one suitable male, whereupon the two mate inside the bower. Young females, it appears, respond most to the quality of a male's bower, whereas more experienced birds tend to go by his display.

Job done, the female heads back to the nest to get laying. Her clutch of two to three eggs hatch after 21 days and fledge after a further 21. The male, meanwhile, stays at the bower, keeping it spick and span and leaping into performances at the first hint of another passing female.

Satin bowerbirds inhabit woodland and forest around eastern coastal Australia, with a separate isolated population in the northern rainforest. Males are solitary, but females and young form small flocks. They feed mostly on fruits, plus insects or leaves in season.

At a glance

Length: 27–33cm
Weight: 204g
Food: fruit all year, plus insects in summer and leaves in winter
Reproduction: 2–3 eggs; 21-day incubation
Habitat: eucalypt forest and woodlands and nearby open areas; rainforest in the north
Distribution: east and southeast coastal Australia, from southern Queensland to Victoria; Atherton tablelands
Status: Least Concern

73. Temminck's tragopan

Tragopan temminckii

Horns and a bib are hardly the facial adornments of your average bird. But this fantastical pheasant has a breeding display of lurid naked flesh that would put even a tropical sea slug to shame.

Fantasy pheasant

Male tragopans – as with many pheasants – are gorgeous creatures, and this species is no exception. His bright orange-crimson plumage is embellished with exquisite dots, pearl-grey above and white below, while his face is a shocking electric-blue. Female plumage is subtler, with brown and grey mottling serving as camouflage on the nest.

More eye-popping than the male's plumage, however, are the fleshy facial adornments that he inflates to bizarre effect during the breeding season. These comprise a vivid blue bib – known as a lappet – that is emblazoned with bright scarlet and violet markings, like some tribal mask, and two bright blue horns above his eyes. The whole get-up appears more tropical sea slug than bird.

Pumped up

Courtship gets under way in March and lasts for about a month. The male has two kinds of display. In the 'lateral display' he simply stands alongside the female and leans in towards her, fluffing up his feathers to make himself look bigger. In the 'frontal display', however, the action gets weirder. First he jerks his head to reveal the fleshy horns and bib. Then, beating his wings and vibrating his horns frenziedly, he allows the lappet gradually to expand and unfold over his breast and, with his bill buried in its fleshy folds, starts calling. This performance

continues for over a minute until the horns and lappet disappear back under the feathers and the bizarre apparition once again becomes a bird.

A female undertakes all parental duties alone. She makes her nest in the low branches of a tree,

sometimes taking over the nest of another bird. Her clutch of three to five eggs is laid in early May and incubated for 26–28 days. The chicks develop quickly and can fly just days after hatching – though they stick with mum for up to six weeks, until they can feed themselves and make it to safety in the trees.

Tragopans – when not strutting their stuff – are shy birds that stick to dense stands of rhododendron and bamboo on the Himalayan slopes. They migrate vertically with the seasons, spending cold winters at lower altitudes then moving back up with the spring. This species is primarily a ground feeder, foraging for flowers, moss, seeds and other plant matter, plus the occasional insect, but it is still more arboreal than most pheasants and will take to the treetops when pressed.

Temminck's tragopan is not currently considered threatened. However, habitat loss through over-grazing and understorey clearance is reducing its range, while its feathers and eggs remain targets for hunters and collectors.

At a glance

Length: 64cm (male); 58cm (female)
Weight: male 1.3–1.4kg; female 900–1,000g
Food: plant matter, including flowers, leaves, moss, berries, seeds; some insects
Reproduction: 3–5 eggs; 26–28 days incubation
Habitat: evergreen and mixed montane forest from 1,000–3,300m, with dense stands of rhododendron and bamboo
Distribution: eastern Himalayas, including eastern India, China, Bhutan, Myanmar, Vietnam
Status: Least Concern

74. Magnificent frigatebird

Fregata magnificens

This sinister-looking seabird is the original Pirate of the Caribbean, striking terror into other birds as it pursues them over the waves. On its breeding grounds, however, it offers a quite different – and decidedly bizarre – spectacle.

Winged wonder

The frigatebird's exceptionally long and angular wings can measure 2.3m across. With its forked tail and black plumage it creates an unmistakable silhouette high in a tropical sky. In fact, this species has the largest wingspan-to-body weight ratio of any bird, its plumage weighing more than its skeleton. No surprise, then, that it is a largely aerial operator, often travelling hundreds of kilometres without landing. Its habit of riding oncoming weather fronts has long alerted sailors to changing weather patterns.

This is one of five species in the family Fregatidae, which is allied with gannets and pelicans in the order Pelecaniformes – its long, hooked bill betraying this affinity. Females are larger than males and identified by their white underbelly.

Smash and grab

Frigatebirds are best known for their piratical pursuit of other seabirds, such as tropicbirds and boobies, harrying them until they abandon their catch. This feeding strategy, known as kleptoparasitism, explains their alternative name of 'man-of-war bird'. Studies show, however, that they obtain only a small proportion of their food in this way. The rest – mostly flying fish, squid and other marine life – they pluck from the surface using their long bill.

Whatever the method, all food is taken in flight. Frigatebirds cannot land on the water as their plumage lacks waterproofing oils and so they would become too waterlogged to take off. They are also very clumsy on land.

Balloon dance

The preposterous courtship display of frigatebirds is in stark contrast to their rakish elegance in flight. Males spread their wings, point their bills skywards and inflate a pouch of skin on their throat – the gular sac – into a monstrous scarlet balloon. At the appearance of a female overhead, they quiver their wings and vibrate their bill against this balloon to produce a distinctive drumming sound.

Once a pair have got together and cemented their bond for the season, they build a nest, the male collecting the material and the female assembling it. Frigatebirds breed just once every two years and are exceptionally diligent parents. The two eggs hatch after 40–55 days' incubation. For the first three months both parents feed the helpless chicks, after which the female continues alone for another eight months. While she's off searching for food the youngsters enter a kind of energy-efficient shutdown, hanging their heads in the hot sun as though dead but waking up the moment she returns with the next meal.

Magnificent frigatebirds breed in colonies on remote islands in the Atlantic, the Caribbean and off the Pacific coast of America. At other times they wander far across the tropical oceans, occasionally turning up in temperate waters.

At a glance

Length: 89–114cm; 196–244cm wingspan
Weight: 625–1,640g
Food: flying fish, squid, jellyfish and other marine surface life
Reproduction: 2 eggs once every 2 years; chicks fledge after ±11 months
Habitat: tropical oceans; breed on remote tropical islands
Distribution: breeds Florida, Caribbean, Cape Verde, Mexico to Ecuador; disperses over tropical Atlantic, Pacific and Indian oceans
Status: Least Concern

75. Southern cassowary

Casuarius casuarius

What was that rumble in the jungle? Could it perhaps have been the mating call of a cassowary? Before you plunge in to investigate, bear in mind that this is the world's second-biggest bird we're talking about, with a dinosaur's helmet and a kick like a dagger-shod mule. Might be more prudent to keep your distance.

Big bird

There's no mistaking a cassowary. For a start, there's its sheer size: approaching 2m tall and weighing 60kg or more, it is second only to the ostrich in the overgrown budgie stakes. Then there's its outrageous appearance: a shaggy black mound of feathers surmounted by a naked, bright-blue neck that sports two pendulous scarlet wattles and – on top – a bizarre shark's fin of a helmet. It's a bird all right, but not as we know it.

The southern, or double-wattled, cassowary is one of three species found in Australia and New Guinea. All belong to the ratite group, which means that – like their cousins, the emu and ostrich – they are flightless. Putting aside sheer weight, this failing is evident in their hair-like feathers, which lack the stiffened quills vital to getting airborne. Their skeleton also lacks the keeled sternum that, in flying birds, anchors the big pectoral muscles required to power the wings.

But with legs like these who needs to fly? A cassowary's powerful limbs can power it through the rainforest tangle at impressive speed. Each ends in a three-toed foot equipped with wicked claws – especially the inner one, which is a 15cm dagger. An unhappy cassowary can deliver lethal, disembowelling blows with these feet; human fatalities have been recorded and, indeed, *The Guinness Book of Records* lists this as the most dangerous bird in the world. The fearsome reputation, however, belies the reality that attacks are rare. In fact this naturally shy and elusive creature is only considered dangerous where hand feeding has habituated it to humans. Such feeding is (surprise, surprise) not encouraged.

Hard hat or amplifier?

The role of the cassowary's casque is cloaked in scientific controversy. It is not bony, as you might imagine, but consists of a spongy, cellular material coated in a keratinous skin, and is surprisingly flexible. For a long time scientists thought it served primarily as a crash helmet, protecting the bird's skull from collisions with tree trunks as it barrelled through the undergrowth. Other suggestions have included its possible role as a sexual signal in courtship display or as a tool for rooting through leaf-litter. Most recent, however, is the theory that it is connected to the bird's booming mating call. This call is the loudest of any bird, though its very low frequency of about 32Hz makes it almost inaudible to us. The spongy internal structure suggests the casque might help either to amplify this call or to assist the bird in detecting the calls of others – much as has been suggested for various dinosaur species, such as *Corythosaurus*, that sported similar structures.

Seeds of success

Whatever the explanation for the cassowary's bizarre bonce, there is no doubting the bird's importance to rainforest ecology. Cassowaries feed primarily on fruit, which they take from the forest floor or low branches. Their droppings help spread the seeds for a kilometre or more and are vital dispersal agents for many rainforest trees. Indeed, tests have proven that germination rates for several tree species, including *Ryparosa*, increase by up to 90% if their seeds pass through a cassowary. This feathered fertiliser is thus seen as a 'keystone' species, its fate inextricably tied to that of the rainforests where it lives.

Cassowaries themselves are relatively slow breeders. A female lays a clutch of three to eight large pale-green eggs directly onto the forest floor, whereupon she leaves the male to take over incubation duties. He tends the clutch for around two months, sitting on the eggs and hardly budging from position. After the eggs hatch the male continues to take care of his brood for another nine months and is a formidable deterrent to any would-be predator.

Curiously, the stripy yellow-brown camouflage livery of cassowary chicks is remarkably similar to that of young ostriches and emus – despite the differences between their respective parents. It takes the youngsters two years to moult into their black adult plumage, and another year before they reach breeding maturity. As adults they lead a solitary life, except when breeding and tending young, and in captivity they have lived more than 40 years. Cassowaries are threatened by the loss of their rainforest habitat, as well as by road traffic, feral pigs (which compete for food), dogs and humans. Their population was estimated at 10,000–20,000 in 2002, with around 2,000 in Australia, where the species is endangered.

At a glance

Size: 1.5–1.9m tall; 50–60kg, exceptionally over 70kg
Food: primarily rainforest fruits; also other plant matter, fungi, invertebrates and small vertebrates
Reproduction: 3–8 eggs; male performs all parental duties
Habitat: tropical rainforest, including swampy areas and riverbanks; also adjacent fruit plantations
Distribution: northern Queensland (Australia) and southern New Guinea
Status: Vulnerable

76. Anoles
Anolis spp

Birds may think they've cornered the market in the colours of seduction. But feathers are not the only way to strut your stuff. Male anoles do it with dewlaps, dazzling the ladies with a fancy flash of throat flap.

Colour chart
First up, these lizards are not chameleons, despite often being referred to as such. They belong to the diverse Polychrotidae family of New World lizards, centred upon the Caribbean and Central America. Indeed with over 370 species the *Anolis* genus is more diverse than any other genus of reptile, bird or mammal.

Anoles are slim and long-tailed, with adhesive toe pads similar to those of geckoes that help them to clamber around steep surfaces. Most are predominantly brown or green, but can change colour according to temperature or emotion – which helps explain the 'chameleon' misnomer. Females and young usually have a pale stripe down the spine.

The dewlap is a flap of erectile cartilage. Invisible when the lizard is at rest, it flips out in a flash of colour – like a flag suddenly unfurled – during courtship or threat displays. In some species both sexes boast this feature, though it is always larger in the male. Some males also raise a dorsal crest, or 'roach', to enhance the effect.

Duelling dewlaps
The breeding season starts in late spring and lasts four to five months. Males take up prominent positions, often head down on a conspicuous branch or post, from which to proclaim their patch.

They expand the dewlap, bob their head and perform intimidating press-ups. Battles between rivals can involve much butting and biting, and males will even take on their own reflection.

The same display technique is used to attract a mate. A female that pauses to admire is pursued and overhauled, her suitor seizing her by the neck before mating. Two weeks later she seeks out a warm place in the leaf-litter for her eggs. She lays one every week or so up to a total of 10–14, depending on the species. These hatch after 60–90 days and the hatchlings leave immediately to establish their own territories.

Niche to their own
Anoles are largely arboreal, some living among bushes and foliage close to the ground, others higher up. They eat insects, spiders and even the hatchlings of other anole species – in short, any prey they can cram into their mouth.

The way in which this group of lizards has adapted to fill a variety of ecological niches makes it a classic case study of adaptive radiation. A different species has evolved for virtually every island or habitat type within the group's range. Their dewlaps have followed suit, with each species having its own unique colour or pattern.

Anoles are also great colonisers and have taken readily to new niches. The brown anole, one of several species to

At a glance
Length: average 8–18cm; knight anole *Anolis equestris* can exceed 30cm
Food: arthropods, including crickets, spiders, moths; hatchlings of other *Anolis* spp
Reproduction: 10–14 eggs, according to species
Habitat: bushes, trees and the ground below; rocks, walls and buildings
Distribution: southeastern USA, Caribbean, Central America, South America. Many escaped or released in USA (Florida, Hawaii)
Status: varies by species

have colonised Florida, has adapted to living on the lower trunk of trees and ground below, thus displacing the native green anole that has shifted its niche to the upper trunk and canopy.

77. Fiddler crabs

Uca spp

If natural selection generally favours symmetry, then these bizarre crabs are the exception that proves the rule. Waving their one grossly outsized pincer like a baseball catcher's mitt, it's a wonder they don't tumble over.

Pincer power

Fiddler crabs belong to the Ocpypodidae family of crabs. There are more than 100 species, all inhabiting mangroves, mudflats and other intertidal habitats along tropical coasts. They are smallish, generally brownish in colour and, like all crabs, have four pairs of walking legs and two pincers at the front.

In males, however, one of these pincers is many times the size of the other – as though the crab is holding a fiddle in one claw and using its smaller pincer as a bow. This outsized member is often brightly coloured,

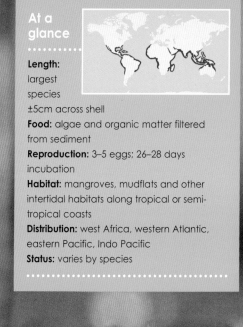

making it all the more conspicuous. Either the left or the right claw can develop in this way. If it breaks off, then the smaller claw will grow to replace it while a normal-sized pincer will regenerate in place of the broken one.

Waving, not drowning

Fiddler crabs dash around on the mudflats as they pursue a frantic life of feeding, fighting and courtship. They often occur in great numbers, each individual with its own burrow and small patch of surrounding territory. The burrow provides a refuge at high tide and a place to keep gills wet (and thus oxygenated) when the tide is out.

Feeding takes place on the surface. The crabs use their small pincers to scrape up sediment and transfer it to their mouth, sifting out algae, bacteria, decaying marsh plants and other organic matter. They spit out the residue as a small pellet, thousands of which litter the mudflats at the end of low tide.

The male's outsized claw, however, is no use for feeding. In fact males feed at half the rate of females so must spend double the time doing so. The sole purpose of this outsized appendage is sexual display. Males wave them in the air to attract the attention of females.

Mister Right

Females make the mate selection. Their choice may depend upon the male's claw size or his rate of waving. Whatever, the process follows a strict protocol. As a female wanders towards a displaying male, he darts towards her then nips back down into his burrow. She follows, but then, more often than not, soon reappears and moves on to the next one. One female may visit over 20 burrows before finding one that ticks all the boxes – whereupon she stays put.

Mating takes place underground. The male emerges the next day and seals in his partner with sand before scuttling off to find a new burrow. The female incubates the eggs under her body for two weeks, before emerging to carry them down to the water. Egg release coincides with a nocturnal high tide, so the larvae wash far out to sea. Here they develop in their planktonic state before returning to take up a new life on the mudflats as tiny crabs. Fiddler crabs can live for two years, moulting once or twice each year as they grow. Females breed every two months, while males can mate every day.

At a glance

Length: largest species ±5cm across shell

Food: algae and organic matter filtered from sediment

Reproduction: 3–5 eggs; 26–28 days incubation

Habitat: mangroves, mudflats and other intertidal habitats along tropical or semi-tropical coasts

Distribution: west Africa, western Atlantic, eastern Pacific, Indo Pacific

Status: varies by species

5 PASSING IT ON

All animals need to breed, otherwise their species would quickly fizzle out. It all kicks off with mating, and the meeting of sperm cell and egg cell that ignites new life. But that's only half the story. Before any animal can pass the genetic baton from one generation to the next, that new life has to be born and raised. Nature has tackled these twin challenges with some surprising strategies.

Born or hatched?

All animals pursue one of two strategies when producing young: oviparous animals lay an egg while viviparous animals give birth to live young. In fact, the only real difference between the two approaches is in where the offspring develops before it emerges – inside or outside its mother's body.

We tend to think animals fall into fairly clear categories according to their breeding behaviour. Take mammals: these warm-blooded, hairy creatures that nurse their young on milk all bear live young, right? Wrong. The platypus (page 118), like its relative the echidna (page 72), is a monotreme; that is to say, an egg-laying mammal. The female does not have teats, so her baby, known as a puggle, laps up the milk that oozes onto the fur of her belly.

So far, so weird. But surely birds are more straightforward. They make a nest, lay an egg, brood it until it hatches, then feed the chick until it's old enough to head out alone – right? Well, most do, but there are many that pursue rather different strategies. The malleefowl (page 124), for instance, does not sit on its eggs but instead buries them under an enormous mound of sand and rotting vegetation, which it maintains at exactly the right temperature for the eggs to incubate successfully. Once they hatch, its responsibilities are over. The parents have no contact with the scrawny little chick, which they leave to make its own way in the world.

The common cuckoo chick (page 125) is another one that never meets its parents. That's because the female cuckoo lays her eggs in the nest of other species, the host birds, whose own progeny is supplanted – literally, kicked out of the nest – by this super-sized interloper. The young cuckoo, having eaten its hosts out of nest and home, sets out alone in the world, none the wiser about its parentage. This strategy, known as brood parasitism, is practised by a number of bird families around the world.

Nesting alternatives

Birds, of course, are not the only creatures that make nests for their eggs. A range of species, from stickleback to Indian python, constructs some kind of shelter for both protection and incubation. The giraffe-necked weevil of Madagascar (page 129) uses its preposterously long neck to roll up a leaf into a tube, which serves as a perfectly secure chamber for its single egg.

Some of the strangest arrangements occur among amphibians. The male Surinam toad of South America (page 127) drags the fertilised eggs over the back of the female and presses them down – as though planting seedlings – into the spongy flesh. The skin grows over the eggs and the tadpoles develop inside, eventually breaking out to freedom through the skin of their own mother's back.

On the same continent, the male Darwin's frog (page 127) gathers up the newly hatched tadpoles, over whose development he has presided since the departure of the female, and scoops them into his mouth. They find their way down to his vocal sac, where they develop on the few nutrients they can find there, until they are large enough for him to regurgitate back out into the outside world.

▶ Owls, such as this snowy owl, are notoriously fearless in defence of their nest and young.

▲ A baby Hermann's tortoise, like many reptiles, hatches from its egg good to go. It will never know its parents.

Bringing up baby

Childcare concerns vary enormously from one species to another according to their reproductive strategy. Some animals, from orang-utan to albatrosses, take a long time to reach sexual maturity and then breed very slowly, one pair raising just a handful of young in its lifetime. Others race through their development and are breeding within just a few weeks, producing large numbers of young which, in turn, go on to do the same. There is a trade-off here: the former, in painstakingly producing just a few young, can devote more time and resources to their upbringing, and have a high success rate in raising their progeny; the latter offer no such care and attention to their large litters or broods, so infant mortality is very high.

There can be few more devoted parents than the male emperor penguin (page 122), which broods a single egg on its feet through the freezing dark of an Antarctic winter – the single most brutal climatic challenge on the planet. The pair-bonding rituals that greet the changeover, when the female returns with food from the ocean just in time for the egg to hatch, attest to the value of close relationships when it comes to raising young in testing conditions.

Norway lemmings (page 120), by contrast, keep breeding at an astonishing rate: a youngster becomes sexually mature at just one month, and – in a good season – may bear half-a-dozen litters of six to eight young. Small wonder that these prolific rodents sometimes outstrip their resources and are forced into mass migrations in search of pastures new.

Population explosions can play an interesting role in the anti-predator protection strategy of a species. The periodical cicada (page 129) synchronises its breeding so that the nymphs, which have spent a staggering 17 years turning into adults underground, all emerge in their millions in exactly the same place at exactly the same time. The effect is to flood the market. Countless individuals may perish, but the sheer numbers overwhelm predators and the casualty rate is proportionally reduced.

While it may take the periodical cicada 17 years to mature – pretty much the same time-span as a human being (though, admittedly, we generally hope to stagger on for more than a couple of weeks after emerging from adolescence) – one bizarre species of Mexican salamander never grows up at all. The axolotl (page 126) is the Peter Pan of the amphibian world, remaining in a perpetual larval state – although this doesn't stop it breeding. Talk about having your cake and eating it.

▲ This female Socotran scorpion, carrying her babies on her back, is among a surprising number of invertebrates that exhibit maternal care.

78. Platypus
Ornithorhynchus anatinus

It's a hoax. At least so thought the British Museum's George Shaw when, in 1798, he first got his hands on a platypus skin. He even tried to unpick it with scissors, believing a duck's bill and feet had been stitched to a mammal's body. Had he known the full truth – that not only is this a perfectly bona fide mammal, but also that it lays eggs, sports venomous spurs and uses electricity to detect food – the distinguished scientist may simply have keeled over.

Ducking the issue

The platypus is the size of a rabbit, with the flattened tail of a beaver, the webbed feet of an otter and, of course, that celebrated bill – which is not hard like a bird's, but rubbery, with the nostrils on top and the mouth underneath. Indeed, the creature looks such an odd mix of parts that some have quipped it can only have been designed by committee.

This species, along with the echidnas (page 72), is one of just five monotremes. These ancient animals, confined to Australia and New Guinea, are warm-blooded, grow fur and produce milk, like other mammals. But, like reptiles, they lay eggs and have a single cloaca for reproduction and excretion ('monotreme' means 'with one hole').

Platypuses are semi-aquatic, as even Shaw must have guessed from the feet and tail, with exceptionally dense fur that provides fine insulation. They have a normal body temperature of 32°C, compared with the 37–38°C typical of placental mammals, and fare equally well in tropical and near-freezing waters.

More reptilian affinities can be seen in their rolling, lizard-like gait, which comes from having legs positioned at the sides. The curved spur at the back of a male's hind foot can deliver a venom strong enough to kill a dog and probably serves to settle disputes between rivals.

Electricity bill

The platypus lies up by day in a short 'resting burrow', hidden beneath waterside vegetation. At dusk and dawn – and sometimes on overcast days – it emerges to forage along the bottom of quiet waterways for insects, crustaceans and other aquatic prey. Uniquely among mammals – again – it swims using an alternate rowing motion of its front feet; its rear feet held against the tail to help in steering.

A foraging platypus closes its eyes, ears and nostrils, and trusts to its bill. This unique appendage is not only sensitive to touch but also covered with electro-receptors that can detect slight electrical impulses generated by its prey and work out exactly where they are coming from. This explains why it sweeps its head side to side – like a metal detector – while foraging.

Cheek pouches store the catch until the platypus surfaces to breathe, whereupon it grinds up the food between hard pads in its jaws. Although it generally surfaces after a minute or so, its oxygen-rich blood enables it to stay down much longer if necessary. A platypus needs to eat about 20% of its weight each day, which means about 12 hours are spent looking for food. As an insurance against lean times, it can also store fat in its tail.

Hatching a plan

The platypus's breeding season lasts from July to October, during which a male may mate with several females. After mating he disappears, leaving a female to dig her nursery burrow and produce the young alone. This burrow can be up to 20m long. She drags in leaves and other bedding material using her curled tail, walls herself in to keep out predators, then lays her clutch of one to three eggs inside. These are small and leathery, like reptile eggs.

The eggs develop *in utero* for about 28 days and so hatch only ten days after they are laid, incubated

meanwhile between the female's belly and her curled-up tail. A baby platypus, or puggle, emerges poorly developed but grows fast on its mother's milk, which – as she lacks teats – it laps from her abdomen. It is weaned at four to five months. When leaving to feed, the mother plugs the tunnel entrance with soil. At four months they start to follow her.

Platypuses may live at least 11 years in the wild. Their natural predators include snakes, water rats, goannas and birds of prey. Greater threats are of human origin, including habitat destruction, pollution and introduced predators. In Tasmania there are also concerns about a local susceptibility to the fungal disease *Mucormycosis*. Nonetheless the species has lost little range since the first Europeans arrived in Australia. Today it retains an important role in national culture, enshrined on the 20-cent coin and as an emblem of New South Wales.

At a glance

Length: 43cm (female); 50–60cm (male)

Weight: 0.7–2.4kg (males larger); Tasmanian population twice as heavy

Food: insects, crustaceans, worms, small fishes and frogs

Reproduction: 1–3 eggs, hatch after 10 days; young weaned at 4–5 months

Habitat: undisturbed waterways, from cool highlands to tropical forests

Distribution: eastern Australia, from base of Cape York Peninsula (Queensland) to Tasmania, and including Australian Alps

Status: Least Concern

79. Norway lemming

Lemmus lemmus

Is it true? Does this cute-looking rodent *really* perform mass suicide leaps from Norwegian cliff tops? OK, Scandinavian winters can be depressing, but in any species other than our own topping yourself is generally an evolutionary no-no. Might there, perhaps, be another explanation?

Below the snow

Lemmings, of which there are more than 25 species, are essentially arctic-adapted voles, with rotund bodies and very short tails. This species is found in northern Scandinavia and adjacent parts of Russia, and has long silky fur, attractively blotched in orange, black and white. It uses its sharp, constantly growing incisors to nibble on a diet of sedges, grasses and moss.

Few habitats are tougher than the tundra. Conditions lurch between a long, dark, freezing winter and a brief, damp, sunlit summer. The lemming's secret is its 'subniveal' lifestyle: it is adapted to living *under* the snow. Thus it doesn't hibernate, but remains active all winter in its nests and runs, finding food by burrowing through the snow and feeding on its stores of nibbled grass.

In spring, when the snow starts to collapse, the lemmings head for lower ground – a reverse movement to that of most arctic or alpine species. Then, in autumn, they move back up again, leaving before frost and ice have covered the lowlands but not before the first snow has fallen on the uplands.

Norwegian wouldn't

Lemmings generally get together only to mate.

But in the right conditions – usually long summers followed by short winters (every three or four years) – their population can increase explosively. Few mammals can outbreed lemmings. A female is sexually mature at less than a month and can produce a litter of six to eight every four weeks. Each of her female young will itself breed within a month, as will their young, and theirs, and so on.

As the booming population outstrips its resources, the older, stronger lemmings oust the younger ones. The refugees disperse in search of pastures new – sometimes being forced by the topography into narrow corridors, where the build-up of numbers can lead to aggression and panic. On occasion, such as when crossing lakes, many may die (although lemmings swim well). But never do they end it all by deliberately flinging themselves off cliff tops into the sea.

So how did the suicide myth arise? No doubt occasional mass migration events have been misinterpreted over the years. But one thing that didn't help was the 1958 Disney film *White Wilderness*, which showed the hapless rodents leaping to their death. In this case the camera definitely did lie: the lemmings had been launched off a cliff using a turntable.

At a glance

Length: 13–15cm (plus 2cm tail)
Weight: 28–113kg
Food: grasses, sedges and mosses
Reproduction: female matures at one month; produces litter of 6–8
Habitat: tundra: high ground in winter, low ground in summer; often near water
Distribution: northern Scandinavia and adjacent Russia
Status: Least Concern

In any case, suicide seems an unlikely option for a rodent that spends much of its time trying to escape the many tundra predators – from snowy owls to Arctic foxes – that depend upon it for food. Survival is simply too hard to think of throwing it all away.

80. Kiwis
Apteryx spp

Few birds look less bird-like than New Zealand's celebrated national emblem. But while kiwis may be sadly lacking in the wings department, their eggs would win first prize in any farmers' market.

Makeshift mammals

Kiwis are the smallest of the flightless 'ratite' group of birds, so named for lacking the keeled breastbone of flying birds. They were long presumed related to New Zealand's enormous moas, now extinct, but recent DNA studies suggest closer ties to Australia's cassowary and emu. Today scientists recognise five species, of which the great spotted kiwi is the largest and the little spotted kiwi the smallest.

These pear-shaped, chicken-sized birds have a long bill, powerful legs and no tail. Their tiny, useless wings are hidden beneath bristly, hair-like feathers (*Apteryx* means 'without wing'). Indeed, as they scurry across the forest floor, they look rather more like furry mammals than birds. And this is no coincidence: with New Zealand having no native terrestrial mammal species, other than a couple of bats, kiwis are among several flightless birds that have evolved to fill the vacant niches.

Kiwis are largely nocturnal – although may have been less so before the arrival of humans. They forage on the forest floor for worms, insects and other juicy invertebrates using their highly sensitive bill. This appendage is unique among birds in having the nostrils located at the tip, which gives it the strongest sense of smell in the bird world and allows kiwis to sniff out prey even when underground.

Eggs-tremely big

Male kiwis are aggressive in defence of their territory and form a monogamous lifelong bond with their partner. The courtship season is June–March, the birds calling by night then meeting in their burrows by day.

Once mated, the female produces what is, proportionally, the biggest egg in the bird world – up to a quarter of her weight, and six times bigger than that of an equivalent-sized chicken. This beauty takes 30 days to develop and places huge demands on her. At first she eats three times her usual amount, but in the last few days before laying she stops eating altogether, as there is simply no space left for her stomach. She may even squat in puddles to relieve the discomfort.

The egg is laid in August–January. Some species lay one per season; others two or three. Incubation – generally the male's job – lasts 63–92 days, according to species. The chicks are immediately abandoned by their parents. After ten days they venture out of their burrows, whereupon they must now run the gauntlet of New Zealand's many introduced predators. Fewer than 25% survive their first six months.

Kiwis have long played an important role in New Zealand folklore and, since the nickname given to soldiers during World War 1, have become emblematic of the nation. Nonetheless, their fortunes took a turn for the worse the moment that humans first set foot on the islands, with introduced mammals – from wild pigs to ferrets – finding their eggs and hatchlings easy prey. Today all species are subject to intensive conservation programmes.

At a glance

Length: 25–50cm (females larger); varies with species
Weight: 0.9–3.3kg; varies with species
Food: worm, insects and invertebrates; also small amphibians, seeds and fruit
Reproduction: lays 1–3 (according to species) large eggs Aug–Jan; incubation 63–92 days
Habitat: originally subtropical and temperate native forest; now also adapted to tussock, sub-alpine scrub and mountains
Distribution: endemic to New Zealand; each species with its own limited range
Status: Near Threatened to Critically Endangered (varies with species)

81. Emperor penguin

Aptenodytes forsteri

You think *your* life is hard? Try swapping places with the emperor penguin. Not only does this bird live in the coldest place on earth; it also chooses the dark, frozen depths of winter as its breeding season. And to get the job done, it must starve itself for up to three months.

Deep freeze

The emperor penguin is the largest of the world's penguins, reaching 1.2m tall and weighing 35kg or more – though its weight falls by nearly half during the long winter fast.

Temperatures in the Antarctic winter regularly fall below –50°C, and winds of 150km/h batter the icy terrain. Nonetheless, this penguin maintains a constant body temperature of 39°C. Its tiny, blade-like outer feathers are packed more closely together than on any other bird. By holding them erect it can trap an insulating layer of air in the soft down underneath, which keeps body heat in and water out. Constant preening keeps the whole system in order, while a thick layer of fat adds extra insulation.

Warm company helps too. Emperor penguins huddle together to shelter from the elements. This dense mass of birds is in constant rotation, with individuals moving from the outside to the centre, so that all share the benefit.

Paddle power

An emperor penguin's paddle-like wings power it along underwater with great speed and agility. It feeds in the open ocean, eating mostly fish, plus some krill and squid. Prey is seized in the sharp bill and the barbed tongue prevents it from slithering out.

This penguin's favourite hunting ploy is to dive below fish to spot them swimming against the ice above. It can descend to more than 500m and stay down for 18 minutes. Solid bones help it withstand the pressure, and its blood can transport oxygen at unusually low concentrations. Meanwhile it shuts down non-essential metabolic functions and reduces its heartbeat to just five beats per minute.

Balancing act

The emperor penguin is the only species to breed during the Antarctic winter. In March, as winter

starts to bite, the adults trek from the ocean to their colonies, some 50–120km away across the pack ice, tobogganing on their bellies where the gradient allows. Males perform their 'ecstatic' display to attract a mate, lowering their head before uttering their courtship call. Once a female responds, the two stand face to face, raising and lowering bills in a formal bonding ceremony that pairs them up for the season.

The female lays a single egg of 460–470g. Though this may sound large, at just 2.3% of the female's weight it is proportionally the smallest of any bird. She then carefully transfers the egg onto the male's feet. This is the hazardous bit, as a dropped egg will not survive any contact with the freezing ground. Her mate immediately snuggles it beneath his thick fold of warm belly skin.

Now the female heads back to the sea to feed, leaving the male to incubate the egg alone. He stays at his post, huddled among his companions, for an astonishing 64 consecutive days, the egg not once leaving his feet while he endures the very worst of the world's hardest climate. And all this without food; by the time the egg hatches he will not have eaten for over three months.

Changing the guard

The egg hatches just as the females return in mid-July to early August. Each locates her mate by his call, recognising its unique pattern from among thousands. She immediately takes over, feeding the chick by regurgitating food from her stomach.

Now it's the male's turn to head for the sea to feed. He's back after three weeks, though, and both parents tend to their growing chick together. Youngsters are covered in silver-grey down. At seven weeks they huddle into crèches for warmth, but the parents continue to feed them. By the beginning of summer (December–January), parents and young abandon the colony *en masse* and return to the sea. This time the trek is shorter, as the melting pack ice has brought the sea nearer.

Emperor penguins may live to 20 years or more, though only 19% survive their first year. Giant petrels prey on chicks, while leopard seals and orcas snatch inexperienced youngsters entering the water. Today there are 400,000–450,000 spread across 40 separate colonies. The species is at risk from climate change and dwindling food supplies, while intrusive tourism is also a worry.

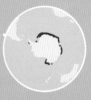

At a glance

Length: 1.1–1.22m
Weight: 22–45kg
(average: 38kg for male; 29.5kg for female)
Food: fish (especially Antarctic silver fish), krill and squid
Reproduction: breeds in Antarctic winter; single egg, incubated on male's feet, hatches after 64 days
Habitat: pack ice and polar ocean
Distribution: endemic to Antarctic; vagrants recorded as far north as New Zealand and South Georgia
Status: Least Concern

82. Malleefowl

Leipoa ocellata

Some parents show their devotion in strange ways. This curious Australian bird dedicates its life to building and tending enormous nesting mounds that give its chicks the perfect start in life. Yet it never lays eyes on its own offspring.

Big foot

The malleefowl is the largest of the megapodes, or 'mound-builders', a ground-dwelling family named for their large feet. It is a chicken-sized bird, coloured creamy-white below and mottled rufous and grey above.

This shy and largely solitary species inhabits the mallee of southern Australia, a semi-arid habitat of dense low-growing eucalypt scrub, where it uses its powerful feet to scratch for seeds, fruits and other food. It trusts to its camouflage to escape detection, melting quietly into the scrub at any hint of danger, and takes off only when pursued by a predator – or flying up to its roost in a tree.

Building big

Malleefowl pair for life, although the male and female spend little time together except when mating and tending the nest. The mound is the work of the male, who starts building at around four years. He scrapes a long depression in an area of open ground, which he fills with leaves, bark and other organic matter, mixing it with sand as he does so. He piles them up and scrapes on more sand until the finished mound measures up to 1m high and 4–5m across.

The male tends his mound like a gardener tends a compost heap, turning and mixing it to encourage

decay. In August (the end of winter) he digs an egg chamber. Once conditions are right, usually after rains have helped kick-start the decomposition process, the female starts to deposit her eggs in the chamber – one at a time, at 5–15-day intervals. The final clutch may number anything from 3–30. Each large, thin-shelled egg is about 10% of the female's weight.

The heat generated by the rotting vegetation incubates the eggs. The male continues to tend the mound in order to maintain the temperature at the required 33°C. He modifies it according to conditions, scraping off sand if it becomes too hot and piling back on if conditions cool down. It's a full-time job that can last 50–100 days.

Eventually the chicks break out and dig their way to the surface. This can take anything from 2–15 hours. Within minutes of emerging and opening their eyes for the first time, they tumble down the mound and disappear into the scrub. Within two hours they can run fast and after a day they can fly. This is just as well because, with no parent in sight and no siblings hatching at the same time, they're on their own.

Malleefowl were once widespread across Australia but have declined since the arrival of Europeans. They are vulnerable to invasive predators, such as the red fox, while habitat destruction and climate change present a serious threat, especially through drought and bushfires.

At a glance

Length: 55–60cm
Weight: 1.5–2kg
Food: seeds, flowers, fruits, tubers, fungi and invertebrates
Reproduction: female lays 3–30 eggs inside incubation mound; chicks hatch after 50–100 days and head out alone
Habitat: mallee scrub and heath
Distribution: scattered across southern Australia, including central New South Wales, northwestern Victoria, South Australia and southern Western Australia
Status: Vulnerable

83. Common cuckoo

Cuculus canorus

Cu-ckoo! Cu-ckoo! **The distinctive major third of this migratory bird may inspire Swiss clock-makers and herald summer for correspondents of** *The Times*. **But to many a wary songbird the sound means trouble.**

Hawk alarm

The common cuckoo is a slim, pigeon-sized bird with a long tail, pointed wings and soft, dove-grey plumage, barred underneath rather like a hawk's. Its silhouette also recalls that of a bird of prey, though its thin bill quickly reveals its true identity. Females are browner.

This species is a widespread summer visitor to Europe, arriving in late April from its winter quarters in southern Africa and leaving again by September. Like many of the cuckoo family (Cuculidae), it has a taste for noxious, hairy caterpillars. It is best known, however, for its habit of laying its eggs in other birds' nests. This behaviour is known as brood parasitism and, though not true of all cuckoos, is a standard breeding strategy among species of the Old World subfamily Cuculinae.

Nest cheat

It was Edward Jenner, he of vaccination fame, who first described this curious breeding behaviour. The cuckoo, he discovered, is an 'obligate brood parasite'. This means that, however much its behaviour may offend our delicate moral sensibilities, evolution has given it no choice.

The strategy is quite simple: once a male has attracted a female with his call and the pair have

mated, they then seek out the nests of suitable 'host' birds, such as dunnock, meadow pipit and reed warbler. It may be that the male's hawk-like appearance intimidates these birds or that, conversely, it draws them out to mob him. Either way, the minute a nest is left unguarded a female cuckoo slips in. She needs just ten seconds in which to push out one of the host's eggs, lay her own in its place and then discreetly slip away.

When the host returns it finds one new, larger egg in among its clutch. But the markings resemble those of its own, as all female cuckoos specialise in parasitising certain host species and have evolved eggs to match. Thus the host thinks no more of it and continues to brood the whole clutch. Big mistake. The cuckoo chick hatches first and instinctively ejects all the other eggs – or hatchlings – heaving them out of the nest with its back. Soon it is enjoying the undivided attention of its new foster parents, who ignore their own progeny dumped on the ground below.

The imposter chick needs this attention, as it has a lot of growing to do. With a persistent begging call and colourful gape, it coerces its hosts into providing a constant supply of food. It grows fast: in just 14 days it is already three times the size of its exhausted foster parents. Still they continue to feed it until, at 20–21 days (twice as long as its hosts take to fledge), it leaves the nest and strikes out alone.

At a glance

Length: 32–34cm

Weight: 115g

Food: insect larvae – especially hairy caterpillars – and other invertebrates

Reproduction: brood parasite; female lays eggs in nest of host birds (eg: dunnock, meadow pipit, reed warbler), which rear chick as their own

Habitat: open country: heaths, farmland, open woodland

Distribution: breeds Europe and Asia, east to Japan; winters in sub-Saharan Africa and southeast Asia

Status: Least Concern

84. Axolotl
Ambystoma mexicanum

This weird-looking creature is the Peter Pan of the amphibian world. Why grow up, after all, when life is so much better as a larva?

Arrested development
'Axolotl' is thought to derive from the Aztec *nahuatl*, meaning 'water dog'. While this amphibian is certainly no dog, its appearance and lifestyle are so bizarre that you can forgive a little confusion.

In fact, the axolotl is a salamander. Like all its kind it has four limbs and a tail. But the first thing you'll notice are the three feathery gills that project from behind its broad head on either side. This is a feature you'd normally associate with tadpoles at an early stage of development, as is the long caudal fin running the length of its tail and the small lidless eyes sunk into the side of the head.

At a glance

Length: 15–45cm (average 23cm)
Weight: 60–227g
Food: aquatic worms, insects and small fish
Reproduction: male deposits sperm for collection by female; female lays eggs 24 hours later; embryo transforms into a larva but never reaches adult stage
Habitat: stagnant freshwater lakes at high altitude
Distribution: endemic to Lake Xochimilco, Mexico
Status: Critically Endangered

What you're looking at, however, is very much an adult – or as close as this amphibian will ever get. The axolotl never grows up: it is a classic example of 'neoteny', a phenomenon by which an animal remains in a life-long larval stage, never undergoing the physical transformation to adulthood.

Not that this holds the axolotl back. It continues growing, sometimes reaching 30cm or more. And in this state of arrested development it reaches full sexual maturity, breeding like any other amphibian, and may live more than 12 years. It never comes on land and continues to use its gills to breathe underwater.

Axolotls are from the central highlands of Mexico and are closely related to tiger salamanders, which develop normally and can live happily on land. Neoteny is associated with high altitudes. It is not irreversible, however. Occasionally axolotls mature naturally into a full adult state, and scientists can bring about this transformation by treating them with the hormone thyroxine.

Lakes and labs
The axolotl has long been a hot topic of laboratory research, and scientists have discovered that it has remarkable healing powers. An axolotl that loses a limb will quickly generate a new one, without forming the scar tissue that inhibits this process in humans. It can even regenerate structures as complex as parts of its brain and spinal chord. Some scientists think that studies of this species may yet yield medical benefits for our own.

Sadly, although it thrives in captivity, the axolotl is now critically endangered in the wild. The lakes of Xochimilco and Chalco, where it was once found, have largely vanished beneath the vast sprawl of Mexico City, and the tiny population that remains is threatened both by pollution and predation from invasive fish, such as the African tilapia.

85. Darwin's frog
Rhinoderma darwinii

The male of this small, unassuming amphibian has a fair claim to the title 'Dad of the Year'. His approach to childcare, however, might seem a little hard to swallow.

Baby face

Charles Darwin brought back the frog that now bears his name when he returned on *The Beagle* from South America. It can't have seemed his most exciting find, being simply a pointy-snouted amphibian with a blotchy belly. But it's what it does that gets naturalists excited.

Look at a male in the breeding season and you will notice his chest appears curiously puffed-out.

That's because it's full of tadpoles. This 'chest' is, in fact, his vocal sac – the inflatable organ with which he called to attract a female in the first place. Having mated with her and then watched over her eggs, he gobbled them up just as they were ready to hatch. The growing tadpoles now stay inside his vocal sac for up to 70 days, feeding off the remains of the egg yolk. Once they develop into froglets he simply opens his mouth and lets them out.

Darwin's frogs live in the leaf-litter around streams and boggy areas, feeding on insects and other small invertebrates. When faced by a predator they will flip over and play dead, revealing the striking pattern on their belly.

At a glance

Size: 2.2–3.1cm (snout to vent)
Food: insects and other invertebrates
Reproduction: female lays ±40 eggs; tadpoles develop inside vocal sac of male
Habitat: moist leaf-litter in cool, temperate forests
Distribution: central and southern Chile; parts of western Argentina
Status: Vulnerable

---

86. Surinam toad
Pipa pipa

Strange looks are not the half of it with this amphibian. This is a creature whose babies hatch, literally, from its back. The female's body is, effectively, a flesh-and-blood maternity ward.

Skin deep

This toad's angular, mud-green body looks just like another dead leaf at the bottom of the pond. Look closer, however, and you'll notice two lidless eyes and large, webbed hind feet. The unwebbed front toes sport tiny star-shaped appendages that can sense approaching prey in the murk. Hence the dead-leaf look: this amphibian's deadly camouflage allows it to snap up any prey that comes within range. It surfaces only for air, never coming onto land at all.

Come courtship time, Surinam toads spring into action. A male attracts a mate with a curious underwater clicking. He then clasps her in the 'amplexus' embrace and the two somersault to the surface, the female releasing her eggs for the male to fertilise.

At a glance

Size: 10–13cm; max. 20cm
Food: small fish, worms and other freshwater organisms
Reproduction: eggs hatch from pockets in dorsal skin of female
Habitat: the bottom of murky fresh waters
Distribution: Amazon Basin, including Peru, Guyana, Surinam and Brazil
Status: Least Concern

Now comes the strangest part. The male spreads the fertilised eggs across the female's back and uses his movement to embed them in the soft, spongy skin. Within 24 hours this skin has begun to swell around the eggs, and by ten days each has sunk into its own little pocket and is covered by a thin membrane. The female's back now looks like a fleshy honeycomb. Under the surface the eggs hatch and after 12–20 weeks the youngsters emerge as miniature toadlets.

87. Dung beetles
Scarabaeidae spp

The world's strongest animal has chosen an odd material on which to flex its muscles. But while dung may not appeal to our species, it gives a beetle larva a nutritious start in life. And the good news is, there's plenty of it about.

Family ties
Dung beetles belong to the superfamily Scarabaeoidea (scarabs), which comprises thousands of species. Some, the 'tunnellers', bury dung wherever they find it. Others, the 'dwellers', live in the stuff permanently. The best known, however, are the 'rollers', which roll up their supply into a perfect ball.

Typical rollers are big, chunky beetles, with a spade-like head shield, powerful front limbs and long hind limbs for propelling their prize. Under their shiny wing cases they have long folded wings that get them straight to the freshest dung pile (except for South Africa's Addo flightless dung beetle, which has to foot it). Colours vary between species, from shiny black to metallic green and even iridescent pink.

Dung roaming
'Rollers' thrive wherever there are mammals to provide dung – typically large herbivores, such as buffalo. Most find their target by flying upwind towards the smell, although a few will hitch a ride on the provider. They then pile in, using their head and front legs to dig out their own supply. Huge numbers may gather; one heaving heap of elephant excrement harboured more than 16,000 dung beetles.

Securing a ball is a serious challenge amid the hurly-burly of the heap. With competition intense and theft rife, only the strongest prevail. And strength is something that these insects have in spades. The male of one species, *Onthophagus taurus*, can pull 1,141 times its own body weight, the equivalent of a person pulling six fully laden double-decker buses.

Having a ball
A dung ball is not only a personal food supply. A male uses it to woo a mate. If she accepts, the pair rolls the ball away together – the male doing most of the legwork while the female rides on top or follows behind. They take a straight line, irrespective of obstacles, until they reach a patch of soft soil, where they bury their precious cargo.

The pair mates underground. The male then heads off in search of new partners, leaving the female to lay a single egg inside her ball, known as a 'brood ball'. She coats it with a mix of dung and saliva that hardens to form a protective case. When the larva hatches it feeds on the plant fibre in the dung. It develops through several stages, before pupating for three to four months then emerging with the rains as an adult beetle.

Dung beetles are found on every continent except Antarctica, but the 'rollers' are most prolific on the African savanna, where the great herds provide an abundant supply of the brown stuff. They play a vital ecological role in recycling waste and enriching soil. While we may titter at a life cycle based on dung, to the ancient Egyptians these animals were sacred, their labours symbolising the sun's daily progress across the sky.

At a glance

Size: largest species up to 6cm (varies with species)
Food: mammalian dung
Reproduction: female lays 1 egg in each brood ball, inside which larva completes underground metamorphosis into adulthood
Habitat: from desert and grassland to forest and farmland
Distribution: every continent except Antarctica
Status: varies by species

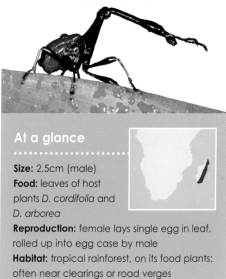

88. Giraffe-necked weevil

Trachelophorus giraffa

Yes, it's another mind-bogglingly weird creature from Madagascar. And there are no prizes for guessing how this insect got its name – though guessing what it does with its eponymous appendage might prove a little trickier.

Roll your own

The Attelabidae – or leaf-rolling weevils – are a widespread family, with more than 2,000 species around the world. They are included within the 'primitive weevils' group (Orthoceri) because of their straight antennae, located at the base of the rostrum. This species, which is one of the largest, is

At a glance

Size: 2.5cm (male)
Food: leaves of host plants *D. cordifolia* and *D. arborea*
Reproduction: female lays single egg in leaf, rolled up into egg case by male
Habitat: tropical rainforest, on its food plants; often near clearings or road verges
Distribution: central and eastern Madagascar
Status: Least Concern

remarkable for the male's enormously elongated neck, which takes up more than half his total length and is neatly hinged in the middle like some toy mechanical digger. The children's-toy impression is enhanced by his shiny red elytra (wing cases). The female's neck is less than half the length of the male's.

The giraffe-necked weevil is endemic to the rainforests of Madagascar, where it can be found resting on the foliage of its host plants *Dichaetanthera cordifolia* and *Dichaetanthera arborea*. Rival males nod their necks up and down in a ritualised display, the loser retreating and backing off. This bizarre feature is not just for show, however. Having mated, a successful male uses his neck to roll up a leaf into a tube, which forms an egg case. The female lays a single egg inside and the larva, when it hatches, feeds on the leaf.

---

89. Periodical cicadas

Magicicada spp

An insect's life is short and sweet, right? Well, consider the life of a periodical cicada: 17 years stuck underground before it ever tastes adulthood, and then it's all over in three weeks.

Perfect timing

The seven *Magicicada* species, known as periodical cicadas, live in eastern North America. Like all cicadas, males attract a mate by generating an ear-splitting noise using organs called tymbals in their hollow abdomen. After mating, a female lays around 600 eggs on young twigs. These hatch six to ten weeks later and the nymphs drop to the ground, burrowing down to 30cm or more.

All cicada nymphs develop slowly, but periodical cicadas are exceptional: 13 years for the four southern species and a staggering 17 years for the three northern ones. They feed on the juices of plant roots and pass through five development stages before finally exiting to adulthood.

Then comes the strangest bit. In any one location, the whole population is synchronised to emerge at exactly the same time in the same year. It happens on a spring evening; countless millions of adults

crawl up and festoon the foliage. They are easy prey for everything from lizards to squirrels, but sheer numbers defeat the predators, ensuring that the majority survives and the cycle starts all over again.

At a glance

Size: 3–4cm
Food: pierce plants to suck liquid; adults from twigs and larvae from roots
Reproduction: eggs laid in twigs; larvae develop underground, taking 17 years to reach adulthood
Habitat: canopy of deciduous trees
Distribution: eastern United States
Status: Least Concern

6 LIVING TOGETHER

No animal is an island. In a world where food and other resources can be thin on the ground and predators lurk around every corner, it pays to have friends. Many species rely upon the company of their own kind, forming lasting relationships that are the key to their survival. Others may strike a deal with a different species altogether.

▲ Starling flocks move with perfect synchronicity, forming fabulous gyroscopic patterns.

We generally think of primates as the most evolved of the social mammals – though perhaps we *would* say that, being primates ourselves. Certainly the siamang (page 136) demonstrates many of the key attributes of the social mammal: communication skills – their dawn songs serve both for group bonding and territorial defence; and parenting skills – both adults care for the youngster, and adolescents hang around to help out with childcare before they finally set out to establish their own families.

Close-knit social groups also create a learning environment, where the inexperienced can benefit from the example of their peers. It takes young chimpanzees, for instance, several years of watching their elders before they can crack open a nut with a rock, and studies of the Japanese macaque (page 137) have revealed how the achievements of one especially enterprising individual are gradually passed on to the whole troop.

All for one

It is easy to imagine that the most evolutionarily 'advanced' animals top the pinnacle of the socially skilled. But before we primates become too smug and self-congratulatory, we would do well to look a little further down the scale.

The most impressive social structures of all are probably those of social insects, such as ants, bees and termites, where individuals are organised by caste – soldier, worker and so on. Through their collective effort the colony is capable of building structures that rival our cities, both in their scale and complexity. Leafcutter ants (page 146) do not only build and organise vast colonies but even grow their own food – a kind of fungus, cultivated on leaves that the foraging hordes carry back to the colony and feed to the growing larvae.

Such insect societies are known as 'eusocial'. One of the trickier concepts for us to grasp is their

Living together

The benefits of living in a group are clear enough: more willing hands – or paws, bills, mandibles, whatever – to look after young, find food and raise the alarm. In the case of the sociable weaver (page 143), teamwork results in an enormous communal nest, with hundreds of birds each occupying individual chambers within one huge thatched apartment. Building never stops, and the constant comings and goings within the colony mean the whole community shares any news of good new foraging sites – or approaching predators.

A crowd without order can be a recipe for chaos, so truly social animals live within strictly organised structures, where everybody knows their place. With the spotted hyena (page 134), it is the dominant females that hold the most authority. These intelligent predators may not meet our idea of the caring, sharing type, but their large clans constitute highly sophisticated societies, governed by complex codes and rigid hierarchies, in which an individual will fare far better than were it to take its chances alone. Close co-operation allows them to thrive where other carnivores fail.

selflessness: the extent to which individual ambition is sacrificed for the collective good. In honey ants (page 147), for example, a caste of workers turn themselves into living larders, dispensing sweet nectar from their grossly engorged bodies to other members of the colony then dying when their job is done. And it is not only insects that function in this way. The naked mole rat (page 138) is an unusual example of a eusocial mammal, with a society – just like that of ants – that is organised by caste and presided over by a queen. Only the queen breeds: other adults, despite being perfectly fertile, suppress their reproductive urges in order to carry out their duties for the colony.

You scratch my back ...

Symbiosis, which – loosely translated – means 'living together', describes the way in which animals can form relationships across species boundaries as a means of beating the competition.

These relationships can take different forms. Mutualism describes a relationship that is advantageous to both parties. This is common between animals and plants – for instance, a hummingbird visits a specific flower to feed on nectar, carrying pollen from one bloom to another and thus pollinating the plant while it gets its meal. The clownfish/anemone arrangement (page 144) offers a classic example of a much rarer phenomenon: mutualism between two animals. The fish finds protection among the stinging tentacles of the anemone, to which it is immune, while providing a clean-up service to its host. The greater honeyguide (page 142) offers another: the bird leads people to a bees' nest, so that its emissaries break in and pull out the comb and both parties can share the reward.

Not all symbiosis is win–win. Commensalism describes a relationship in which only one party appears to have an interest – such as that enjoyed by remoras (page 145), which hitch a ride on sharks and other large marine creatures in order to feed on their host's leftovers. Parasitism describes a relationship in which one party exploits another –

▶ Ants offer protection to aphids while tending them for their honeydew.

and to its detriment. Ticks are a classic example, leaching blood from their host and providing nothing in return except discomfort and disease.

Nature's arrangements are seldom quite as clear-cut as the textbooks would like, however. Oxpeckers (page 140), for instance, were once hailed as a classic example of mutualism; these birds feed on ticks from the hides of large mammals and so, it was long assumed, offered a personal grooming service in exchange for a meal. But research now suggests that the oxpeckers have a taste for blood and – more parasite than partner – spend much of their time opening up and feeding from wounds on their host's hide.

It is in our social behaviour, above all, that we humans often think of ourselves as somehow above the rest of the animal kingdom: the complexity of our societies, the subtleties of our personal interactions and our capacity to act in the interests of others. Look a little harder at the animal kingdom, though, and you'll find it has long had all these bases covered.

▼ Safety in numbers is the meerkat maxim, with all taking turns at sentry duty.

90. Spotted hyena
Crocuta crocuta

Hyenas have never cut it as cuddly toys or conservation pin-ups. On the contrary, whether as the demons of African folklore or the cowardly bad guys of Disney's *Lion King*, they have long inspired little but our fear and loathing. More's the pity, as these intriguing animals have social skills that would put many of their critics to shame.

Identity crisis

Scientists had formerly grouped hyenas with both cats and dogs before assigning them their own family, Hyaenidae. In fact the fossil record shows that hyenas evolved from arboreal, civet-like ancestors some 26 million years ago. Some extinct species were the size of lions.

The spotted hyena, at up to 75kg, is the largest of today's four species. By conventional standards, it is not a thing of beauty. Its distinctive front-heavy profile slopes down from powerful neck and shoulders to oddly slight hindquarters, while its greyish-fawn coat is smudged with indistinct black spots that fade as it gets older.

Females are larger than males. But telling the two sexes apart is tricky, as the female's sexual organs look identical to the male's – the clitoris enlarged into a 'pseudo penis' and the labia fused into 'pseudo testes'. No wonder that many cultures, from Africa to ancient Greece, believed hyenas to be hermaphrodites.

Waste not, want not

Our revulsion for spotted hyenas owes as much to their lifestyle as their looks. We don't, as a rule, go a bundle on scavengers, despite their vital ecological role in recycling waste, and this animal is nature's ultimate dustbin. It tracks down carcasses over great distances, using its loping, energy-efficient gait, and following clues such as the calls of lions or the sight of descending vultures. Its immensely powerful jaws – some 40% stronger than a leopard's – can tear through the thickest hide and split open a giraffe's tibia, while powerful stomach acids can handle the most putrid flesh. Nothing goes to waste. Indeed, a single hyena can eat 15kg at a sitting and consume a gazelle fawn in two minutes flat.

But spotted hyenas do not simply live on leftovers. They are skilled predators in their own right and, working together, can bring down prey as large as zebra, often pursuing it for several kilometres. Behaviour varies with conditions: those in Tanzania's Ngorongoro Crater obtain more than 80% by hunting; those in South Africa's Kruger Park only about 50%.

This species once ranged from western Europe to China, but today is restricted to sub-Saharan Africa. Here it occurs in most habitats, except rainforest and desert, but is numerous only in protected areas with abundant prey. It is the dominant predator wherever lions are absent.

Hyenas have long fired our imaginations. Some African societies associate them with witchcraft, others with funeral rites. The Beng people of west Africa hold that if you come across a hyena corpse with its anus everted (as one does) you must pop it back in or else become inflicted with perpetual laughter. These canny opportunists can grow surprisingly bold where they have lost their fear of people, often raiding campsites for food and, occasionally, even snatching people from villages. You underestimate them at your peril.

Hyenas compete fiercely with lions and when the odds are in their favour (a ratio of at least four to one) can sometimes turn the tables on the big cats, although lions may attack and even kill them. Other predators, such as leopards and cheetahs, usually abandon their kill when faced with those massive jaws.

Girls on top

Spotted hyenas live in clans that vary in size from ten to 60 or more individuals, depending on abundance of prey. Each comprises strict matriarchal hierarchies, presided over by a dominant female, whose cubs enjoy special privileges. Tail, ears, mane and posture are all deployed in a complex body language to convey rank and emotion. Indeed hyenas show primate-like social skills in their ability to recognise such subtleties as, for example, kinship ties between third parties in the clan.

Voice is also vital. Individual hyenas may forage alone, but always keep in contact with other clan members using their far-carrying whooping calls. This allows them to summon reinforcements quickly, such as when hunting larger prey or contesting a kill. Large gatherings generate a chorus of ghoulish cackling, as individuals renew bonds and jockey for position.

Hyenas mark their territory by 'pasting' a pungent secretion from the anal gland on strategically located vegetation. They also use communal latrines, easily located by their white, bone-filled droppings (known to wittier game rangers as 'bush meringues').

Denning down

Breeding takes place year-round, with an average litter of one to two cubs born in an underground den. One drawback of the female's extraordinary genitals is a constricted birth canal, which means that mortality rates are high among both cubs and first-time mothers. Unusually for carnivores, young hyenas are born with open eyes and sharp teeth, and siblings battle fiercely for supremacy. Their mother nurses them on a highly protein-rich milk for up to 16 months. They reach sexual maturity at three years, females remaining with the clan while males move out to try their luck elsewhere.

At a glance

Length: 120–185cm
(plus 25–35cm tail)
Weight: 45–85kg
(females ±12% bigger)
Food: wide variety of prey, from birds to mammals as large as zebra (mean weight ±100kg); scavenges from refuse and carcasses
Reproduction: 1–2 cubs born after ±110 days' gestation: weaned at 16 months; mature at 3 years
Habitat: open country, from grassland and semi-desert to open woodland
Distribution: sub-Saharan Africa, except for Namib Desert and Congo Basin, largely in protected areas
Status: Least Concern

91. Siamang
Symphalangus syndactylus

If gibbons are indeed 'funky', then this one must be the James Brown of the primate world. Not only does it hurtle across its treetop stage with the abandon of a trapeze artist, but it also possesses one of the most histrionic singing voices in the animal kingdom – and has the throat to show for it.

Arms and the gibbon

Gibbons are apes, distinguished from monkeys by their lack of a tail. The siamang is the largest species, recognisable by its uniform black coat and – more remarkably – its gular sac, a large, naked throat pouch that it can inflate to the size of its head.

Like all gibbons, the siamang uses its preposterously long arms to 'brachiate' hand-over-hand through the rainforest canopy, moving at breakneck speed and sometimes flinging itself 15m or more between trees. Its hands function as hooks and, uniquely among gibbons, have the second and third digits fused for a stronger grip.

A siamang's short back legs are used more for carrying things than getting around. It can walk upright on the ground, holding up its arms for balance, though in the wild has little need to leave the canopy. Unlike other apes it does not make a sleeping nest, but tough pads on its buttocks, called ischial callosities, help cushion it against the branches as it catches some kip.

Unhinged melody

Siamangs live in a tight-knit family group of around six, comprising one dominant male and female, their offspring and a sub-adult or two. Each defends its home by singing. Every morning, at 09.00–10.00, the male and female climb to the top of a large tree and perform their far-carrying duet. The female starts off, alternating a series of barks with low booms that resonate in her throat sac. The male then joins in with a synchronised sequence of screams. The duet rises in pitch until it ends with the male's thunderous throat-pouch boom.

This performance warns other troops to avoid the home territory. It may be reprised again before dusk, or whenever one group encounters another – especially when fruiting trees encourage gatherings. A vigorous shaking of branches leaves nobody in any doubt about the singers' location.

Canopy carrier

A female siamang gives birth to a single naked youngster after a seven-month gestation. For the first few months it clings to her abdomen as she moves around the canopy. Males help with the carrying, although the infant will always return to its mother to sleep and nurse. At two years it is independent, but remains with the family, not becoming sexually mature until the age of seven.

Siamangs live in the rainforests of Thailand, Malaysia and Sumatra, where they feed on fruits, leaves, nuts and small animals, the diet varying by season and location. Their droppings are important in dispersing the seeds of rainforest plants. Unfortunately much of their habitat is being lost to deforestation, notably for palm oil plantations, while the illegal pet trade continues to take its toll.

At a glance

Length: ±1m (arm-span more than twice body length)
Weight: 14kg
Food: fruit, young leaves, flowers, seeds and other plant matter; also eggs, insects and small animals
Reproduction: 1 young born after 7-month gestation: weaned at 2 years
Habitat: lowland and montane rainforest, up to 3,800m
Distribution: southeast Asia; Thailand, peninsular Malaysia and Sumatra (Indonesia); Sumatran population may constitute a separate subspecies
Status: Endangered

92. Japanese macaque

Macaca fuscata

Not all monkeys leap around jungles, munching bananas. This one likes nothing better than relaxing in a nice thermal spa – which is especially therapeutic when the temperature outside is 15 below.

Winter warmers

'Snow monkey' is an apt alternative name for this stocky, short-tailed primate, which inhabits the forests of central and northern Japan. Apart from humans, no primate lives further north, and to fend off the winter chill it has developed a thick winter coat of grey-brown fur, which it moults during the warm summers. Its naked face, by contrast, is almost human in its expressiveness.

This monkey, like most macaques, feeds on everything from fruits and roots to eggs and crabs. The spa habit is unique to a population in the Nagano Mountains, an area fed with thermal springs. Remarkably, this behaviour was unknown until 1963, when one female that plunged in to retrieve some soybeans found the warm waters to her liking and stayed put. Soon the rest of her troop copied, and the habit spread. Indeed, so popular did it become that macaques started invading human spas. Eventually they were given a resort of their own, at a special sanctuary called Snow Monkey Park.

Monkey see and monkey do

Taking warm baths is not all that these intelligent monkeys have taught one another. In a separate population on Koshima Island, one young female – known to researchers as Imo – learned to rinse sweet potatoes in the sea rather than brushing off the dirt by hand. She soon discovered that the saltwater added a tasty seasoning. The habit soon passed to her siblings and, before long, the entire troop was at it.

Imo did not stop there: soon she had learnt to ball up a handful of wheat and sand from the beach and toss it in the water, so she could pick off the floating grain. Studies of these monkeys have since shed new light on how primates other than ourselves can invent new behaviour and learn by example from others.

Pooling rank

Troops of Japanese macaques can number anything from 20–100, with females outnumbering males by three to one. A dominant male presides over each group, but hierarchies are matrilineal, with infants inheriting their mother's rank. Lower-ranking individuals tend to hang around on the fringes, often denied access to the warm pools. Males leave their troop when they mature; females stay all their lives, forming strong bonds.

During the breeding season a female may mate with around ten males, which she selects carefully.

At a glance

Length: 79–95cm (tail 10cm)
Weight: 10–14kg (male); 5.5kg (female)
Food: omnivorous: fruits, seeds, flowers, roots and other plant matter; insects, eggs, crabs even fish
Reproduction: 1 young born after 173-day gestation: weaned at 2 years
Habitat: various forest types, including deciduous, coniferous and semi-tropical, up to 1,650m
Distribution: Japan, in 4 separate populations
Status: Least Concern

Her single infant is not weaned until two years, by which time its hard-pushed mother will also be coping with the demands of its adolescent, but still dependent, siblings. Females mature at 3½ years; males a year later.

93. Naked mole rat
Heterocephalus glaber

Not so much a furry mammal as a wrinkled frankfurter with teeth, this extraordinary subterranean rodent has the social life of a termite and the temperature regulation of a frog. And that's not the half of it.

Skin deep

Naked mole rats – also known as sand puppies – are among about 20 species in the Bathyergidae family, confined to Africa. Neither rat nor mole, these burrowing rodents have a closer evolutionary affinity to porcupines and guinea pigs.

This species inhabits arid savanna regions of east Africa. Like all mole rats, it lives in a labyrinth of burrows. But while other mole rats have a decent covering of fur, this one's wrinkled pinkish-yellow skin is virtually hairless. It also has four enormous teeth, two above and two below, that protrude in front of its closed lips.

Grotesque, perhaps, but these traits are specialised adaptations to a life of burrowing. The teeth do the digging, powered by jaw muscles that take up nearly 25% of the animal's body mass, while the loose, naked skin allows it to twist and turn in narrow tunnels without any clogging of fur. Its short, thin legs can propel its cylindrical body equally fast backwards or forwards – like a tube train – and its tiny eyes, though almost blind, can sense a change in air currents and thus detect any intrusion from the surface.

Going underground

Naked mole rats live in colonies of anything from 20 to 300, in a burrow system that may measure 5km in total extent. These burrows comprise main highways (wide enough for two animals to pass), plus numerous side tunnels, breeding chambers, toilet chambers and so on. Excavation involves a kind of nose-to-tail chain gang: the 'diggers', in front, chisel away with their teeth; the 'sweepers', behind, shift the soil back down the tunnel; and the 'volcanoers', at the back, kick it out onto the surface, forming distinctive conical molehills.

These rodents feed mostly on large plant tubers. They do not consume the whole thing at once but nibble away from the inside, leaving the outside intact and thus allowing the tuber to regenerate. By 'farming' their food in this way, the colony can subsist on a single tuber for months. They are also coprophagous – in other words, they will eat their own faeces.

Air supply

To cope with the suffocating conditions underground, naked mole rats use oxygen minimally and have a blood supply that can maximise its uptake. They also have a very slow metabolism – only two-thirds that of an equivalent-sized mouse. This means that they cannot regulate their internal temperature like other mammals. If conditions get too cold they will huddle together; too hot, and they will retreat to cooler burrows deeper down.

Stranger still, naked mole rats have an amazing insensitivity to pain. Research has revealed that their skin lacks the key neurotransmitter 'substance P', which means, among other things, that they cannot feel acid. This is thought to help them withstand the build-up of acid in their body tissues that results from the high carbon dioxide concentrations in their poorly oxygenated tunnels.

Queen's rules

Naked mole rats are – along with the Damara mole rat – one of only two 'eusocial' mammals.

This means that, like social insects such as ants or termites, their society is structured around a caste system. At the top is the queen and just below sit the two or three males with whom she breeds. Remarkably, these are the only animals in the whole colony with a sex life. All the rest are workers who, though genetically fertile, remain permanently celibate. They suppress their reproductive behaviour in the presence and authority of the queen.

The workers – as with ants or termites – are loosely divided by job: soldiers defend the colony from predators and rival colonies; tunnellers tunnel. All members of the colony use scent to recognise one another and distinguish friend from foe, and will top this up with a regular roll in the burrow's toilet chamber.

A female gives birth to her litter of anything from three to 12 pups (with a staggering maximum of 28 recorded) once per year after a 70-day gestation. The young weigh just 2g at birth. The queen nurses them for one month, after which workers help feed them on faeces until they are old enough to eat solids. Naked mole rats, due to their slow metabolism, are the longest-lived rodent.

Monarchy and anarchy

A colony of naked mole rats functions like a single organism, so selflessly does each individual serve the whole. Workers will share food and even, when required, sacrifice themselves for the common good – such as by confronting a predator. It is the queen's authority that keeps things running smoothly; she will prod and shove workers into action and come down hard on any other females with ideas above their station.

When the queen dies, however, everything changes. The colony is plunged into turmoil, sometimes for months, as other females engage in a violent struggle for succession. Once the new ruler takes the throne, her rivals quickly slip back into their subordinate positions and order is restored.

At a glance

Length: 8–10cm
Weight: 30–35g; queen may exceed 50g
Food: tubers; faeces (their own)
Reproduction: litter of 3–12 pups (exceptionally up to 28) born after 70-day gestation; weaned at 1 month
Habitat: arid savanna and semi-desert; underground
Distribution: east Africa, Kenya, Somalia, southern Ethiopia
Status: Least Concern

94. Oxpeckers
Buphagus spp

Valet or vampire? The jury is out on these African birds, which make their living on the back of large, hairy mammals. Once hailed as a model of win-win mutualism, it now seems that this arrangement may be more one-sided than the birds' hosts would like.

Fitting the bill

Oxpeckers make up the family Buphagidae, which is closely related to starlings. There are two species, whose names – red-billed (*Buphagus erythrorhynchus*) and yellow-billed (*B. africanus*) – indicate how best to tell them apart. Both are starling-sized, with brown plumage and strong feet. In addition to its bill colour, the red-billed also has a distinctive yellow eye-ring and a darker rump than its cousin.

These birds are widespread across sub-Saharan Africa, preferring open bush and savanna habitats. In truth, however, their habitat is the hides of the large mammals on which they spend most of their time, feeding, preening, roosting, courting, mating and even gathering nest material – hair – from their hosts. These mammals range from impala, at the bottom of the scale, to giraffe, at the top. The yellow-billed oxpecker has a preference for the large, grey and hairless, such as hippos and rhinos, but both species may use a variety of hosts – and in regions where their distributions overlap, the two may even line up on the same animal.

Large mammals living in African grasslands are infested with ticks and other ectoparasites, such as botfly larvae. This is both a great irritant to the host and a great potential food source to an enterprising bird. And watching oxpeckers at work, as they swarm over the hides of their hosts, probing

At a glance

Length: 19–22cm
Weight: 42–59g
Food: ectoparasites and blood, gleaned from hide of mammal hosts
Reproduction: 2–3 eggs (exceptionally 5); fledge after 1 month
Habitat: open woodland and tropical savanna, with large game or livestock present
Distribution: east and southern Africa (both species); west to Senegal (yellow-billed)
Status: Least Concern

into every orifice and deftly scissoring out the parasites with their bills, the deal would appear to be straightforward: the birds get a free meal; the host gets a personal grooming service. Mutualism at its very essence. Isn't nature wonderful?

Bloodlust

Look a little closer, though, and you'll see that oxpeckers devote much of their attention to any wounds they can find on their host's hide. Indeed, their pecking and probing actually serves to keep open wounds that would otherwise heal. Oxpeckers, you see, have a taste for blood. And many of the fat, engorged ticks they remove have already filled up on the stuff.

It's not just blood. These birds spend a lot of time probing into ears, for earwax, and picking out dead skin flakes – dandruff – from their host's hair. In other words, they are making more of a meal of their host than the parasites it carries, which rather suggests that the bird itself is the real parasite.

Studies have been inconclusive. One conducted on domestic cattle in Zimbabwe concluded that those exposed to oxpeckers lost no more ticks than those that weren't, and also that their wounds took longer to heal. A study of impala, however, suggested that individuals receiving attention from oxpeckers tended to groom themselves less than those that weren't. Some animals do appear actively

to assist the oxpeckers – zebra, for instance, by lifting their tail. Either way, most hosts tend to tolerate the discomfort and indignity, with the exception of elephants, which will swat the birds away with an irritated trunk. The oxpeckers, meanwhile, are also choosy, and eschew the hides of long-haired antelope, as well as certain other species, such as topi.

Help at the hole

The only time that oxpeckers abandon their hosts is when they breed. They nest during the rainy season, choosing holes or cavities – sometimes in walls – and lining their nest with grasses and hair that they pluck from the hide of their hosts. Both species lay two to three eggs, on average. They are co-operative breeders: one or more immature birds from a previous brood help their parents feed their chicks, which remain in the nest for up to a month.

After fledging, the young continue to beg for food for another month, often while perched on the backs of their hosts. Outside the breeding season both species form small, noisy flocks.

Whatever the benefit or otherwise of oxpeckers to large African mammals, people walking in big game country often have cause to be grateful to these birds. whose rattling alarm calls can be a helpful warning of something big and possibly belligerent lurking behind the next bush.

95. Greater honeyguide
Indicator indicator

This bird's names – both the scientific and vernacular – spell out its secret. It is a veritable pied piper of the African bush, leading followers with a merry tune to a precious but risky food source, and then cashing in on their brave efforts.

Honey trap

Honeyguides (family Indicatoridae) are small, unremarkable-looking birds, distantly related to woodpeckers, that live in the woodlands of Africa and Asia. There are 17 species in all, but this is one of only two that perform the trick for which the family is named.

Traditional African societies have long known about the greater honeyguide and learned to respond when it comes calling. The bird flits through the bush from tree to tree, keeping up its incessant chattering 'guiding call' and flashing its white outer tail feathers as a come-on, until it has led its followers to the bees' nest. Then it falls silent, leaving the followers to shin up the tree and extract the honey – a job only for the experienced, who know how to subdue the irate bees by smoking them out.

The bird itself does not eat honey. Its interest is in the grubs and beeswax (honeyguides are among the few birds that can digest wax), and it takes its fill from what its followers leave behind. It is also thought to perform the same guiding service for the honey badger (*Mellivora capensis*), a voracious thick-skinned carnivore with an appetite for honey, although there is still a lack of conclusive evidence for this behaviour.

When no assistance is on hand, the greater honeyguide will go it alone, entering hives early in the morning, when the bees are still torpid, or feeding on nests already ransacked by honey badgers. It may also feed on swarming termites and other flying insects, often joining mixed-species flocks to do so.

Nest cheat

When it comes to breeding, the greater honeyguide is equally adept at exploiting others. Like many cuckoos it is a nest parasite, which means the female lays her eggs in the nests of other birds – primarily hole-nesters such as woodpeckers, barbets and kingfishers. She lays in batches of three to seven, up to a total of 20 in a season. The young hatch with a hook on the bill that they use, while still blind and featherless, to puncture the host's eggs and kill its chicks.

Life is not all easy for greater honeyguides. They have been found stung to death beneath beehives, and often endure attacks from other birds that catch them snooping around their nests. Nonetheless they are much appreciated by many traditional peoples across Africa, for whom they provide a free and delicious source of protein.

The service, however, does come with one caveat. According to African folklore you should *always* leave behind a gift of honeycomb for your avian guide, or next time it will lead you to a buffalo or a black mamba.

96. Sociable weaver
Philetairus socius

Among the guild of master builders that is the weaver-bird family, first prize for sheer scale goes to the sparrow-sized sociable weaver. Its monstrous communal haystack of a construction is the largest tree nest in the bird world, measuring up to 5m across and weighing more than a tonne.

High-rise haystack
Sociable weavers live in the dry semi-desert of the Kalahari, where summers are blistering but winter nights can be freezing. Like many weavers, they nest in colonies. Unlike other species, however, they do not build one nest per pair but instead create a mass thatched apartment complex that can house over 300 birds in up to 100 individual chambers.

Construction starts with a platform of strong twigs built in the fork of a large tree, such as a camelthorn (*Acacia erioloba*). Stiff grass stalks are then used to build up the body. There is no actual weaving; the birds simply push the stalks into the structure, which hangs together from sheer weight.

Each chamber opens downwards, leaving the underside of the nest honeycombed with openings. The entrance tunnels may be 25cm long and 7cm wide, with a 10–15cm nesting chamber at the end, lined with fur, plant fluff or other soft material. Spiky grass stalks stuck into the tunnel walls help repel intruders such as marauding snakes, notably cape cobras and boomslangs, which swallow their fair quota of nestlings.

Sociable weavers seldom venture more than a kilometre from their nest. They never stop building, and the nest remains home until they die (or, as sometimes happens, the supporting branch crashes to the ground). Its dense insulating thatch shields the birds from both the baking summer sun and the cold winter nights. Some nests have remained occupied for over 100 years.

Family and friends
This species' breeding cycle – like that of many birds that live in arid regions – is triggered by rainfall. It makes the most of good times, raising four broods per cycle. A female lays up to two to six eggs in the chamber, the chicks hatching after 13–14 days and fledging after another 21–24. Immature birds will provide food for their younger siblings, while parents may even feed their neighbours' young next door.

This spirit of hospitality even extends to strangers, with other small birds, including chats, tits and lovebirds, often taking over vacant chambers. One notable tenant is the diminutive but ferocious pygmy falcon, which helps provide protection for the colony, though may – ungratefully – snatch the odd fledgling. Larger birds, including owls, eagles and vultures, often roost on the roof.

At a glance

Length: 14cm
Weight: 26–30g
Food: insects, especially harvester termites; some seeds
Reproduction: breeds with the rains; up to four broods per breeding cycle.
Habitat: arid savanna woodland and semi-desert
Distribution: Botswana, Namibia and northwestern South Africa
Status: Least Concern

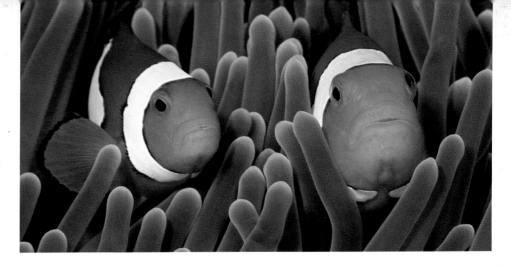

97. Clownfish
Amphiprion spp

Relax, you've found Nemo. But – Pixar version aside – do you really know what this jaunty little fish is doing in a bed of deadly stinging anemone tentacles? And can you even be sure that 'he' isn't, in fact, 'she'?

Colours of a clown

There are around 28 different species in the genus *Amphiprion* that go by the name of clownfish, or clown anemone fish. These attractive reef fishes are well known from pet shops (they do well in captivity) and, in more recent years, as the stars of the animated movie *Finding Nemo*.

All clownfishes are boldly marked, their bodies typically divided into contrasting bars or zones of white against orange or red, with black piping outlining their rounded fins. They are among the more conspicuous inhabitants of coral reefs across the Indian and Pacific oceans, invariably seen darting amongst the tentacles of sea anemones.

Fraternising with the anemone

But wait. Sea anemones? Don't they have deadly stings? Well, yes they do – deadly enough to kill many other fish. But clownfish have come to a remarkable arrangement with their venomous hosts. Their skin secretes a protective mucus coating that allows them to move among the stinging tentacles with impunity. Thus they can use the anemone as a refuge from predators, while also getting to polish off its leftovers.

In return for its hospitality, the anemone receives a clean-up service from the clownfish, which gets rid of algae, harmful invertebrates and dead tentacles. The fish's faecal matter also provides valuable nutrients to the anemone, while its constant

movement among the tentacles improves water circulation. It is even thought that the bright colours of the clownfish may lure other fish close enough for the anemone to ensnare them.

The science behind this arrangement is not entirely understood. One theory suggests that as the protective mucus is based on sugars, not proteins, the anemone does not recognise the fish as food and thus holds fire with its nematocysts (sting cells). Whatever the explanation, this win–win deal remains a classic example of symbiosis.

Most clownfish species have evolved this arrangement with only one particular species of host anemone. All are highly territorial, living in groups around a single anemone, which they defend aggressively from others.

Gender benders

Male and female clownfish form strong bonds. They lay their eggs in batches of hundreds or even thousands (depending on species), on rocks or coral beside their host anemone. Both parents guard the eggs for six to ten days until they hatch. The babies spend two weeks floating among the plankton community in the open sea, before settling on the reef and looking for a new anemone host, where they will remain for the rest of their lives.

In any community of clownfish the breeding female is dominant, followed by the mating male and finally the non-mating males. Bizarrely, all clownfish are born male. But as they grow and establish hierarchies, the dominant male switches sex to become female. If the dominant female dies, the next mating male turns into a female and chooses a new partner. And so on. This process is known as sequential hermaphroditism.

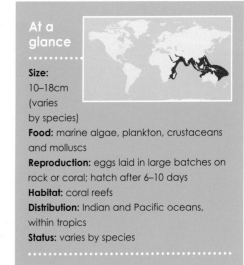

At a glance

Size: 10–18cm (varies by species)
Food: marine algae, plankton, crustaceans and molluscs
Reproduction: eggs laid in large batches on rock or coral; hatch after 6–10 days
Habitat: coral reefs
Distribution: Indian and Pacific oceans, within tropics
Status: varies by species

98. Remoras
Echeneidae spp

Most creatures flee from sharks. Remoras stick – literally – to their sides. These fish are nature's ultimate hangers-on, saving valuable energy by latching onto their hosts and feeding off the scraps they leave behind.

Forming attachments

Eight species of remora – sometimes known as suckerfish – make up the family Echeneidae. All are slim bony fish, brown, black or grey in colour, that are unremarkable apart from a strange oval structure on top of their head. This organ, the suctoral disk, is a modification of the spiny dorsal fin. It comprises 22–26 slat-like structures that can open or close to provide suction.

A remora swims up to a large marine creature, such as a shark, whale or turtle, and uses this disk to attach itself. It then hangs on for the ride, feeding from its host's leftovers or making short sorties after small marine titbits. By sliding backwards against the skin of its host it can increase the suction, locking on tighter. Conversely, by sliding forwards it can release itself.

Different species attach themselves to different hosts, and some may remain in place for up to three months. The smaller species may latch on inside the mouths of large fish, such as mantas or sunfish, where they can more easily hoover up scraps. It is not clear how much the host benefits from the arrangement – although the remora may remove bacteria and parasites from its skin.

Tropical wanderers

Remoras are found primarily in tropical seas, although they may hitch a ride on a host that wanders into more temperate waters. Spawning occurs during the spring and early summer. The eggs are fertilised externally and their tough shell keeps them from drying out, even if washed up on land. Hatchlings are approximately 5mm long. They live as part of the plankton for the first year, until they develop a sucker disk at about 1cm. At 3cm long they are fully formed, and head out to find the nearest convenient host.

Some traditional fishing communities, notably in the Indian Ocean, have used remoras as 'fishing fish'. They attach a line to one they have captured and then, when they come within sight of a turtle, release it into the sea. The remora usually swims straight to the turtle and attaches itself, whereupon the fishermen are able to drag in their catch – or at least bring it within harpooning range.

At a glance

Length: 30–90cm (varies by species)

Food: parasites; copepods; any leftover scraps from host

Reproduction: spawns in open ocean; hatchlings find host at 3cm long

Habitat: warm and tropical oceans; may be carried by hosts into more temperate zones

Distribution: worldwide

Status: Least Concern (all species)

99. Leafcutter ants

Acromyrmex and *Atta* spp

Leafcutter ants harvest more greenery in the forests of Latin America than any other animal, getting through up to 20% of all vegetation. Not surprisingly, they can do serious damage to crops, but farmers have learnt to deter them by sprinkling refuse from their nests around tree trunks or over seedlings.

Ants are justly celebrated for their industry. But these ones have also mastered agriculture – not just harvesting their food, but growing it too. They are both the living secateurs of the rainforest and its underground fungus farmers.

Ground force

Forty-one species in two separate genera, *Acromyrmex* and *Atta*, go by the name 'leafcutter ant'. The two genera differ in minor anatomical details, but share a similar lifestyle. Vibrating their powerful jaws at up to 1,000 times per second, they slice off sections of living leaves – up to 20 times their own weight – and carry them back to their nest. Columns swarm across the forest floor, a bobbing procession of mini green flags marking their progress as they hold their trophies aloft.

You might think these ants were simply gathering food. But the adults feed purely on leaf sap. Instead, the sections of leaf are used to cultivate a fungus that they feed to their larvae. The ants chew up the leaf pieces into a pulp, which they store with their faeces and fungus spores, until new strands of fungus begin to grow on it.

This is textbook mutualism. The fungus, from the Lepiotaceae family (different ant species cultivate different fungi species), relies on the ants; it can't survive outside their nest nor reproduce without their assistance. The ant larvae, in return, have their food supply constantly on tap. The relationship is highly tuned. Ants tend the fungi carefully, removing pests and clearing away all waste to keep the colony healthy. The fungi can even communicate via chemicals that a particular leaf is toxic, so the ants don't choose that plant again.

Workers unite

The underground nests of leafcutter ants are enormous, holding up to eight million ants in a structure that can cover anything from 30–600m². The colony is organised by caste, with a queen, a few winged males and the rest non-reproducing worker females. Jobs are assigned by size: the smallest workers brood the larvae and tend the fungus gardens; others cut and collect the leaves, or patrol the terrain and protect the foragers; the largest are soldiers, who defend the nest and clear the trails. The queen, meanwhile, spends all her time producing eggs.

When the time is right, winged males and females take to the air *en masse* in nuptial flights. A female mates with multiple males in order to acquire the 300 million or so sperm she will need to found a new colony. On the ground she loses her wings and goes off in search of a suitable underground lair, carrying with her a tiny piece of the fungus mycelium, tucked into an oral cavity.

At a glance

Length: soldiers up to 1.6mm; workers much smaller

Food: adults feed on leaf sap; larvae on Lepiotaceae fungus cultivated in nest

Reproduction: metamorphosis from egg to adult takes place underground over 6–10 weeks

Habitat: lowland tropical forests

Distribution: South and Central America; southern USA

Status: Least Concern

100. Honey ant
Camponotus inflatus

Many animals that live in arid regions will store away food for harder times. But storing it away inside the bodies of your companions? These curious ants take the idea of a personal larder to extremes.

Full to bursting

Five different groups of ants are known as honeypot or honey ants, and have independently evolved a similar lifestyle in different parts of the world. The best known is *Camponotus inflatus* of Australia. Similar species are found in arid regions of western North America and southern Africa. All get their common name from the grotesquely swollen abdomen of specialised workers – known as repletes – which functions as a living storage vessel, providing vital sustenance to other members of the colony.

Honey ants forage on desert flowers for their sugary nectar and return with it to the nest to share with others. The repletes gorge themselves with this nectar, which they keep undigested in a part of the abdomen called the gaster. They swell to the size of grapes and attach themselves to the ceiling of their underground nests with their claws, where they hang like amber beads until their supplies are needed.

Nectar is not all these ants store. Other liquids and animal juices all help swell their distended abdomens. When the food supply dries up in the surrounding desert, the other workers solicit food from the repletes by stroking their antennae and causing them to regurgitate their bounty. The distended gaster never contracts to its original shape so the repletes die once their supply is exhausted.

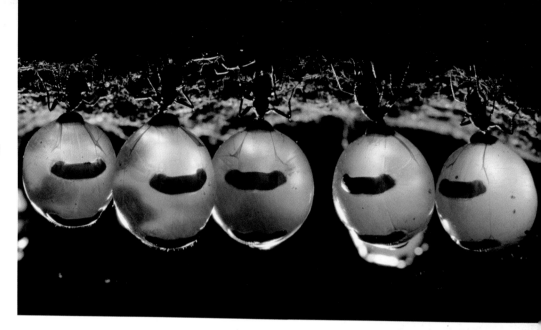

Takeover bids

Honeypot ants live in underground colonies, which may extend 2m below the surface. Like most ants, they have highly structured and stratified societies. Most consist of a single queen, a large number of her worker daughters and a few winged males. The workers are assigned tasks according to size, and it is the larger ones that develop into repletes.

Neighbouring colonies often contest territorial disputes. These are usually resolved by display, but when one colony becomes much larger it may raid the smaller one. The raiders kill all the workers and the queen, but drag back the larvae, pupae and repletes to their own nest, where they are co-opted into the new colony.

After it rains, swarms of honey ants set out on their nuptial flights. The small winged males die off after mating. The larger females tear off their wings then scurry away in search of a suitable burrow in which to lay their eggs. If they can avoid the numerous predators, they may found a new colony.

Traditional desert peoples value honey ants as an occasional source of nutrition, digging them out, biting off the head and squeezing out the sweet contents of the abdomen. In Australia honey ants figure prominently in Aboriginal culture, and the name of the Western Desert Art co-operative, Papunya Tula, means 'honey ant dreaming'.

At a glance

Length: 6–12mm
Food: nectar; also liquids from insects, carrion
Reproduction: life cycle, from egg to adult, takes place underground
Habitat: from true desert to semi-desert and arid woodland
Distribution: Australia; similar species found in southern Africa and western North America
Status: Least Concern

Conservation contacts

You will find further information about the animals in this book from the following organisations. You will also find many ways in which to become involved in their conservation, and that of wildlife in general.

ARKive (www.arkive.org) A website with an ark of media material about endangered species, including information, photos and films.

Birdlife International (www.birdlife.org.uk) A global partnership of conservation organisations that strives to conserve birds, their habitats and global biodiversity, working with people in more than 100 countries and territories.

Conservation International (2011 Crystal Dr, Suite 500, Arlington, Virginia 2220, USA; www.conservation.org) Works on projects worldwide that adopt a highly focused approach, concentrating on biodiversity hotspots.

David Shepherd Wildlife Foundation (61 Smithbrook Kilns, Cranleigh, Surrey GU6 8JJ, UK; www.davidshepherd.org) Founded by the famous wildlife artist, DSWF funds long-term projects in Africa and Asia to protect critically endangered mammals in the wild. Raises funds through subscription, donation and art-based events.

Durrell Wildlife Conservation Trust (Les Augrès Manor, La Profonde Rue, Trinity, Jersey JE3 5BP, Channel Islands, UK; www.durrellwildlife.org)

Founded by the famous conservationist Gerald Durrell, this organisation works with endangered species and has strong in-country education and staff training programmes.

IUCN: World Conservation Union (Rue Mauverney 28, Gland 1196, Switzerland; www.iucn.org) The world's largest conservation network, it aims to influence, encourage and assist societies throughout the world to conserve the integrity and diversity of nature, and to ensure the equitable and ecologically sustainable use of natural resources. The IUCN publishes an official red list of threatened species at www.iucnredlist.org.

Marine Conservation Society (MCS) (www.mcsuk.org) UK charity dedicated to the protection of the marine environment and its wildlife. Includes information about marine resources and current threats.

Royal Society for the Protection of Birds (RSPB) (The Lodge, Sandy, Beds SG19 2DL; www.rspb.org.uk) A UK-based conservation charity, with over one million members and a wide network of reserves. Promotes environmental education and wildlife-friendly land management, and supports conservation projects worldwide.

TRAFFIC International (219a Huntingdon Rd, Cambridge CB3 ODL, UK; www.traffic.org) Tackles illegal trade in endangered species, including their parts and products.

Whale and Dolphin Conservation Society (Brookfield Hse, 38 St Paul St, Chippenham, Wiltshire SN15 1LJ, UK; www.wdcs.org) A global voice for the protection of whales, dolphins and their environment. The world's most active charity dedicated to the conservation and welfare of cetaceans.

Wildlife Conservation Society (2300 Southern Blvd, Bronx, New York 10460, USA; www.wcs.org) An international organisation based at the Bronx Zoo that works to save wildlife and wild lands through careful science, international conservation, education and resource management.

World Wide Fund for Nature (WWF) International (Gland Av du Mont Blanc, 1196 Gland, Switzerland; www.wwf.org or www.panda.org) WWF works for a future in which humans live in harmony with nature, operating in more than 100 countries worldwide.

Zoological Society of London (ZSL) (www.zsl.org) Encompasses London and Whipsnade zoos and is at the forefront of research and field-based conservation.

For more about endangered species, many of them as bizarre as you like, see *100 Animals to See Before you Die* (Garbutt and Unwin, Bradt Travel Guides), the companion volume to this book.

◀ *Bizarre indeed: a tussock bird eyeballs a southern elephant seal.*

Acknowledgements

This book was the brainchild of Hilary Bradt, lifelong champion of the bizarre and eccentric, who was inspired by a snout-to-snout encounter with a leaf-nosed snake in Madagascar (see page 83). I am, as ever, grateful for her encouragement.

I would also like to thank all the Bradt team, including Helen Anjomshoaa, Donald Greig and Adrian Phillips, for their support and – as deadlines shot past – their patience. And especially Anna Moores, for steering the book towards its conclusion with unflappable energy, great editorial expertise and life-saving good humour. Barry Kew also did a great job with the proofreading and index.

Chris Lane at Artinfusion conjured up his usual magic with the designs, even when under great pressure, and was a pleasure to work with. The maps are also Chris's work, with some help from David McCutcheon and advice from Marianne Taylor, though any inaccuracies are entirely my own. Jean Hosking at Frank Lane Picture Agency (www.flpa-images.co.uk) was very helpful in sourcing images. I'm also grateful to Kristie Cannings at Photoshot (www.photoshot.com), and to Ken Catania (star-nosed mole) and Stephen Cunliffe (African Jacana) for providing their excellent photographs. Thanks also to Stella Martin for expert advice on the Australian species.

I am indebted to all the scientists and naturalists out there who, over the years, have unlocked the secrets of these amazing creatures, captivating those of us – like me – who sometimes find our own species rather disappointing. Their many wonderful books have sustained and inspired me and have been invaluable in the writing of this one. Thanks, also, to all the dedicated conservationists working to protect wildlife around the world. And, of course, a nod of appreciation to the animals themselves, without which life would be a great deal duller.

Finally there's my personal back-up team. I'd like to thank my parents for inspiring my love of wildlife, my wife Kathy, for her support and editorial wisdom, and my daughter Florence, for keeping my eyes open to the natural world. The final days of this book consumed a family holiday as surely as an African egg-eating snake swallows its prize, and special gratitude goes to Fiona Gemmell and Keith Parrish for their understanding, and to Elspeth Macdonald and Roddy Paul for their help and hospitality. Bizarre animals, the lot of them, and I'd have it no other way.

Mike Unwin – June 2010

Picture credits

Credits are listed in chronological order specifying the position of the image on the page where necessary. For front and back cover credits, see page 2.

P4: Tui De Roy/Minden Pictures/FLPA; p6: Norbert Wu/Minden Pictures/FLPA; p7: Albert Visage/FLPA; p8–9 Silvestris Fotoservice/FLPA; p10: Piotr Naskrecki/Minden Pictures/FLPA (top), Cyril Ruoso/Minden Pictures/FLPA (bottom); p11: Dietmar Nill/FN/Minden/FLPA; p12: Frans Lanting/FLPA; p13: Michael & Patricia Fogden/Minden Pictures/FLPA; p14: Claus Meyer/FLPA (top); Foto Natura Stock/FLPA (bottom); p15: Merlin D Tuttle/Bat Conservation International/www.batcon.org; p16: Cede Prudente/Photoshot (top), A. N.T. Photo Library/Photoshot (bottom); p17: Jurgen & Christine Sohns/FLPA (both); p18: Michael & Patricia Fogden/Minden Pictures/FLPA; p19: Frans Lanting/FLPA (top), Michael & Patricia Fogden/Minden Pictures/FLPA (bottom); p20: David Hosking/FLPA; p21: Stephen Cunliffe (top), Winfried Wisniewski/FLPA (bottom); p22: Flip De Nooyer/FN/Minden/FLPA; p23: Flip De Nooyer/FN/Minden/FLPA (both); p24: Francois Merlet/FLPA (main), D Zingel Eichhorn/FLPA (inset); p25: Konrad Wothe/Minden Pictures/FLPA; p26: S & D & K Maslowski/FLPA; p26–7: Konrad Wothe/Minden Pictures/FLPA; p28: Stephen Dalton/Photoshot (top); Michael & Patricia Fogden/Minden Pictures/FLPA; p29: Michael & Patricia Fogden/Minden Pictures/FLPA; p30: Cede Prudente/Photoshot (main), Mark Moffett/Minden Pictures/FLPA (bottom); p31: Stephen Dalton/Photoshot (main), Chris Mattison/FLPA (bottom); p32: Jurgen & Christine Sohns/FLPA (main), Cyril Ruoso/Minden Pictures/FLPA (bottom); p33: NORFANZ founding parties (top), Michael & Patricia Fogden/Minden Pictures/FLPA (bottom); p34–5: Reinhard Dirscherl/FLPA; p36: Flip Nicklin/Minden Pictures/FLPA (top), Duncan Usher/Minden Pictures/FLPA (bottom); p37: Nigel Cattlin/FLPA (top), Kevin Schafer/Minden Pictures/FLPA (bottom); p38–9: Tui De Roy/Minden Pictures/FLPA (both); p40: Ken Catania; p41: ZSSD/Minden Pictures/FLPA (top), Wendy Dennis/FLPA (bottom); p42: Flip Nicklin/Minden Pictures/FLPA; p42–3: Flip Nicklin/Minden Pictures/FLPA (main); p43: David Hosking/FLPA (top), Flip Nicklin/Minden Pictures/FLPA (bottom); p45: Frans Lanting/FLPA; p46: Michael Durham/Minden Pictures/FLPA (both); p47: Jurgen & Christine Sohns/FLPA (top), Sunset/FLPA (bottom); p48: Wendy Dennis/FLPA (main), Frans Lanting/FLPA (top); p49: Mark Jones/Minden Pictures/FLPA (main), Tui De Roy/Minden Pictures/FLPA (top); p50: Frans Lanting/FLPA (top); p50–1: David

Hosking/FLPA; p52: ZSSD/Minden Pictures/FLPA; p53: William S Clark/FLPA; p54: Mark Bowler/Photoshot (top), Martin Harvey/Photoshot (bottom); p55: Chris Mattison/FLPA (bottom); p56: Michael & Patricia Fogden/Minden Pictures/FLPA (left & middle), Chris Mattison/FLPA (right); p57: Chris Mattison/FLPA; p58: Albert Visage/FLPA (both); p59: Reinhard Dirscherl/FLPA (top); p61: Chris Newbert/Minden Pictures/FLPA (bottom); p60–61: Reinhard Dirscherl/FLPA (main); p60 & 61: Fred Bavendam/Minden Pictures/FLPA; p62: Norbert Wu/Minden Pictures/FLPA; p63: Norbert Wu/Minden Pictures/FLPA (both); p64: Wendy Dennis/FLPA (main), Mark Moffett/Minden Pictures/FLPA (top); p65: Michael & Patricia Fogden/Minden Pictures/FLPA (top), Norbert Wu/Minden Pictures/FLPA (bottom); p66–7: ZSSD/Minden Pictures/FLPA; p68: Reinhard Dirscherl/FLPA (top), Edward Myles/FLPA (bottom); p69: Michael & Patricia Fogden/Minden Pictures/FLPA; p70–1: Sunset/FLPA; p72: Mitsuaki Iwago/Minden Pictures/FLPA; p73: Jurgen & Christine Sohns/FLPA; p74: Frans Lanting/FLPA (both); p75: Andrew Forsyth/FLPA (main), David Hosking/FLPA (inset); p76: Gerry Ellis/Minden Pictures/FLPA (main), David Hosking/FLPA (inset); p77: Thomas Marent/Minden Pictures/FLPA (left), Frans Lanting/FLPA (right); p78: Ingo Arndt/Minden Pictures/FLPA; p78–9: Martin Harvey/Afripics.com (main); p79: Chris Mattison/FLPA (top), Ingo Arndt/Minden Pictures/FLPA (bottom); p80: Dave Watts/Photoshot (left), A.N.T. Photo Library/Photoshot (right); p81: Anthony Bannister/Photoshot (top), Daniel Heuclin/Photoshot (bottom); p82: ZSSD/Minden Pictures/FLPA (top), Chris Mattison/FLPA (bottom); p83: Michael & Patricia Fogden/Minden Pictures/FLPA (top), A.N.T Photo Library/Photoshot (middle), Michael & Patricia Fogden/Minden Pictures/FLPA (bottom); p84: Panda Photo/FLPA (main image), Fred Bavendam/Minden Pictures/FLPA (inset); p85: Norbert Wu/Minden Pictures/FLPA (top), Tom & Therisa Stack/Photoshot (bottom); p86: Chris Newbert/Minden Pictures/FLPA (inset); p86–7: Taketomo Shiratori/Photoshot (top); p87: Chris Newbert/Minden Pictures/FLPA (inset); p88: Sunset/FLPA (both); p89: SA Team/FN/Minden/FLPA (top); p90–91: Tui De Roy/Minden Pictures/FLPA (main); p92: Dickie Duckett/FLPA (top), Winfried Wisniewski/FLPA (bottom); p93: Winfried Wisniewski/FLPA; p94–5: Cyril Ruoso/Minden Pictures/FLPA (all); p96: Thomas Marent/Minden Pictures/FLPA (both); p97: Kenneth Fink/ardea.com; p98–9: Patricio Robles Gil/Minden Pictures/FLPA (main); p99: Yva Momatiuk & John

Eastcott/Minden Pictures/FLPA (inset) p100: Ernie Janes/Photoshot; p101: Terry Whittaker/FLPA (left), Albert Visage/FLPA (right); p102: Bruce Beehler/Photoshot (main), Konrad Wothe/Minden Pictures/FLPA (inset top & bottom); p103: A. N.T. Photo library/Photoshot; p104: Tui De Roy/Minden Pictures/FLPA; p105: Tui De Roy/Minden Pictures/FLPA; p106: Jurgen & Christine Sohns/FLPA (left), Frans Lanting/FLPA (right); p107: Cyril Ruoso/Minden Pictures/FLPA; p108: Terry Whittaker/FLPA (top), R & M Van Nostrand/FLPA (bottom); p109: Michio Hoshino/Minden Pictures/FLPA, Mitsuaki Iwago/Minden Pictures/FLPA (bottom); p110: Malcolm Schuyl/FLPA (left), Hugh Lansdown/FLPA (right); p111: Konrad Wothe/Minden Pictures/FLPA; p112: James Christensen/Minden Pictures/FLPA; p113: Konrad Wothe/Minden Pictures/FLPA; p114–15: Tui De Roy/Minden Pictures/FLPA; p116: Konrad Wothe/Minden Pictures/FLPA; p117: ImageBroker/Imagebroker/FLPA (top), Fabio Pupin/FLPA (bottom); p118: Mitsuaki Iwago/Minden Pictures/FLPA; p118–19: Andrew Forsyth/FLPA (main); p120: Jari Peltomäki; p121: Mark Jones/Minden Pictures/FLPA; p122: Rob Reijnen/Minden Pictures/FLPA (inset); p122–3: Frans Lanting/FLPA (main); p123: Tui De Roy/Minden Pictures/FLPA (inset); p124: Eric Woods/FLPA; p125: David Hosking/FLPA (top), Neil Bowman/FLPA (bottom); p126: Jane Burton/Photoshot; p127: Michael & Patricia Fogden/Minden Pictures/FLPA (top), Piotr Naskrecki/Minden Pictures/FLPA (bottom); p128: Vincent Grafhorst/Minden Pictures/FLPA (top), Chris & Tilde Stuart/FLPA (bottom); p129: Ariadne Van Zandbergen/FLPA (top), Mitsuhiko Imamori/Minden Pictures/FLPA (bottom); p130–31: Ingo Arndt/Minden Pictures/FLPA; p132: Paul Sawer/FLPA; p133: Gary K Smith/FLPA (top), ImageBroker/Imagebroker/FLPA (bottom); p134–5: Suzi Eszterhas/Minden Pictures/FLPA, Mitsuaki Iwago/Minden Pictures/FLPA; p136: Mark Newman/FLPA; p137: Jasper Doest/Minden Pictures/FLPA; p138–9: Ron Austing/FLPA (images); p140: Chris & Tilde Stuart/FLPA (inset); p140–1: Shin Yoshino/Minden Pictures/FLPA; p142: Nigel J Dennis/Photoshot; p143: Winfried Wisniewski/FLPA (main), David Hosking/FLPA (inset); p144: Chris Newbert/Minden Pictures/FLPA; p145: Flip Nicklin/Minden Pictures/FLPA (main), Norbert Wu/Minden Pictures/FLPA (inset); p147: Mitsuhiko Imamori/Minden Pictures/FLPA; p146: Christian Ziegler/Minden Pictures/FLPA (main), Mark Moffett/Minden Pictures/FLPA (inset); p148: Dickie Duckett/FLPA.

Index

Main entries indicated in **bold**.

aardvark 41, 71
adder, African night 57
Africa 32, 71, 79, 94, 97, 113, 139, 140
  southern 64
  sub-Saharan 21, 24, 41, 47, 48, 56, 81, 125, 135, 140, 142
agama, rock 92
Amazon 44, 62
Amazon Basin 14, 51, 54, 85, 127
Andes 20, 49
anemones, sea 144
Angola 29, 97
anoles 112
Antarctic 123
anteater 71, 72
  giant 38–9
ants, honey **147**
  invasive 82
  leafcutter 146
aphids 133
aposematism 69
Araguaia/Tocantins 44
archerfish, banded 58
Arctic Ocean 43
Arctic, Canadian High 43
  Russian 43
Argentina 19, 51, 127
Arizona 26
armadillos 71
Asia 88, 125
  central 24
  southeast 30, 31, 55, 58, 81, 136
Atlantic coast 51, 95
Atlantic Ocean 62, 109, 113
Australia 33, 63, 73, 75, 76, 80, 83, 84, 103, 106, 107, 110, 119, 124, 147
Australasia 32, 58
axolotl 126
aye-aye 45

babirusas 101
  Bola Batu 101
  Buru 101

golden 101
  Sulawesi 101
  Togian 101
baboons 94
badger, honey 142
Bahia 19
Bali 87
Bangladesh 53
basilisk, green 28
  plumed 28
bats, American long-eared 46
  fruit 97
  hammerhead 97
  Madagascar sucker-footed 15
  Mexican big-eared 46
  Rafinesque's big-eared 46
  Townsend's big-eared 46
bears, polar 43
beetles, Addo flightless dung 128
  dung 128
  fog-basking 64
Bhutan 53, 108
birds-of-paradise 102–3
  king 102
  King of Saxony 102
  superb 103
  Wilson's 102
Bird, tussock 148
blobfish 33
Bolivia 23, 25, 49, 54
Borneo 13, 16, 31, 55, 96
Botswana 143
bowerbird, satin 107
Brazil 14, 19, 127
  Amazonian 23
Broken Bay 33
Burma 30
Buru 101
bushmeat trade 94

California 26, 51, 65
Cameroon 95
Cape Verde 109
capuchin, white-fronted 14
Caribbean 51, 109, 112
cassowary 121
  double-wattled 110–11
  southern 110–11
caterpillar, looper 10
catfishes 85

cats 80
  wild 41
Central America 112, 146
chameleons 78–9
  Madagascar dwarf 79
  Namaqua 79
  Oustalet's 79
Chile 20, 127
China 100, 108
cicadas, periodical 129
climate change 123, 124
clownfish 144
cobra, black-necked spitting 81
  brown spitting 81
  Mozambique spitting 81
  red spitting 81
cobras, spitting 81
coconut plantations 45
Colombia 14, 25, 49
colugo, Malayan 16
  Philippine 16
commensalism 133
Congo 95
Congo Basin 94
crabs, fiddler 113
cranes, Japanese 92
crocodile, American 62
crocodilians 52
crustaceans 43
crypsis 68
cuckoo 23
  common 125

Darwin, Charles 31
deer, Chinese water 100
deforestation 15, 16, 45, 55, 74, 77, 94, 104
dogs 72
dolphin, Amazon river 44
doves 23
duck, torrent 20
dunnock 125

eagle 72
  Philippine 16
East Anglia 100
echidnas 118
  long-beaked 72
  short-beaked 72–3
Ecuador 25, 49, 51, 54, 109
eel, electric 85
egg-eater, common 56
  rhombic 55

Eimer, Theodor 40
emu 121
elephant-shrew,
  golden-rumped 7
Equitorial Guinea 95
Ethiopia 139
Europe 24, 88, 125

falcon, pygmy 143
Falklands 99
feather trade 103
fish 43
  angler 59
  clown anemone 144
  hatchet 6
  invasive 126
  splitfin flashlight 63
fishing, drift-net 61
  game 62
  shark 61
  trophy 62
Fjordland 104
flatheads 33
Flinders Island 75
Florida 28, 54, 109, 112
fossa 74
fox 72
  red 124
frigatebird, magnificent 109
frog, Darwin's 127
  leaf-horned 55
  Malaysian leaf 55
  Wallace's flying 31
  water-holding 83
frogfish 59
frogmouth, tawny 76

Gabon 94, 95
galliformes 23
Gambia 56
gannets 109
gecko, common leaf-tailed 77
  mossy leaf-tailed 77
  satanic leaf-tailed 77
geckos, leaf-tailed 77
Georgia 40
gharial 52–3
gibbons 136
giraffe 140
goannas 119
Gould, John 47
Greenland Sea 43

Guacharo Cave 25
guinea pig 138
gulls 50
Guyana 25, 127
habitat destruction/loss 17, 23, 39, 40, 44, 46, 51, 53, 54, 58, 75, 83, 96, 101, 103, 108, 111, 119, 124
hagfish 85
Hawaii 112
heron, black 48
Himalayas 108
hippos 93, 140
hoatzin 22–3
Honduras 19
honeyguide, greater 142
housefly 84
hummingbird, sword-billed 49
hunting 14, 17, 39, 43, 44, 94, 96, 98, 103, 104, 108
hyena, spotted 134–5

Iban people 13
Idaho 82
iguana 28
impala 140
India 53, 58, 79, 108
Indian Ocean 99, 109, 144
Indo Pacific Ocean 58, 113
Indo-Australian archipelago 59
Indonesia 16, 17, 30, 63, 101, 136
Innuit 43
Isla Escudo de Veraguas 19
Ivindo River 95

jacana 28
  African 21
Japan 32, 63, 125, 137
Java 16
Jay, Eurasian 36
Jenner, Edward 125
Jiangsu 100

kakapo 104–5
Kakapo Recovery Plan 104
Kalimantan 96
Kenya 47, 139
kiwis 121
  great spotted 121
  little spotted 121
  North Island brown 4

Koshima Island 137
Kruger Park 134
Lake Chad 71
Lake Xochimilco 126
lemming, Norway 120
lemur 45
   flying 16
Lenbeh Strait 87
lizard 28, 80, 112, 129
   armadillo girdled 82
   desert horned 82
   frilled 80
   monitor 21
   shovel-snouted 29
locomotion 10–11
logging 13, 14
Lopé National Park 94
lyrebird, superb 106

macaque, Japanese 137
Macquarie Island 99
Madagascar 15, 45, 48, 74, 77, 79,
   83, 129
Malaysia 16, 30, 65
malleefowl 124
mandrill 94–5
mangroves 32
mantis, Malaysian orchid 65
Massachusetts 51
mata mata 54
medicinal product trade 43, 52,
   71, 84
Mediterranean 79
meerkats 133
Mexico 26, 28, 82, 109
mimicry, Batesian 57, 69
mockingbird, northern 27
Mojave Desert 27
mole, star-nosed 40
Moluccas 101, 102, 103
mongoose 74
monkey, howler 19
   proboscis 96
   squirrel 14
   woolly 14
monotremes 116, 118
moth, puss 88
mudskipper, barred 32
mutualism 133
Myanmar 53, 108

Nagano Mountains 137

Namaqualand 82
Namib Desert 29, 33, 64
Namibia 29, 33, 64, 143
narwhal 42–3
Nepal 53
New Guinea 73, 80, 103, 107,
   110, 147
New Mexico 26
New Zealand 105, 121, 123
Newfoundland 40
Ngorongoro Crater 134
nightjars 25, 76

Oceania 32
octopus, mimic 86–7
Ogooué River 95
oilbird 25
orca 43, 98, 123
Origin of Species 31
Orinoco river basin 44, 54, 85
otters 21
overfishing 62
overgrazing 108
owl, snowy 117
oxpeckers 140–1
   red-billed 140
   yellow-billed 140

Pacific coast 51
Pacific Ocean 62, 63, 99, 109,
   113, 144
Pakistan 53
palm oil plantations 96
Panama 19, 28
pangolin, Cape 70–71
   common 70–71
   ground 70–71
parrots 104–5
peacock 42
pelicans 109
penguin, emperor 122–3
Peninsular Malaysia 31, 55, 136
persecution 53, 75
Peru 14, 23, 25, 49, 127
pesticides 13
pet trade 54, 55, 58, 77, 82, 84
petrels, giant 123
pheasant 108
Philippines 13, 16, 30
pipit, meadow 125
platypus 72, 118–19
plovers 21

poaching 101
pollution 20, 44, 84, 119
Polynesia 58
porcupine 41, 138
powerboats 51
pythons 41
   African rock 36

Quebec 40

raptors 80, 119
rat, Damara mole 138
   naked mole 138–9
rats 119
rattlesnake 27
raven, common 27
remoras 145
reptile trade 83
rhinos 140
   Sumatran 31
riflebird, magnificent 102
road traffic 27, 39, 76, 111
roadrunner, greater 26–7
rollers 128
Russia 120

Sabah 96
salamander 126
sand puppies 138
sandpipers 21
Sangea River 95
Sarawak 96
Sargasso Sea 59
sawfish, large-tooth 62
Scandinavia 120
scorpion, Socotran 117
seadragon, leafy 84
seahorse 84
seal, leopard 123
   northern elephant 98
   southern elephant 98–9,
   148
Senegal 48, 97, 140
shark, bull 62
   **scalloped hammerhead
   60–1**
shoebill 47
siamang 136
sifaka, Verreaux's 10
silkwood 16
skimmer, African 50
   black 50–1

Indian 50
**sloth, brown-throated
   three-toed 18–19**
   maned 19
   pale-throated three-toed 19
   pygmy three-toed 19
   three-toed 18
   two-toed 18
snails, cone 65
**snake, African egg-eating
   56–7**
   Indian egg-eating 56
   leaf-nosed 83
   milk 69
   paradise tree 30
snakes 80, 119
Snow Monkey Park 137
sole, peacock 68
Somalia 139
songbirds 106
Sonoran Desert 27
South Africa 48, 56, 65, 71, 82,
   134, 143, 147
South America 112, 146
South Atlantic 98
South Georgia 99, 123
Southern Ocean 98
spider, cartwheeling 33
   huntsman 33
   raft 9
   squid 43
squirrels 129
Sri Lanka 79
starlings 132, 140
Stewart Island 104
suckerfish 145
Sudan 47, 48, 56
Sula 101
Sulawesi 13, 87, 101
Sumatra 13, 16, 31, 55, 65, 136
sunbittern 68
Surinam 127
swift 27
   Eurasian 24

Tanzania 47, 124
tarsier, Western 12–13
Tasmania 33, 76, 106, 119
Tasmanian devils 72
tenrec, lowland streaked 74
terns 50
Texas 26

Thailand 16, 30, 136
Tierra del Fuego 20
toad, Asiatic horned 55
   horned 82
Surinam 127
Togian Island 101
tortoise, Hermann's 117
tourism impact 74, 123
tragopan, Temminck's 108
traveller's palm 15
treehopper 89
**treekangaroo, Goodfellow's
   17**
Trinidad 25, 54
trout 20
turacos 23
turtle 145
   snake-necked 54

uakari, bald 14
   red 14
   white 14
Uganda 47, 97
unicorn 42
United States 129, 146, 147

Valdes 99
Venezuela 20, 23, 25, 49
Vietnam 108
viperfish, Sloane's 63
Von Humboldt 25

Wallace, Alfred Russel 31
warbler, reed 125
warthog 41, 71
wasp, Pompilid 33
weaver, sociable 143
weevil, giraffe-necked 129
whale, humpback 37
Whipsnade Zoo 100
witchcraft 71
wombat, common 75

Yangtze River 100

Zambia 47
Zhejiang 100